W9-CXQ-808

Welcome. We've been expecting you.

You are about to embark on a fantastic adventure:

A quest for twelve treasures: over ten thousand dollars in precious jewels. They may be hidden in your city or your local park or even in your own backyard. You might even figure out one of their hiding places without leaving your house. . . .

You are about to learn the answer to an age-old mystery:

Whatever happened to the Fair People: the goblins, dragons, fairies, leprechauns and other fantastic creatures of the Old World?

You are about to meet their descendants:

For the first time, you will see the creatures who are really responsible for all the unexplainable things that happen to you—from the *Maître D'eamon* (who makes sure you get the table near the kitchen) to the *Screaming Mimi* (who loves the sound of a baby crying in your ear). Plus you'll have a chance to send in *your own sightings* of fantastic creatures.

The Secret
A Treasure Hunt
A Mythology for the Modern World

You are cordially invited to participate.

♦ T H E S

Sean Kelly
Ted Mann
Authors

JoEllen Trilling
Sculptress

Developed and Edited by
Byron Preiss

John Jude Palencar
John Pierard
Overton Loyd
Illustrators

Ben Asen
Photographer

Alex Jay
Designer

C R E T ♦

A Byron Preiss Book

ibooks

Habent Sua Fata Libelli

This book is dedicated to
Alexsandr Ginzburg, Yuri Orlov, Anatoly Shcharansky
Andrei Sakharov, Victor Nekipelov, George Vladimovand
all the other voices of freedom in the Soviet darkness

THE SECRET

An ibooks book, November 2014

Cover painting by John Jude Palencar.
Cover and book design by Alex Jay with assistance and support from
Kathy Connolly and Vincent, a one-ear cat.

 The Secret was produced by Byron Preiss Visual Publications, an imprint of J. Boylston & Company, Publishers.

The Editor would like to thank Louis Wolfe, Jack Romanos, Nina Hoffman, Sally Williams, F. X. Flinn, Lucy Salvino, Vincent Liguori, Lisa Nichol, Ian and Betty Ballantine, Paul Fedorko, Stuart Applebaum, Alun Davies, Patrice Clay, Aliene Aizer, Phyllis Mandel, and Joan Brandt for their gracious support, consideration and friendship during the production of The Secret

Special thanks to Barry Denenberg for his editorial help, generous enthusiasm, and care-taking of an unusual endeavor.

The Contributors would like to thank the following parties for providing locations for shooting some of the Fair People: Ms. Emily Dieder of the Riverside Church, New York (Tinkerbelle); The Cheese Cellar Restaurant, New York (Maître D'eamon); Columbia University; Mr. Oswaldo Novaes, Joia Interiors, New York (Evil Neckromancer); Mr. John Doolan and Col. Davis, 7th Regiment U.S. Army, New York (Pre-Revolutionary Warlock); Arthur Cunningham's 94th Street Newsstand; The Friar's Club; Ms. Charlotte Gasperini; and Vincent Sbarbati, The Magic Cue. Many thanks also to Henny Youngman, Monte Irvin, Betsy Bernfeld, Marilyn and John Palencar, Sandi Mendelson, Susan Devins, Clark Bott of Architectural Sculpture (the box castings); and Edmund and Pearl Preiss.

Book Mechanical Production by Tony DiMiceli Graphics. James Gasperini coordinated the photographic sessions for many of the Fair People appearing in the book. The wino in the Djinn Rummy photographs was portrayed by Geoff Prysor. Typography was set by Bailey Typography, Inc., and Jackson Typesetting Company, Inc. The text was set in ITC Souvenir with headings in ITC Bookman. The color separations were made by Seiple Lithograph. JoEllen Trilling's work can be viewed at the Julie Artisan's Gallery, New York. For information about photographic prints of any of the Fair People: Byron Preiss Visual Publications

1230 Park Avenue
New York, New York 10128
Tel: 212-427-7139
bricktower@aol.com • www.ibooksinc.com

CONTENTS

THE TALE, SIMPLY TOLD

A long, long time ago, before the age when Man and Woman sailed in ships to lands they had never seen, there existed in the Old World two empires: that of Man and that of the Fair People.

Man named his abode Civilization, for Man was an acquisitive creature and names were things he could possess. He could not fly on wings of gossamer, like a fairy; nor hide in the gentle slope of a mountain, like a giant; nor throw fire through a gust of wind, like a dragon. So Man often found his strength in words.

The Fair People had no cities or towns or houses. Their home was Nature, and in it they could play or hide or make themselves unseen to Man, who feared Nature, for he could not control it.

What Man could not control, he often sought to change. Thus, over centuries, Man built his cities, and his villages and diminished the Fair People's domain.

Where once lived a goblin, there rose a tavern.

Where once swam a river maiden, a water wheel spun.

Forest to lumber, earth to road . . . Man expanded

his empire and the Fair People were threatened.

From England to Cathay, from Bristol to Bombay, there came a call from the Fair People for a new home, untrammeled by Civilization. Representatives of the Fair People of the Old World were sent to seek it. Elves, fairies, sprites, foletti, duende . . . from thirteen lands they departed the Old World to find a New one.

And they did.

You are about to read of the fantastic passage of the Fair People, who, like Man, arrived on the shores of the New World with dreams of freedom and contentment. You are about to learn of their wonderstones, the twelve treasures brought with them in their passage to the New Found Land: diamond, ruby, pearl, amethyst, emerald, sapphire, peridot, garnet, topaz, aquamarine. . . And you will discover what happened when the Fair People found Man of the New World, who shared their deep love for nature. Best of all, you will learn of your role in the Fair People's story, and the significance of the quest for their treasure in the relationship between Man and the Fair People.

Across North America, twelve treasures are waiting. The key to each requires the proper combination of one treasure painting with one treasure verse. You need only decipher the clues in any pair to learn the

location of a treasure casque. In each casque, waits a key. The return of the key will gain its treasure for you. (If you are unable to retrieve the casque, but believe you have determined its site, you may acquire its treasure by successfully completing the form in the back of the book with a precise description and explanation of your discovery.) Any successful discovery of a treasure will be described in the next edition of *The Secret*.

Finally, you will meet many of the modern descendants of the Fair People who arrived on America's shores. You are cordially invited to inform us, in words or pictures, of your own sightings of Fair People as yet unseen for inclusion in the next edition of *The Secret*.

This is our story, simply told.

The mystery is yours to unravel.

THE PASSAGE TO THE NEW WORLD

The Northern seas are cold and cruel grey;
Across them sailed the fair tall Elven folk.
Southward, the seas are blue, serene and warm;
From that soft mist, with many a merry joke,
Sweet Spirits came. From West, at close of day,
Beneath sails brilliant as a peacock's fan,
Djinni arrived. From sunrise and through storm,
Across the Eastern ocean, last came—Man.

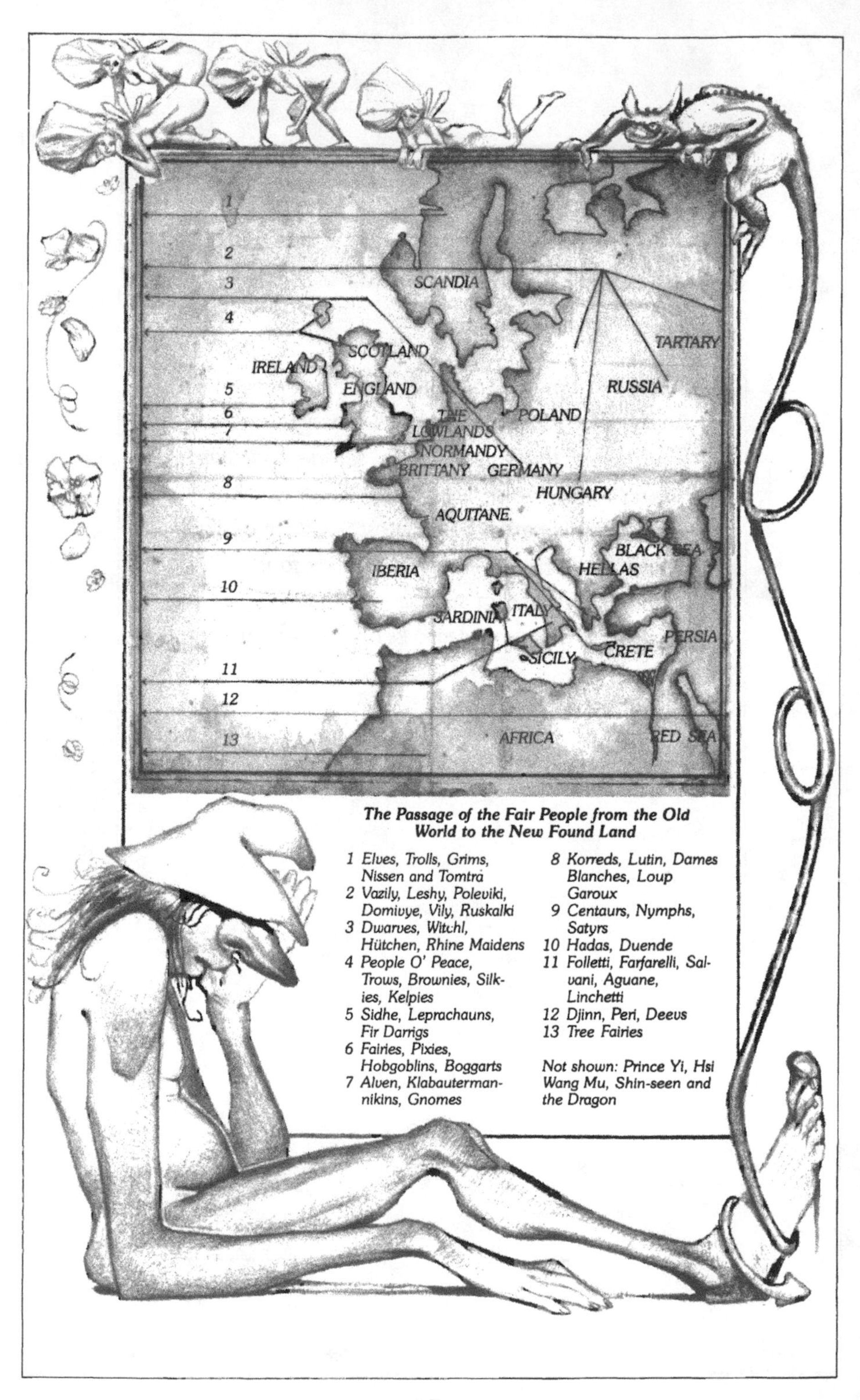

The Passage of the Fair People from the Old World to the New Found Land

1 Elves, Trolls, Grims, Nissen and Tomtra
2 Vazily, Leshy, Poleviki, Domivye, Vily, Ruskalki
3 Dwarves, Witchl, Hütchen, Rhine Maidens
4 People O' Peace, Trows, Brownies, Silkies, Kelpies
5 Sidhe, Leprachauns, Fir Darrigs
6 Fairies, Pixies, Hobgoblins, Boggarts
7 Alven, Klabautermannikins, Gnomes
8 Korreds, Lutin, Dames Blanches, Loup Garoux
9 Centaurs, Nymphs, Satyrs
10 Hadas, Duende
11 Folletti, Farfarelli, Salvani, Aguane, Linchetti
12 Djinn, Peri, Deevs
13 Tree Fairies

Not shown: Prince Yi, Hsi Wang Mu, Shin-seen and the Dragon

Not so awfully long ago, as the stars, who created time, tell it, the Fair People withdrew from the Old World (which they called the Middle Kingdom), migrating across the Ocean Sea to dwell in the hills and forests of the New Found Land.

The first to set foot on its shore (if he said so himself, in the saga he often sang) was Ruddy Alf, a copper-haired *Sea-Troll* of Nortland. It was *he,* he bragged, who left Scandia to brave alone the teeth of the Hell-hounds at sheer cliff's lip of the flat Earth's edge; *he* the hero who pressed a single print from his rein-deerhide boots on the beach there, and *he* who came back to harp on it.

Next, or simultaneously, or (to hear his kin and clan tell of it) years and years before, was Brandan, a *Leprechaun* from Kerry, who zigzagged all the way from the tip of the Dingle to the Brave New World in a sealskin canoe, with naught but poteen for provender.

But most of the Fair People deemed the exploits of Alf and Brandan to be mere myth (even Legends, it seems, look down on legends) and attributed the Discovery of the New Found Land to the Italian fairy Colon Savanelli, an intrepidly nautical *Folleto* out of Genoa.

Savanelli had been commissioned by the Queen

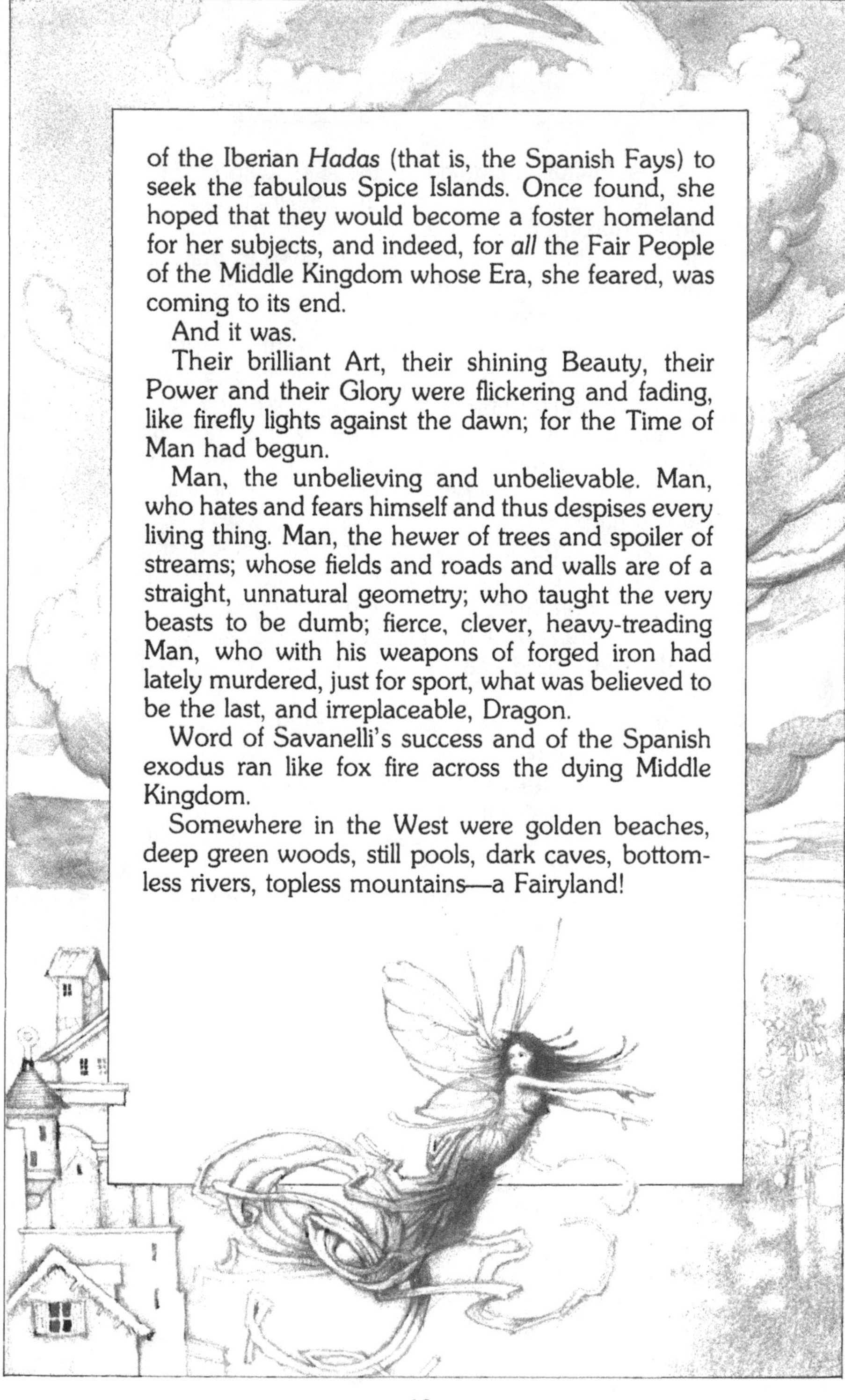

of the Iberian *Hadas* (that is, the Spanish Fays) to seek the fabulous Spice Islands. Once found, she hoped that they would become a foster homeland for her subjects, and indeed, for *all* the Fair People of the Middle Kingdom whose Era, she feared, was coming to its end.

And it was.

Their brilliant Art, their shining Beauty, their Power and their Glory were flickering and fading, like firefly lights against the dawn; for the Time of Man had begun.

Man, the unbelieving and unbelievable. Man, who hates and fears himself and thus despises every living thing. Man, the hewer of trees and spoiler of streams; whose fields and roads and walls are of a straight, unnatural geometry; who taught the very beasts to be dumb; fierce, clever, heavy-treading Man, who with his weapons of forged iron had lately murdered, just for sport, what was believed to be the last, and irreplaceable, Dragon.

Word of Savanelli's success and of the Spanish exodus ran like fox fire across the dying Middle Kingdom.

Somewhere in the West were golden beaches, deep green woods, still pools, dark caves, bottomless rivers, topless mountains—a Fairyland!

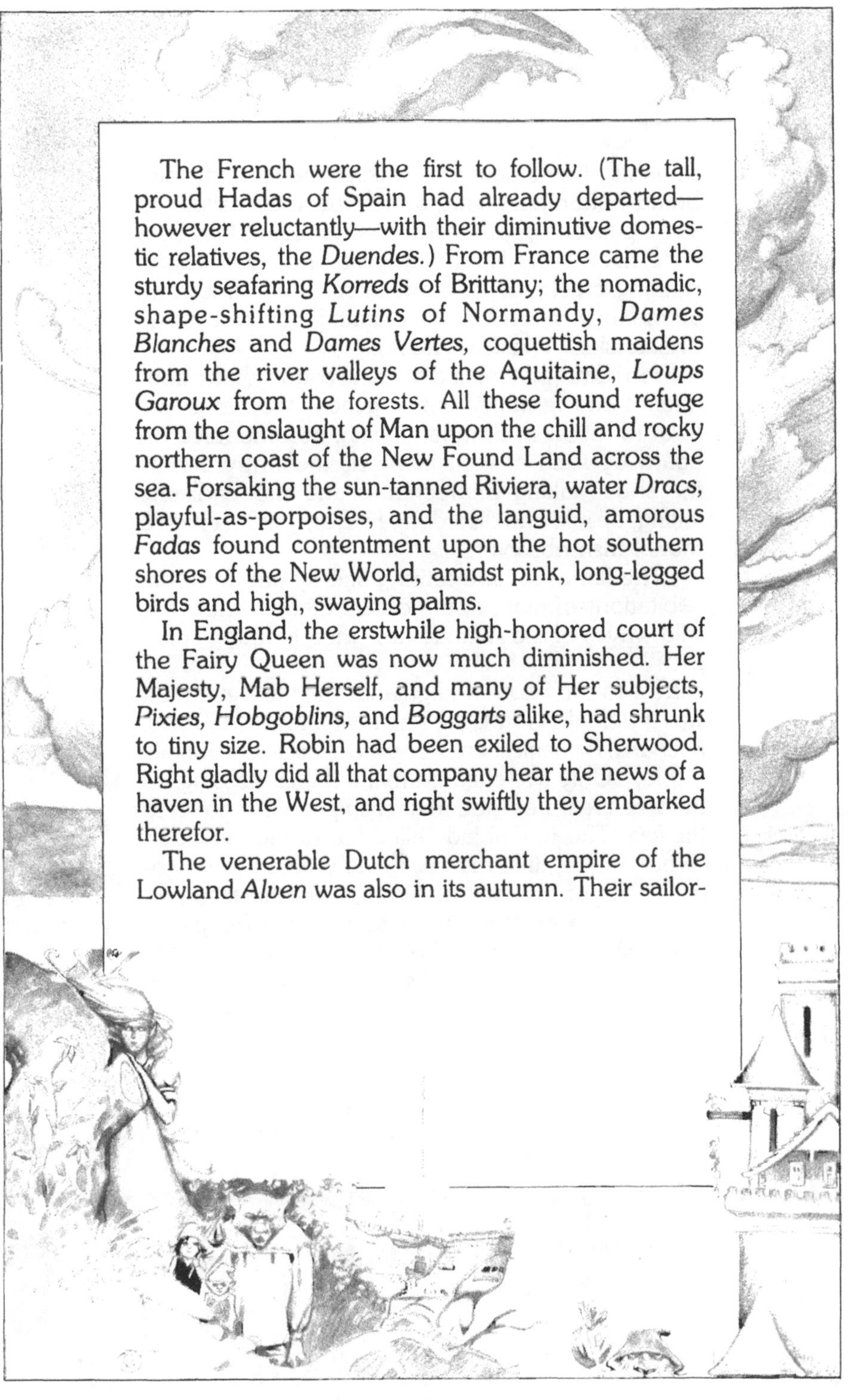

The French were the first to follow. (The tall, proud Hadas of Spain had already departed—however reluctantly—with their diminutive domestic relatives, the *Duendes.*) From France came the sturdy seafaring *Korreds* of Brittany; the nomadic, shape-shifting *Lutins* of Normandy, *Dames Blanches* and *Dames Vertes,* coquettish maidens from the river valleys of the Aquitaine, *Loups Garoux* from the forests. All these found refuge from the onslaught of Man upon the chill and rocky northern coast of the New Found Land across the sea. Forsaking the sun-tanned Riviera, water *Dracs,* playful-as-porpoises, and the languid, amorous *Fadas* found contentment upon the hot southern shores of the New World, amidst pink, long-legged birds and high, swaying palms.

In England, the erstwhile high-honored court of the Fairy Queen was now much diminished. Her Majesty, Mab Herself, and many of Her subjects, *Pixies, Hobgoblins,* and *Boggarts* alike, had shrunk to tiny size. Robin had been exiled to Sherwood. Right gladly did all that company hear the news of a haven in the West, and right swiftly they embarked therefor.

The venerable Dutch merchant empire of the Lowland *Alven* was also in its autumn. Their sailor-

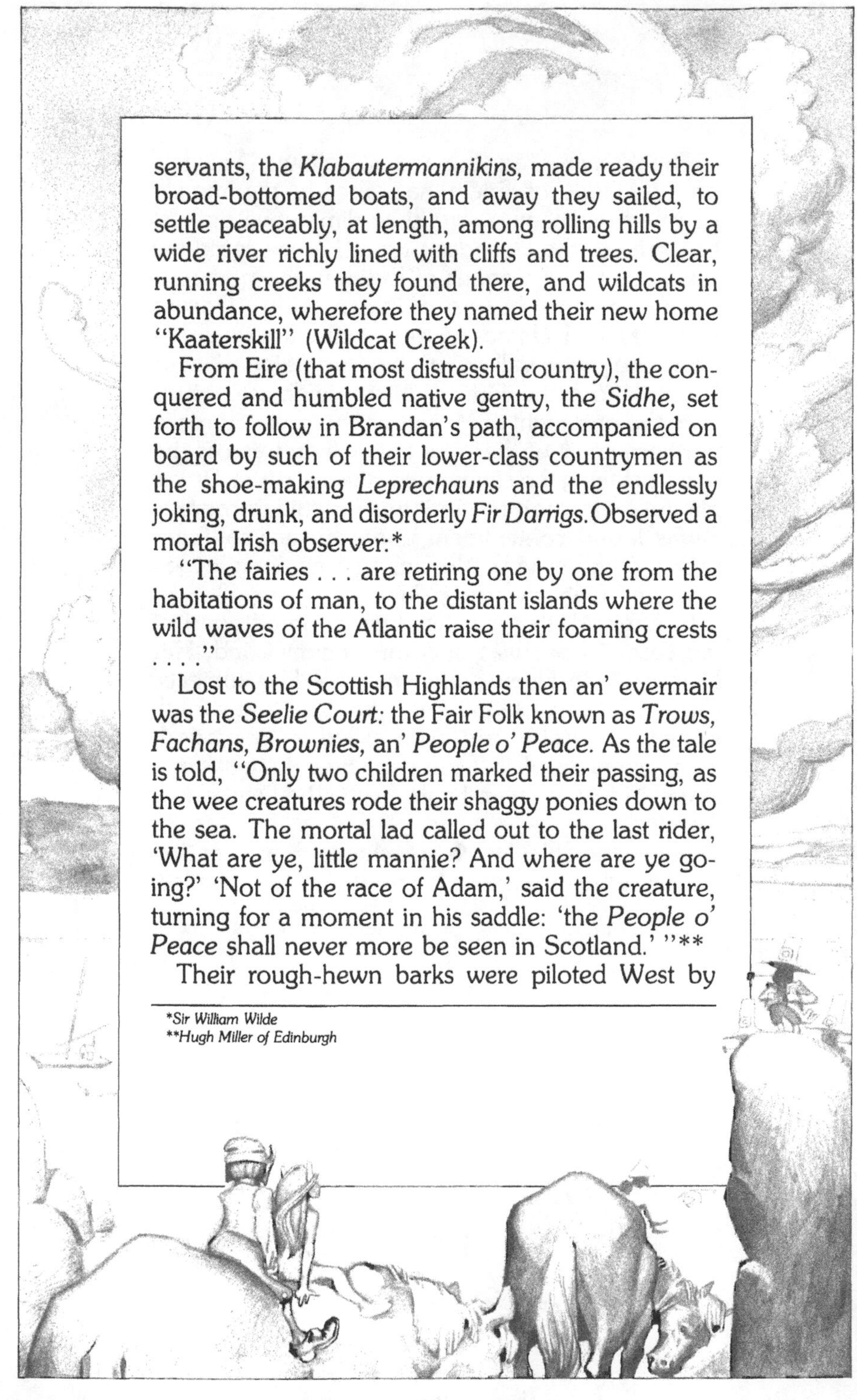

servants, the *Klabautermannikins,* made ready their broad-bottomed boats, and away they sailed, to settle peaceably, at length, among rolling hills by a wide river richly lined with cliffs and trees. Clear, running creeks they found there, and wildcats in abundance, wherefore they named their new home "Kaaterskill" (Wildcat Creek).

From Eire (that most distressful country), the conquered and humbled native gentry, the *Sidhe,* set forth to follow in Brandan's path, accompanied on board by such of their lower-class countrymen as the shoe-making *Leprechauns* and the endlessly joking, drunk, and disorderly *Fir Darrigs.* Observed a mortal Irish observer:*

"The fairies . . . are retiring one by one from the habitations of man, to the distant islands where the wild waves of the Atlantic raise their foaming crests . . . ."

Lost to the Scottish Highlands then an' evermair was the *Seelie Court:* the Fair Folk known as *Trows, Fachans, Brownies,* an' *People o' Peace.* As the tale is told, "Only two children marked their passing, as the wee creatures rode their shaggy ponies down to the sea. The mortal lad called out to the last rider, 'What are ye, little mannie? And where are ye going?' 'Not of the race of Adam,' said the creature, turning for a moment in his saddle: 'the *People o' Peace* shall never more be seen in Scotland.' "**

Their rough-hewn barks were piloted West by

**Sir William Wilde*

***Hugh Miller of Edinburgh*

Silkies and *Kelpies,* over the sea, beyond Skye, to a Nova Scotia . . . .

Down ice green fjords of Scandinavia, and away to the Land of the Eagle, then sailed the *Ellefolk,* in their terrible-prowed longships: the *Nissen* and the *Tomtrå,* those hairy farm-fairies; *Grims* from the stone towers; squat, squinting *Wood-* and *River-Trolls;* and, in the bows, faces set to the cold salt spray, the *Elves* themselves, yellow hair streaming in the wind, blue-gray eyes fixed on the far horizon. Of all the folk of Jotunheim, only some of the *Koboldes* stayed behind, and these proud Tree-Fairies were soon and forever turned to wooden playthings for the children of Man.

Guided on its stately way by the *Rhine Maidens,* a great fleet bearing away strong-thewed *Dwarfs* from the mines, plump and hairy *Witchtln* from the fields, the handsome *Wilden Fraulein* from the marshes, and red-capped *Hūtchen* from the Black Forest forsook Germany and her neighbors for the New World, far across the sea.

Then from the East, from the Far Marches, from the wide snowy Steppes and boundless fertile plains of Russia—travelled the native Fair Folk: *Vazily, Poleviki, Domivye,* and *Vily.* The *Leshy* abandoned the forest tops of Tatary, the *Rusyalki* rose up from the river beds, and all followed the *Forest Fathers* and *Moss Maidens* across the winter prairie to the Black Sea shore and onto waiting ships. Together they emigrated, away to the West.

Cradling Italy, calm as the clouded moon, dark as

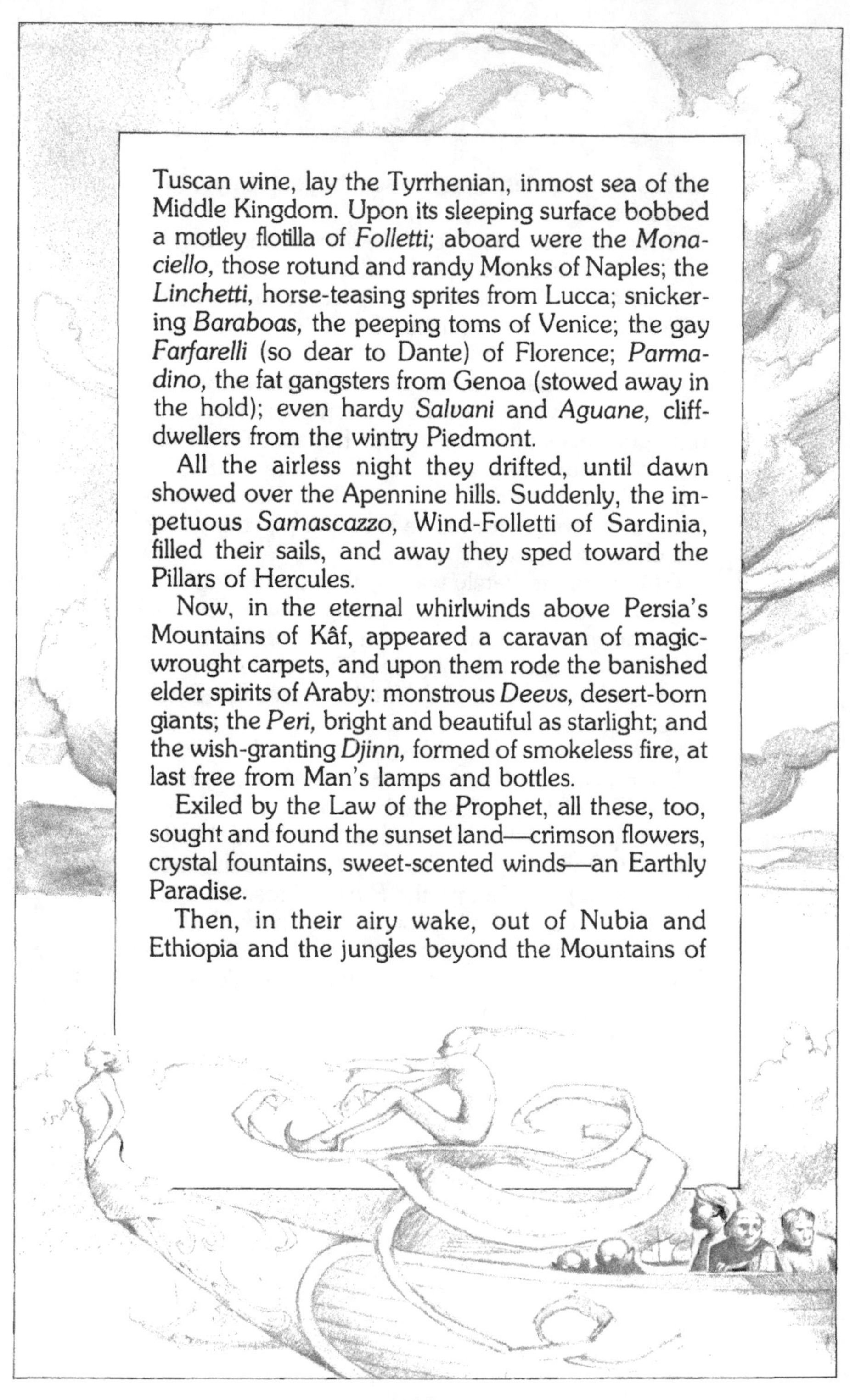

Tuscan wine, lay the Tyrrhenian, inmost sea of the Middle Kingdom. Upon its sleeping surface bobbed a motley flotilla of *Folletti;* aboard were the *Monaciello,* those rotund and randy Monks of Naples; the *Linchetti,* horse-teasing sprites from Lucca; snickering *Baraboas,* the peeping toms of Venice; the gay *Farfarelli* (so dear to Dante) of Florence; *Parmadino,* the fat gangsters from Genoa (stowed away in the hold); even hardy *Salvani* and *Aguane,* cliff-dwellers from the wintry Piedmont.

All the airless night they drifted, until dawn showed over the Apennine hills. Suddenly, the impetuous *Samascazzo,* Wind-Folletti of Sardinia, filled their sails, and away they sped toward the Pillars of Hercules.

Now, in the eternal whirlwinds above Persia's Mountains of Kâf, appeared a caravan of magic-wrought carpets, and upon them rode the banished elder spirits of Araby: monstrous *Deevs,* desert-born giants; the *Peri,* bright and beautiful as starlight; and the wish-granting *Djinn,* formed of smokeless fire, at last free from Man's lamps and bottles.

Exiled by the Law of the Prophet, all these, too, sought and found the sunset land—crimson flowers, crystal fountains, sweet-scented winds—an Earthly Paradise.

Then, in their airy wake, out of Nubia and Ethiopia and the jungles beyond the Mountains of

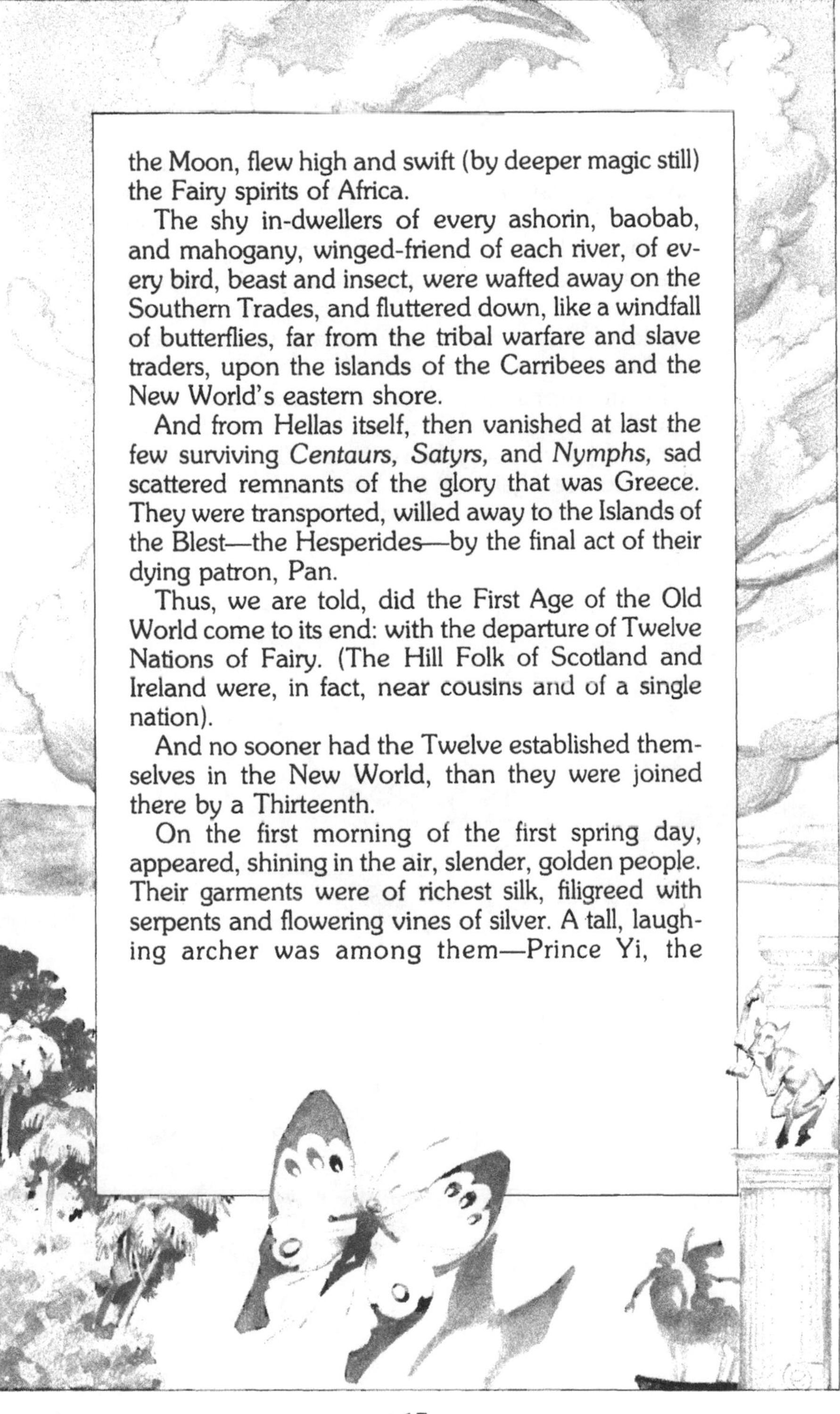

the Moon, flew high and swift (by deeper magic still) the Fairy spirits of Africa.

The shy in-dwellers of every ashorin, baobab, and mahogany, winged-friend of each river, of every bird, beast and insect, were wafted away on the Southern Trades, and fluttered down, like a windfall of butterflies, far from the tribal warfare and slave traders, upon the islands of the Carribees and the New World's eastern shore.

And from Hellas itself, then vanished at last the few surviving *Centaurs, Satyrs,* and *Nymphs,* sad scattered remnants of the glory that was Greece. They were transported, willed away to the Islands of the Blest—the Hesperides—by the final act of their dying patron, Pan.

Thus, we are told, did the First Age of the Old World come to its end: with the departure of Twelve Nations of Fairy. (The Hill Folk of Scotland and Ireland were, in fact, near cousins and of a single nation).

And no sooner had the Twelve established themselves in the New World, than they were joined there by a Thirteenth.

On the first morning of the first spring day, appeared, shining in the air, slender, golden people. Their garments were of richest silk, filigreed with serpents and flowering vines of silver. A tall, laughing archer was among them—Prince Yi, the

Wanderer, bearing the great bow with which he had shot dead nine blazing suns—at his side, his Golden Mother, Hsi Wang Mu, beautiful as the moon, who bore in her hands the peaches of immortality—and Tsao-shen, also, the home-loving imp, his laughing mouth smeared with honey—together with the multitude of *Shiin-seen,* shy, delicate maidens and bright-eyed, bearded sages.

From impossibly distant Cathay they had travelled, bringing with them to safety, to the wonder and joy of every Fairy, what all had thought never to see again—a fire-breathing and terrible, winged and wonderful Dragon.

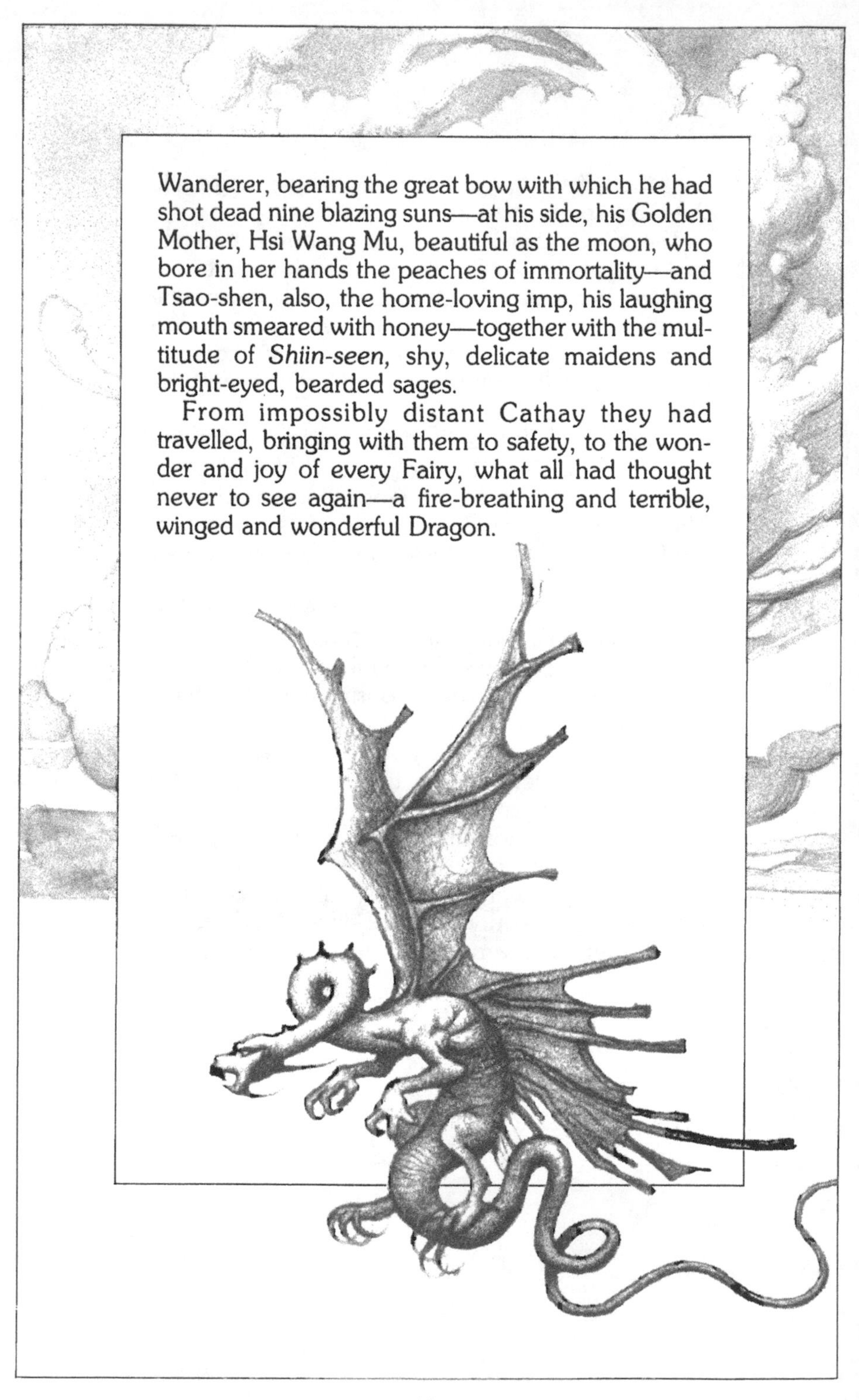

THE LITANY OF THE JEWELS

It is the nature (or perhaps we should say PRETERNATURE) of Fairies to love beautiful things: starshine and flowers, of course, and trees; rushing streams, dew-bright morning spider webs, and music. But of all the desires of the Fair People, there is one thing for which Man shares the same passion: Jewels.

To the Fairies, gold is pretty enough stuff. It reminds them of sunlight dancing on water and of the turning leaves in autumn. (Catch a Leprechaun, they say, and demand of him his golden treasure: you'll sleep a hundred years and wake with dead leaves in your pocket—he keeps his word.)

Likewise, they cherish silver, for it puts them in mind of moonlight and icicles.

But precious stones they value for themselves; perhaps because, like them, gems are earthborn, rare, and beautiful. When it comes to jewelry (and the Fairies are great craftsmen of jewelry)—to rings and pendants, bracelets and necklaces, to broaches and

inlaid dagger hilts, coronets and combs—the Fair People can be jealous, greedy, vain, quarrelsome, possessive, treacherous—almost, in a word, human.

When the Thirteen Nations of the Fair People came to the New Found Land, twelve tribes brought with them their chief pride and treasure: a gem from the Old World, a remembrance of their history and tradition. The Elvish folk of Scandia provided the uncanny casques in which the jewels were kept.

Every Fairy, even the stupidest Goblin among them, knew by heart the Litany of the Jewels:

What are the treasures the Fair Folk bring?
Easily named, and lovingly told:
Fairies of England proudly bear
Garnet, crown-jewel of their Queen.
Brilliant as eyes of Celtic folk,
Cold morning green, their Emerald.
The Hadas of Iberia:
Sapphire, shy as a wild field flower.
Turquoise the Fays of France keep: stone
Rare as a blue midsummer's day.

Dwarves' treasure: purple Amethyst,
Imperial star of Germany.
The Opal of the Lowland Gnomes:
A cloud of shining, shifting smoke.
A Topaz is the Russian prize:
The royal sunstone, frozen fire.
Peridot of old Italy:
Antique, and olivine, and rich.
The Ruby out of Araby:
Scarlet of desert sky at dawn.
Africa's Diamond, earth-born star,
Bright harvest of the midnight rock.
The Nymphs of Hellas cherish sweet
Aquamarine, spring-water clear.
From far Cathay, the dragon's Pearl:
Chaste, perfect as the silver moon.
Each jewel in its weird-wrought casque,
Gift of the Viking craftsmen Elves.
Wonder and glory thirteen-fold:
These are the treasures the Fair Folk bring.

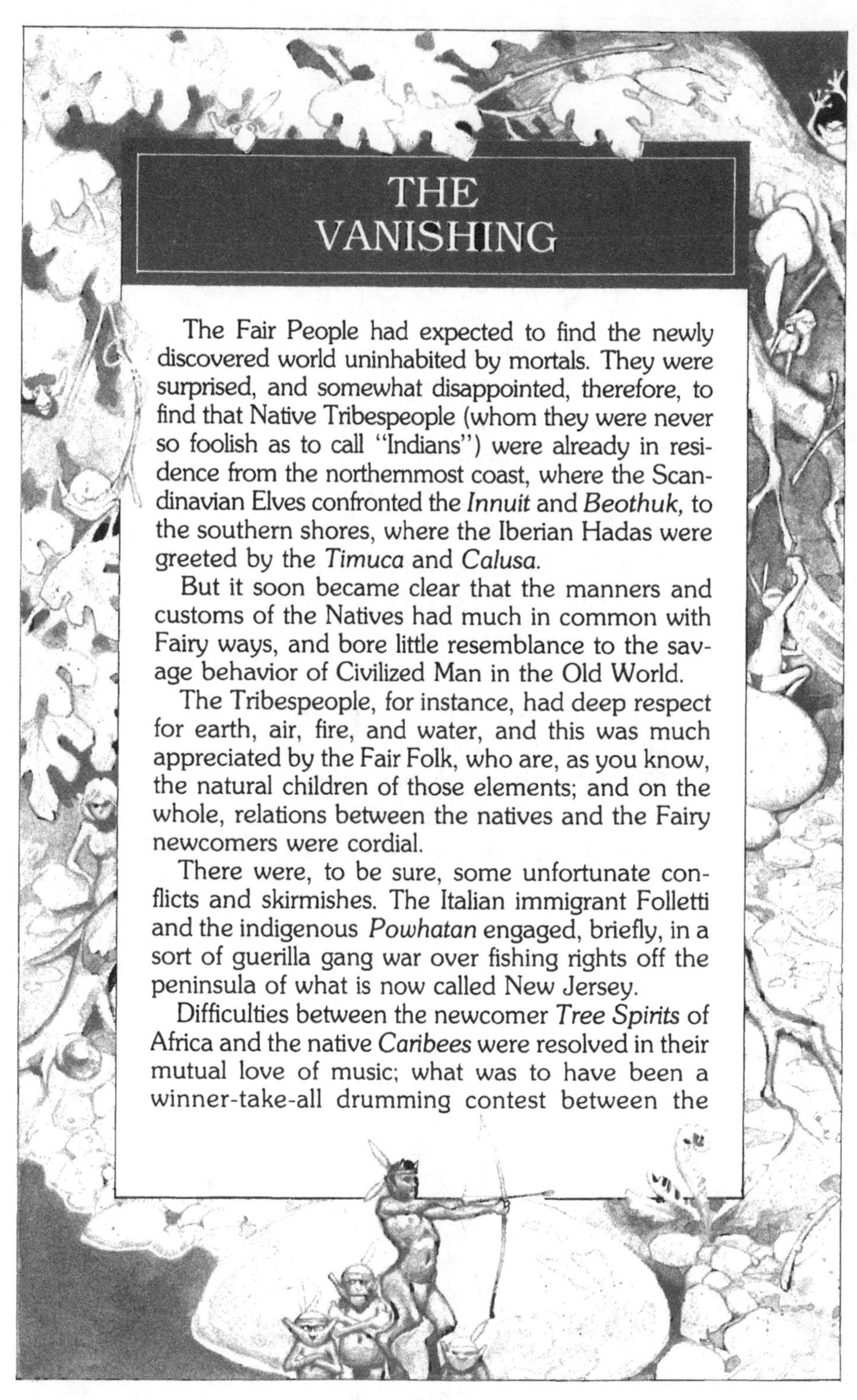

THE VANISHING

The Fair People had expected to find the newly discovered world uninhabited by mortals. They were surprised, and somewhat disappointed, therefore, to find that Native Tribespeople (whom they were never so foolish as to call "Indians") were already in residence from the northernmost coast, where the Scandinavian Elves confronted the *Innuit* and *Beothuk*, to the southern shores, where the Iberian Hadas were greeted by the *Timuca* and *Calusa*.

But it soon became clear that the manners and customs of the Natives had much in common with Fairy ways, and bore little resemblance to the savage behavior of Civilized Man in the Old World.

The Tribespeople, for instance, had deep respect for earth, air, fire, and water, and this was much appreciated by the Fair Folk, who are, as you know, the natural children of those elements; and on the whole, relations between the natives and the Fairy newcomers were cordial.

There were, to be sure, some unfortunate conflicts and skirmishes. The Italian immigrant Folletti and the indigenous *Powhatan* engaged, briefly, in a sort of guerilla gang war over fishing rights off the peninsula of what is now called New Jersey.

Difficulties between the newcomer *Tree Spirits* of Africa and the native *Caribees* were resolved in their mutual love of music; what was to have been a winner-take-all drumming contest between the

champions of both groups was quickly transformed into a month-long party—a "jump-up" on the beach, during which festivities, according to legend, rum was invented.

So long as the Native Peoples would live in harmony with Nature, the "Shining Ones From Over The Big Sea Water" (as they were called) were content to live in harmony with them.

Robin and the Pixies of Britain gave lessons in archery to the *Catawba* braves, who passed their skill in bowmanship along to the neighboring *Cherokee* and *Teton Sioux.* Leshy and Vily, from the forests of Muscovy, instructed the *Mohicans* in woodcraft, teaching them to move silently and invisibly through the trees—a skill which (learned authorities say) the Mohicans possessed to the Last.

The fabulous carpet weaving techniques of the Djinn and Peri were admired and then mastered by the people who were their neighbors in the vast and pleasant desert regions of the New World's Southwest. (It was the sort of place to which the Spirits of Araby were naturally attracted).

Among the native customs quickly adopted by some of the Fairy newcomers was the smoking of To-Bacco—a vice to which the Leprechauns, especially, were susceptible.

How long the Fairy Folk of the Old World dwelt peacefully among the natives of the New, no one knows. There are certainly enough "Indian Myths" to establish the historical veracity of the immigration and cohabitation: stories and poems about "Bright Visitors From a Far Place" abound.

Yet when mortal men of Europe, Africa, and the

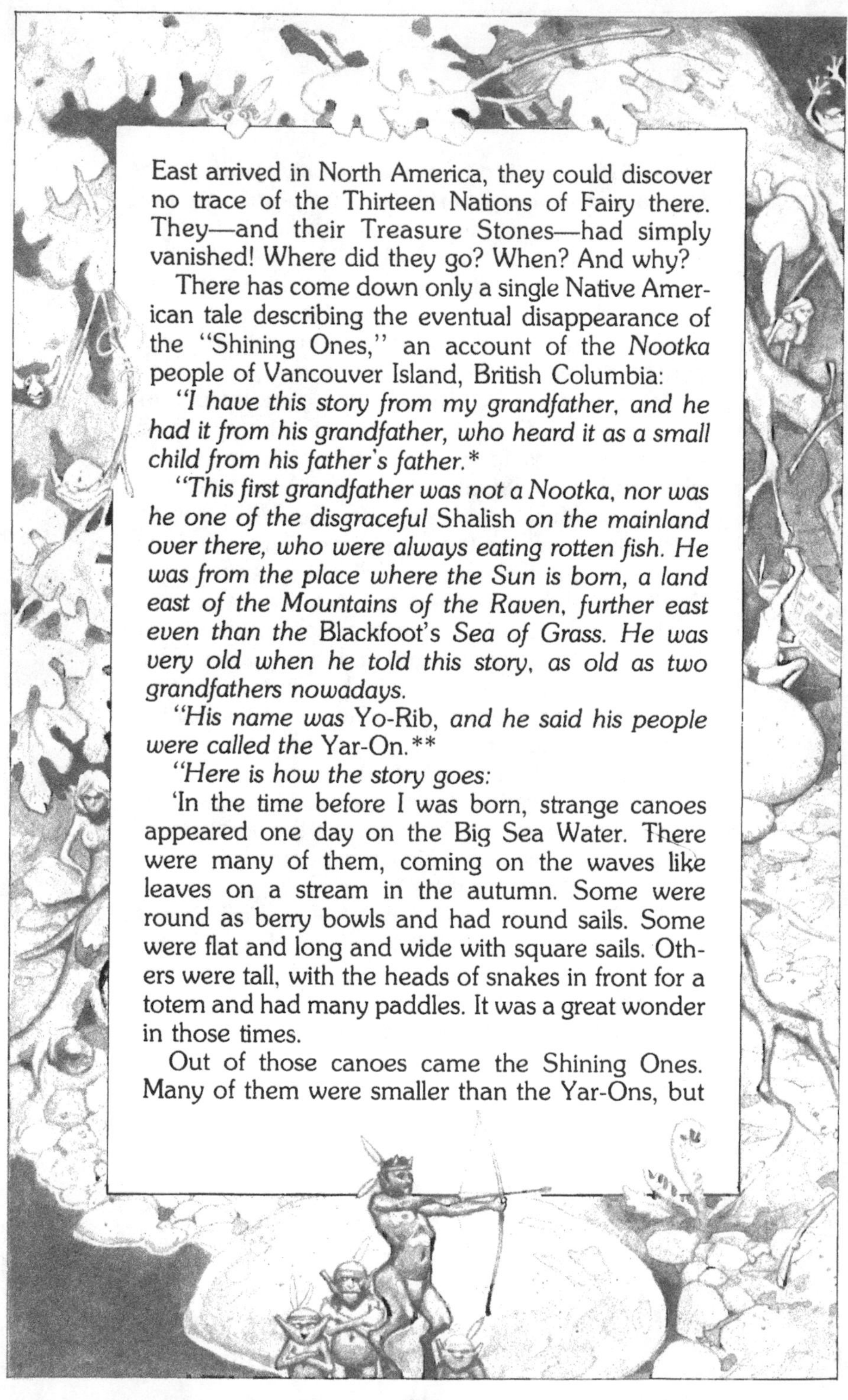

East arrived in North America, they could discover no trace of the Thirteen Nations of Fairy there. They—and their Treasure Stones—had simply vanished! Where did they go? When? And why?

There has come down only a single Native American tale describing the eventual disappearance of the "Shining Ones," an account of the *Nootka* people of Vancouver Island, British Columbia:

*"I have this story from my grandfather, and he had it from his grandfather, who heard it as a small child from his father's father.**

"This first grandfather was not a Nootka, nor was he one of the disgraceful Shalish *on the mainland over there, who were always eating rotten fish. He was from the place where the Sun is born, a land east of the Mountains of the Raven, further east even than the* Blackfoot's *Sea of Grass. He was very old when he told this story, as old as two grandfathers nowadays.*

"His name was Yo-Rib, *and he said his people were called the* Yar-On.**

"Here is how the story goes:

'In the time before I was born, strange canoes appeared one day on the Big Sea Water. There were many of them, coming on the waves like leaves on a stream in the autumn. Some were round as berry bowls and had round sails. Some were flat and long and wide with square sails. Others were tall, with the heads of snakes in front for a totem and had many paddles. It was a great wonder in those times.

Out of those canoes came the Shining Ones. Many of them were smaller than the Yar-Ons, but

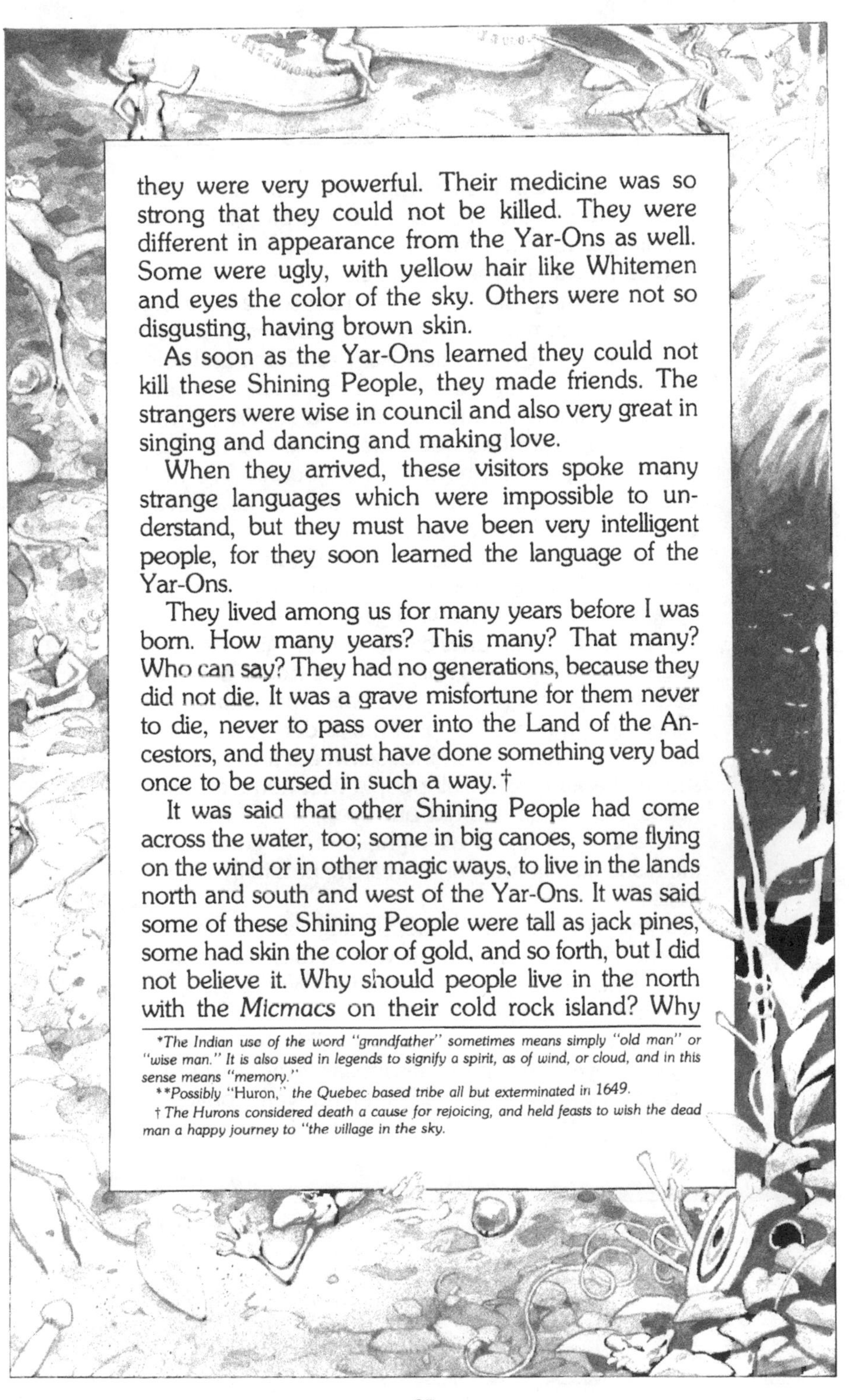

they were very powerful. Their medicine was so strong that they could not be killed. They were different in appearance from the Yar-Ons as well. Some were ugly, with yellow hair like Whitemen and eyes the color of the sky. Others were not so disgusting, having brown skin.

As soon as the Yar-Ons learned they could not kill these Shining People, they made friends. The strangers were wise in council and also very great in singing and dancing and making love.

When they arrived, these visitors spoke many strange languages which were impossible to understand, but they must have been very intelligent people, for they soon learned the language of the Yar-Ons.

They lived among us for many years before I was born. How many years? This many? That many? Who can say? They had no generations, because they did not die. It was a grave misfortune for them never to die, never to pass over into the Land of the Ancestors, and they must have done something very bad once to be cursed in such a way.†

It was said that other Shining People had come across the water, too; some in big canoes, some flying on the wind or in other magic ways, to live in the lands north and south and west of the Yar-Ons. It was said some of these Shining People were tall as jack pines, some had skin the color of gold, and so forth, but I did not believe it. Why should people live in the north with the *Micmacs* on their cold rock island? Why

---

**The Indian use of the word "grandfather" sometimes means simply "old man" or "wise man." It is also used in legends to signify a spirit, as of wind, or cloud, and in this sense means "memory."*

***Possibly* "Huron," *the Quebec based tribe all but exterminated in 1649.*

† The Hurons considered death a cause for rejoicing, and held feasts to wish the dead man a happy journey to "the village in the sky.

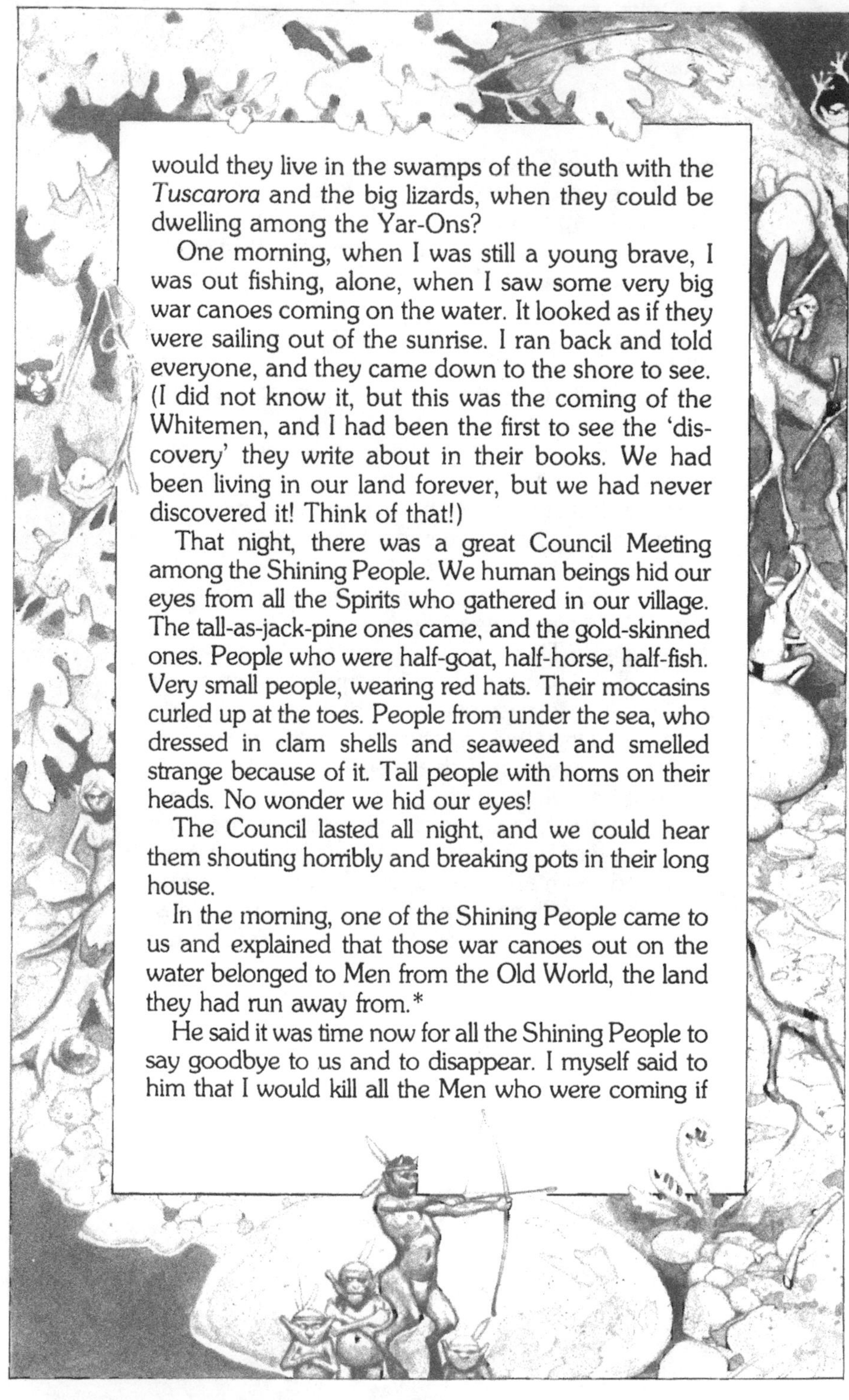

would they live in the swamps of the south with the *Tuscarora* and the big lizards, when they could be dwelling among the Yar-Ons?

One morning, when I was still a young brave, I was out fishing, alone, when I saw some very big war canoes coming on the water. It looked as if they were sailing out of the sunrise. I ran back and told everyone, and they came down to the shore to see. (I did not know it, but this was the coming of the Whitemen, and I had been the first to see the 'discovery' they write about in their books. We had been living in our land forever, but we had never discovered it! Think of that!)

That night, there was a great Council Meeting among the Shining People. We human beings hid our eyes from all the Spirits who gathered in our village. The tall-as-jack-pine ones came, and the gold-skinned ones. People who were half-goat, half-horse, half-fish. Very small people, wearing red hats. Their moccasins curled up at the toes. People from under the sea, who dressed in clam shells and seaweed and smelled strange because of it. Tall people with horns on their heads. No wonder we hid our eyes!

The Council lasted all night, and we could hear them shouting horribly and breaking pots in their long house.

In the morning, one of the Shining People came to us and explained that those war canoes out on the water belonged to Men from the Old World, the land they had run away from.*

He said it was time now for all the Shining People to say goodbye to us and to disappear. I myself said to him that I would kill all the Men who were coming if

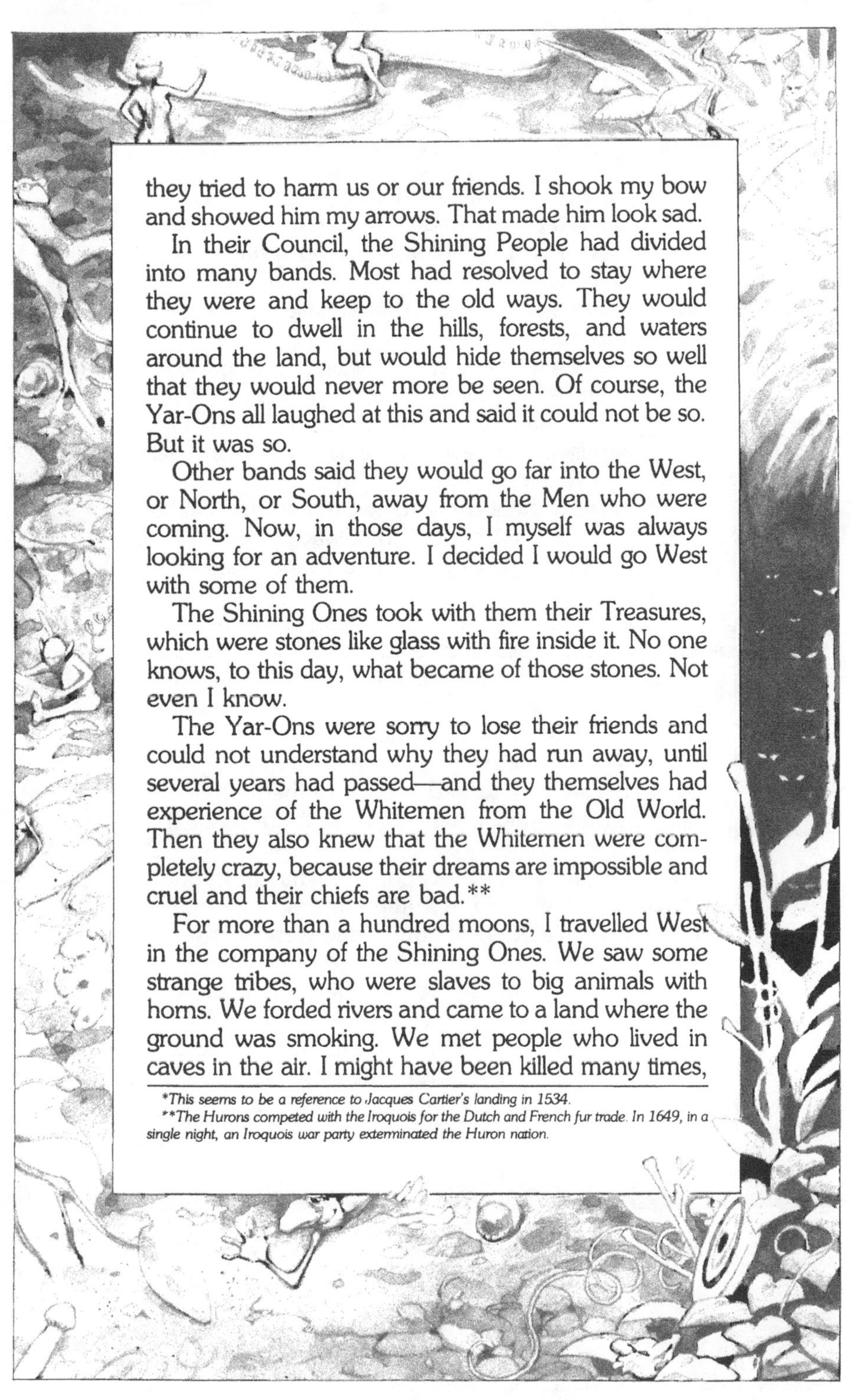

they tried to harm us or our friends. I shook my bow and showed him my arrows. That made him look sad.

In their Council, the Shining People had divided into many bands. Most had resolved to stay where they were and keep to the old ways. They would continue to dwell in the hills, forests, and waters around the land, but would hide themselves so well that they would never more be seen. Of course, the Yar-Ons all laughed at this and said it could not be so. But it was so.

Other bands said they would go far into the West, or North, or South, away from the Men who were coming. Now, in those days, I myself was always looking for an adventure. I decided I would go West with some of them.

The Shining Ones took with them their Treasures, which were stones like glass with fire inside it. No one knows, to this day, what became of those stones. Not even I know.

The Yar-Ons were sorry to lose their friends and could not understand why they had run away, until several years had passed—and they themselves had experience of the Whitemen from the Old World. Then they also knew that the Whitemen were completely crazy, because their dreams are impossible and cruel and their chiefs are bad.**

For more than a hundred moons, I travelled West in the company of the Shining Ones. We saw some strange tribes, who were slaves to big animals with horns. We forded rivers and came to a land where the ground was smoking. We met people who lived in caves in the air. I might have been killed many times,

This seems to be a reference to Jacques Cartier's landing in 1534.

***The Hurons competed with the Iroquois for the Dutch and French fur trade. In 1649, in a single night, an Iroquois war party exterminated the Huron nation.*

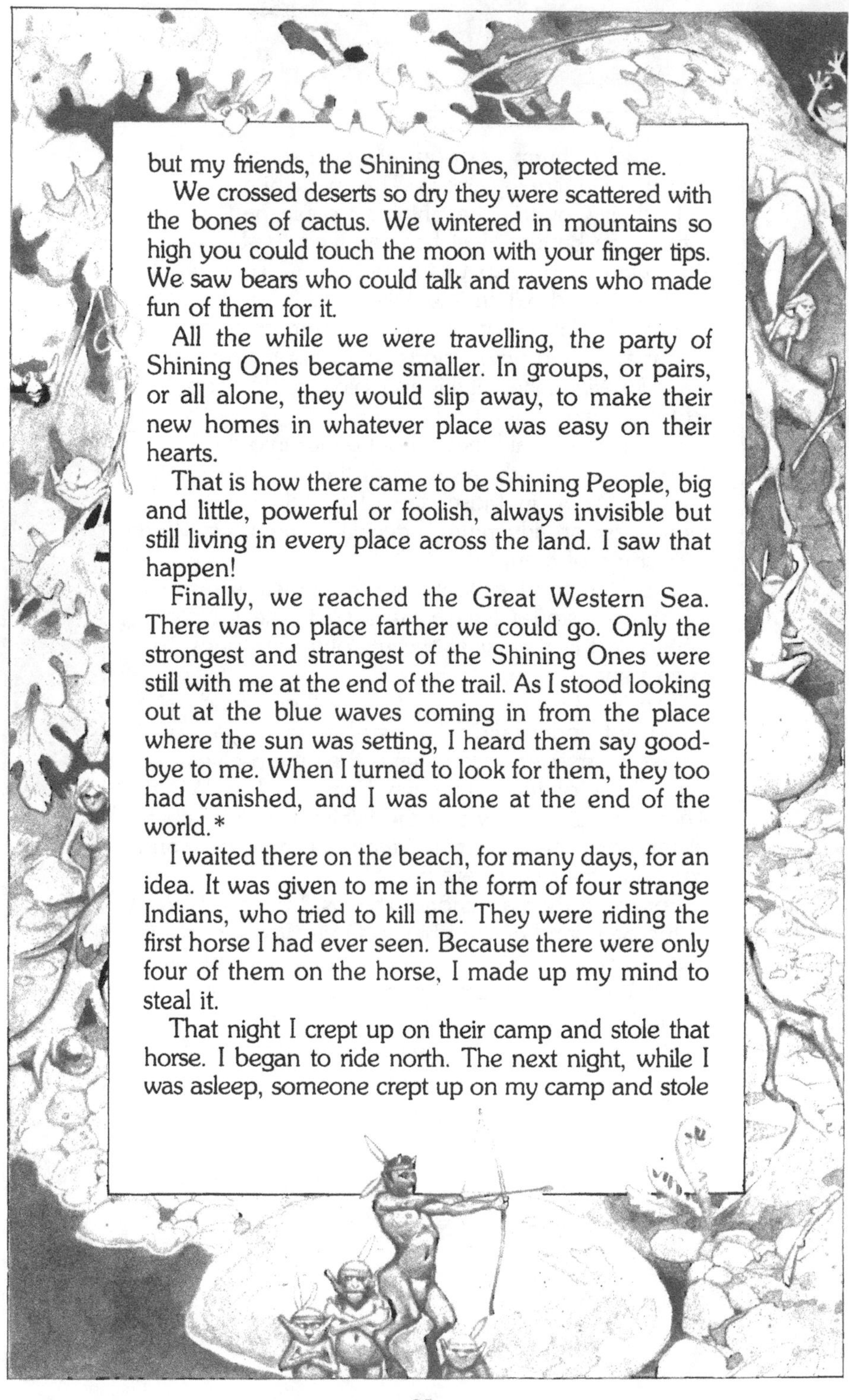

but my friends, the Shining Ones, protected me.

We crossed deserts so dry they were scattered with the bones of cactus. We wintered in mountains so high you could touch the moon with your finger tips. We saw bears who could talk and ravens who made fun of them for it.

All the while we were travelling, the party of Shining Ones became smaller. In groups, or pairs, or all alone, they would slip away, to make their new homes in whatever place was easy on their hearts.

That is how there came to be Shining People, big and little, powerful or foolish, always invisible but still living in every place across the land. I saw that happen!

Finally, we reached the Great Western Sea. There was no place farther we could go. Only the strongest and strangest of the Shining Ones were still with me at the end of the trail. As I stood looking out at the blue waves coming in from the place where the sun was setting, I heard them say good-bye to me. When I turned to look for them, they too had vanished, and I was alone at the end of the world.*

I waited there on the beach, for many days, for an idea. It was given to me in the form of four strange Indians, who tried to kill me. They were riding the first horse I had ever seen. Because there were only four of them on the horse, I made up my mind to steal it.

That night I crept up on their camp and stole that horse. I began to ride north. The next night, while I was asleep, someone crept up on my camp and stole

back the horse. The following night, I took it away again. This went on for some time, with the horse being stolen every night. Finally, I got a good idea. I stole the horse in the afternoon, and got an early start on the trail, so those four Indians were never able to catch up with me.

I rode for many days until at last I came here, to the land of the Nootka. No one here had ever seen a horse, either. They must have thought, seeing me on its back, that I was one of those half-horse men among the Shining Ones, so they let me stay. Here I am.'

That was my grandfather's story."

Like many fabulous, fantastic tales told by Native Americans, this Nootka legend appears to contain some historical truth. The part about the horses, for instance, sounds factual enough . . .

Thus, the tale may explain the mysterious disappearance of the Fair People from this continent. Threatened once again by the coming of Man (with his doubts about Beauty and his faith in Ugliness), the "Shining Ones" fled—into the sea, the hills, the wind, into the wilderness, underground, into diaspora.

Imagine the Leprechauns of Erin (whose earliest roots in the New World were doubtless in Massachusetts) as from their hiding places they watched the Mayflower drop anchor and saw upon its deck a grim-faced throng of Celt-murdering Puritans. . . .

Consider a group of those frugal Lowland Dwarves, the Alven, hovering, invisible, and observing in economic agony while their old friends the *Canarsie* tribe traded Manhattan Island for a handful of trinkets!

**What remained of the shattered Huron nation seems to have later followed the path of these "Shining Ones," wandering through Michigan, Ohio, and Wisconsin. A small band survives in Oklahoma, where they call themselves "Wyandot."*

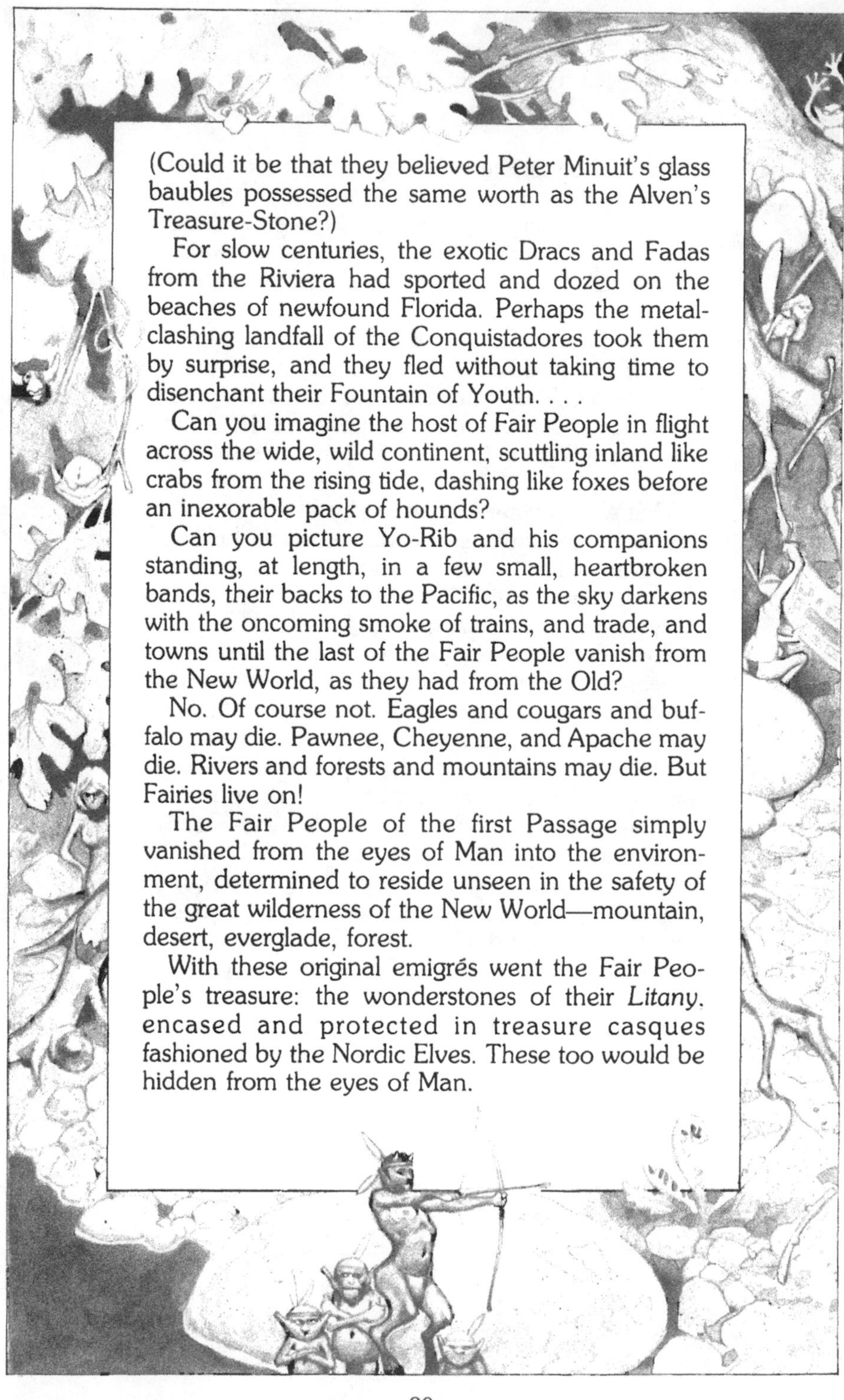

(Could it be that they believed Peter Minuit's glass baubles possessed the same worth as the Alven's Treasure-Stone?)

For slow centuries, the exotic Dracs and Fadas from the Riviera had sported and dozed on the beaches of newfound Florida. Perhaps the metal-clashing landfall of the Conquistadores took them by surprise, and they fled without taking time to disenchant their Fountain of Youth. . . .

Can you imagine the host of Fair People in flight across the wide, wild continent, scuttling inland like crabs from the rising tide, dashing like foxes before an inexorable pack of hounds?

Can you picture Yo-Rib and his companions standing, at length, in a few small, heartbroken bands, their backs to the Pacific, as the sky darkens with the oncoming smoke of trains, and trade, and towns until the last of the Fair People vanish from the New World, as they had from the Old?

No. Of course not. Eagles and cougars and buffalo may die. Pawnee, Cheyenne, and Apache may die. Rivers and forests and mountains may die. But Fairies live on!

The Fair People of the first Passage simply vanished from the eyes of Man into the environment, determined to reside unseen in the safety of the great wilderness of the New World—mountain, desert, everglade, forest.

With these original emigrés went the Fair People's treasure: the wonderstones of their *Litany*, encased and protected in treasure casques fashioned by the Nordic Elves. These too would be hidden from the eyes of Man.

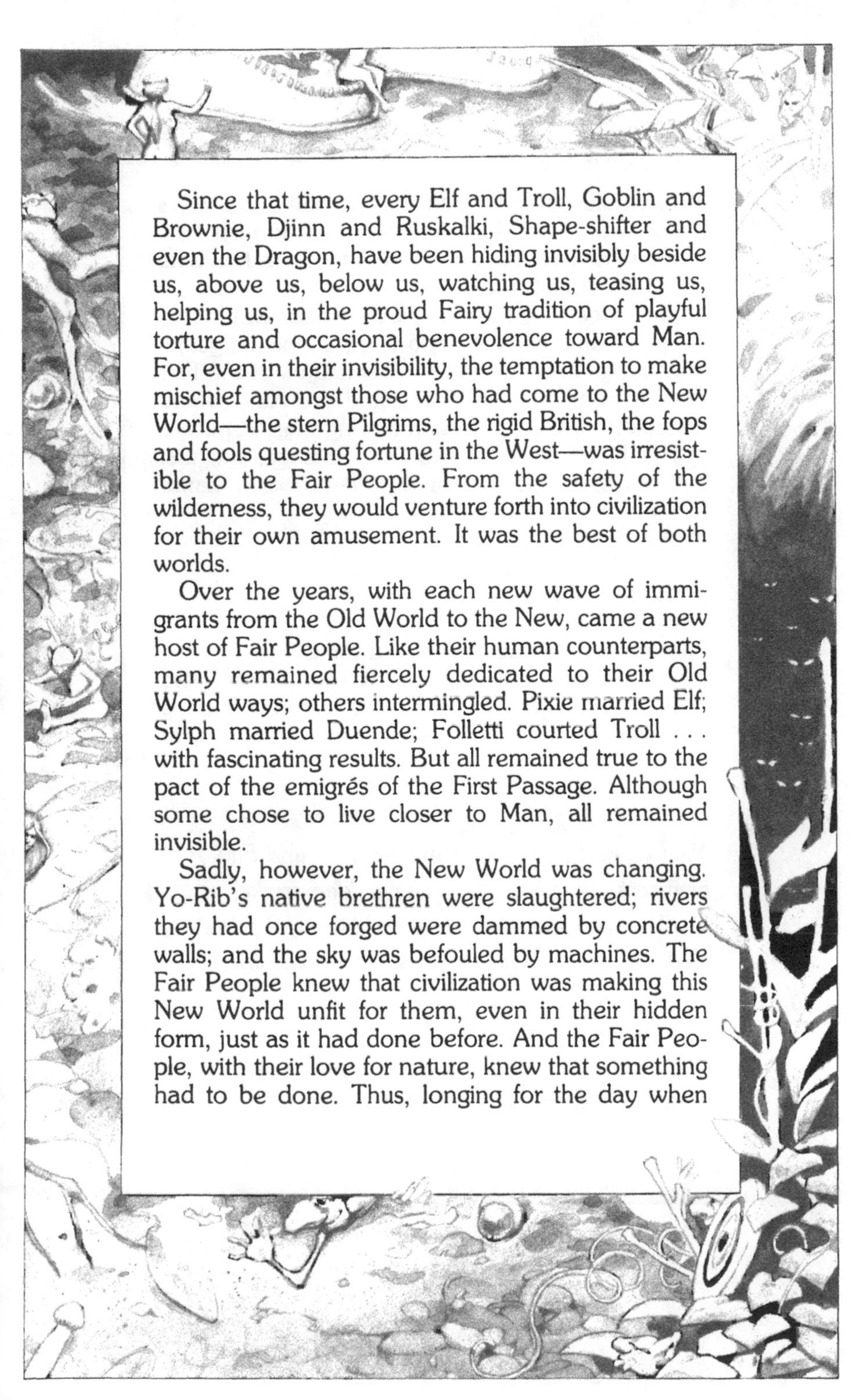

Since that time, every Elf and Troll, Goblin and Brownie, Djinn and Ruskalki, Shape-shifter and even the Dragon, have been hiding invisibly beside us, above us, below us, watching us, teasing us, helping us, in the proud Fairy tradition of playful torture and occasional benevolence toward Man. For, even in their invisibility, the temptation to make mischief amongst those who had come to the New World—the stern Pilgrims, the rigid British, the fops and fools questing fortune in the West—was irresistible to the Fair People. From the safety of the wilderness, they would venture forth into civilization for their own amusement. It was the best of both worlds.

Over the years, with each new wave of immigrants from the Old World to the New, came a new host of Fair People. Like their human counterparts, many remained fiercely dedicated to their Old World ways; others intermingled. Pixie married Elf; Sylph married Duende; Folletti courted Troll . . . with fascinating results. But all remained true to the pact of the emigrés of the First Passage. Although some chose to live closer to Man, all remained invisible.

Sadly, however, the New World was changing. Yo-Rib's native brethren were slaughtered; rivers they had once forged were dammed by concrete walls; and the sky was befouled by machines. The Fair People knew that civilization was making this New World unfit for them, even in their hidden form, just as it had done before. And the Fair People, with their love for nature, knew that something had to be done. Thus, longing for the day when

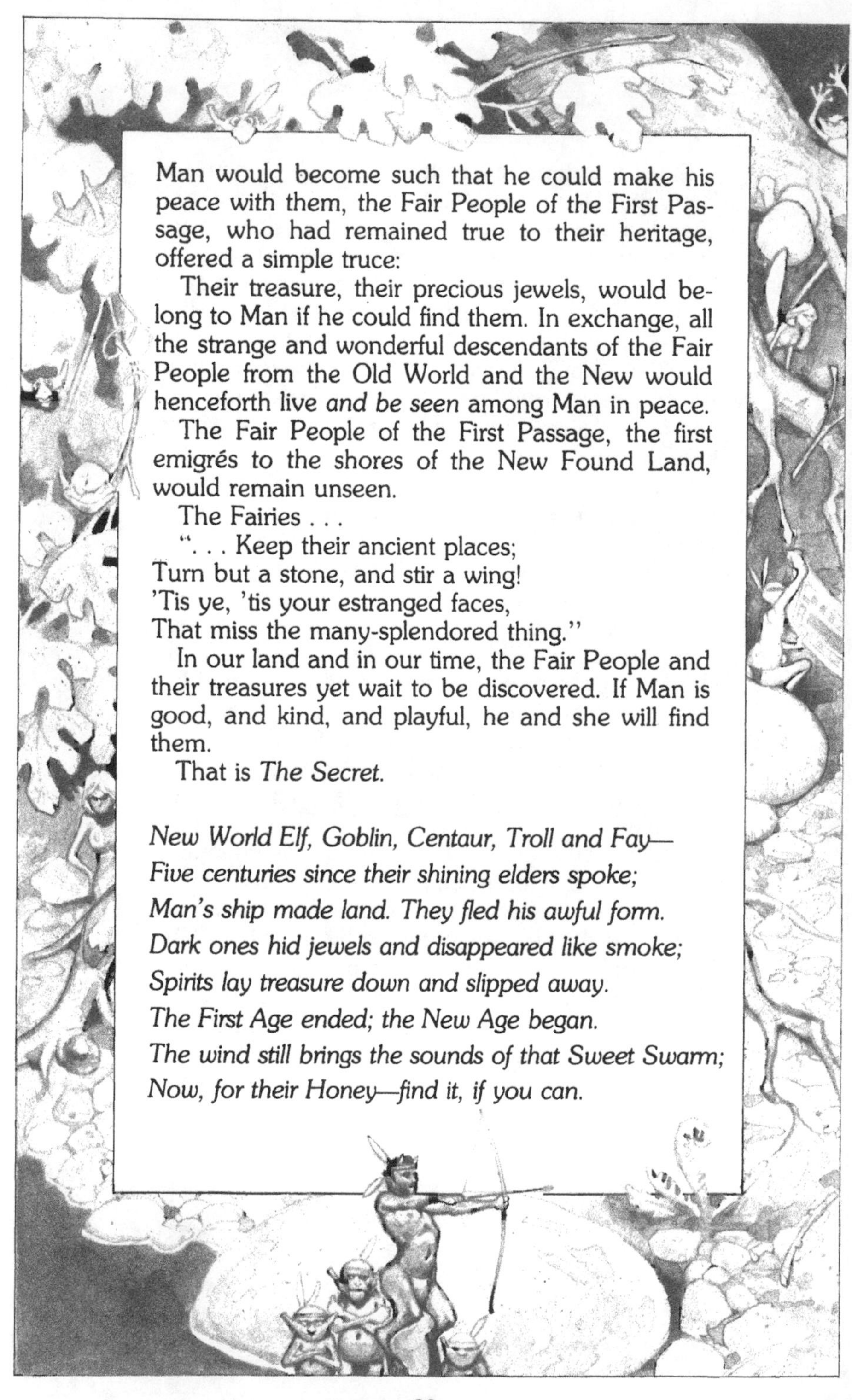

Man would become such that he could make his peace with them, the Fair People of the First Passage, who had remained true to their heritage, offered a simple truce:

Their treasure, their precious jewels, would belong to Man if he could find them. In exchange, all the strange and wonderful descendants of the Fair People from the Old World and the New would henceforth live *and be seen* among Man in peace.

The Fair People of the First Passage, the first emigrés to the shores of the New Found Land, would remain unseen.

The Fairies . . .

". . . Keep their ancient places;
Turn but a stone, and stir a wing!
'Tis ye, 'tis your estranged faces,
That miss the many-splendored thing."

In our land and in our time, the Fair People and their treasures yet wait to be discovered. If Man is good, and kind, and playful, he and she will find them.

That is *The Secret.*

New World Elf, Goblin, Centaur, Troll and Fay—
Five centuries since their shining elders spoke;
Man's ship made land. They fled his awful form.
Dark ones hid jewels and disappeared like smoke;
Spirits lay treasure down and slipped away.
The First Age ended; the New Age began.
The wind still brings the sounds of that Sweet Swarm;
Now, for their Honey—find it, if you can.

THE TREASURE

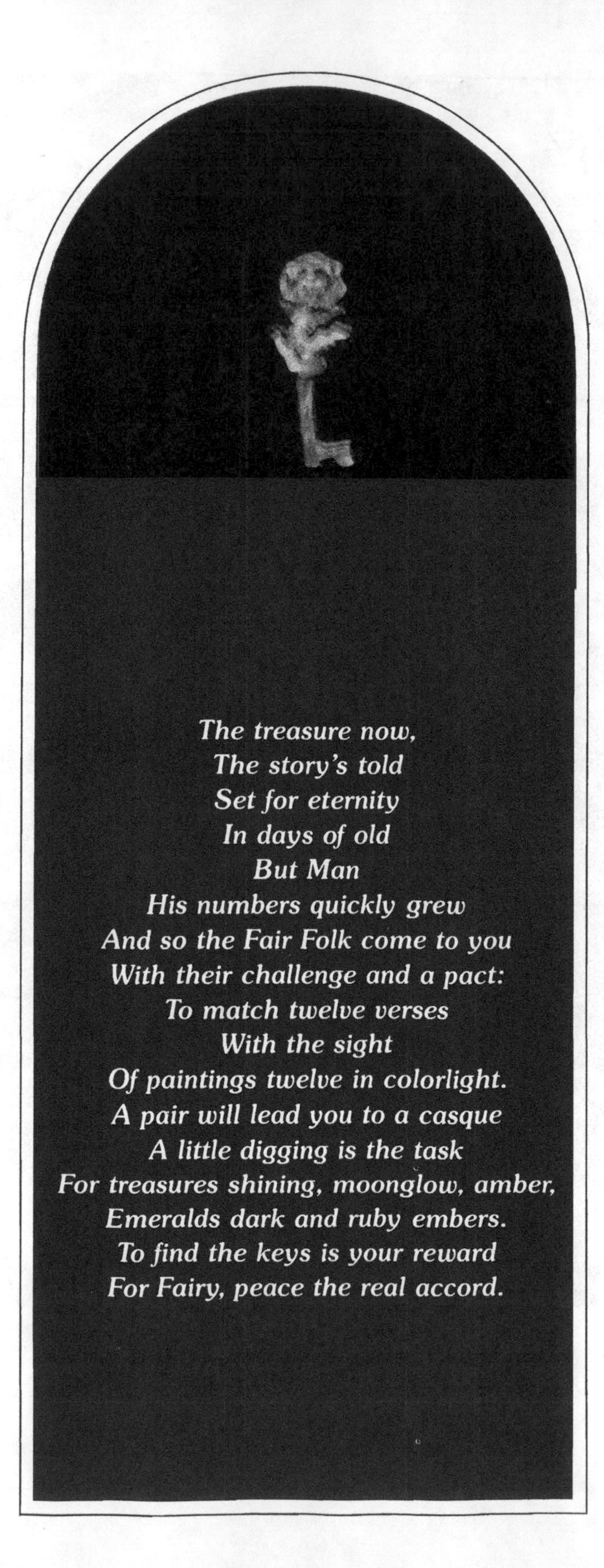

The treasure now,
The story's told
Set for eternity
In days of old
But Man
His numbers quickly grew
And so the Fair Folk come to you
With their challenge and a pact:
To match twelve verses
With the sight
Of paintings twelve in colorlight.
A pair will lead you to a casque
A little digging is the task
For treasures shining, moonglow, amber,
Emeralds dark and ruby embers.
To find the keys is your reward
For Fairy, peace the real accord.

19
PRESERVATION
29

A dozen paintings
Share the clues
Yet Fairy secrets
Come in twos
To sing a happy treasure song
To have a casque to you belong
Wed one picture
With one verse
For Fair Folk's peace
Goodness first.

THE VERSES

THE VERSES

Fortress north
Cold as glass
Friendship south
Take your task
To the number
Nine eight two
Through the wood
No lion fears
In the sky the water veers
Small of scale
Step across
Perspective should not be lost
In the center of four alike
Small, split,
Three winged and slight
What we take to be
Our strongest tower of delight
Falls gently
In December night
Looking back from treasure ground
There's the spout!
A whistle sounds.

At the place where jewels abound
Fifteen rows down to the ground
In the middle of twenty-one
From end to end
Only three stand watch
As the sound of friends
Fills the afternoon hours
Here is a sovereign people
Who build palaces to shelter
Their heads for a night!
Gnomes admire
Fays delight
The namesakes meeting
Near this site.

THE VERSES

If Thucydides is
North of Xenophon
Take five steps
In the area of his direction
A green tower of lights
In the middle section
Near those
Who pass the coliseum
With metal walls
Face the water
Your back to the stairs
Feel at home
All the letters
Are here to see
Eighteenth day
Twelfth hour
Lit by lamplight
In truth, be free.

Beneath two countries
As the road curves
In a rectangular plot
Beneath the tenth stone
From right to left
Beneath the ninth row from the top
Of the wall including small bricks
Seven steps up you can hop
From the bottom level
Socrates, Pindar, Apelles
Free speech, couplet, birch
To find casque's destination
Seek the columns
For the search.

THE VERSES

Lane
Two twenty two
You'll see an arc of lights
Weight and roots extended
Together saved the site
Of granite walls
Wind swept halls
Citadel in the night
A wingless bird ascended
Born of ancient dreams of flight
Beneath the only standing member
Of a forest
To the south
White stone closest
At twelve paces
From the west side
Get permission
To dig out.

Of all the romance retold
Men of tales and tunes
Cruel and bold
Seen here
By eyes of old
Stand and listen to the birds
Hear the cool, clear song of water
Harken to the words:
Freedom at the birth of a century
Or May 1913
Edwin and Edwina named after him
Or on the eighth a scene
Where law defended
Between two arms extended
Below the bar that binds
Beside the long palm's shadow
Embedded in the sand
Waits the Fair remuneration
White house close at hand.

THE VERSES

At stone wall's door
The air smells sweet
Not far away
High posts are three
Education and Justice
For all to see
Sounds from the sky
Near ace is high
Running north, but first across
In jewel's direction
Is an object
Of Twain's attention
Giant pole
Giant step
To the place
The casque is kept.

View the three stories of Mitchell
As you walk the beating of the world
At a distance in time
From three who lived there
At a distance in space
From woman, with harpsichord
Silently playing
Step on nature
Cast in copper
Ascend the 92 steps
After climbing the grand 200
Pass the compass and reach
The foot of the culvert
Below the bridge
Walk 100 paces
Southeast over rock and soil
To the first young birch
Pass three, staying west
You'll see a letter from the country
Of wonderstone's hearth
On a proud, tall fifth
At its southern foot
The treasure waits.

THE VERSES

The first chapter
Written in water
Near men
With wind rose
Behind bending branches
And a green picket fence
At the base of a tall tree
You can still hear the honking
Shell, limestone, silver, salt
Stars move by day
Sails pass by night
Even in darkness
Like moonlight in teardrops
Over the tall grass
Years pass, rain falls.

In the shadow
Of the grey giant
Find the arm that
Extends over the slender path
In summer
You'll often hear a whirring sound
Cars abound
Although the sign
Nearby
Speaks of Indies native
The natives still speak
Of him of Hard word in 3 Vols.
Take twice as many east steps as the hour
Or more
From the middle of one branch
Of the v
Look down
And see simple roots
In rhapsodic man's soil
Or gaze north
Toward the isle of B.

THE VERSES

Pass two friends of octave
In December
Ride the man of oz
To the land near the window
There's a road that leads to
Dark forest
Where white is in color
With two maps
After circle and square
In July and August
A path beckons
To mica and driftwood
Under that
Which may be last touched
Or first seen standing
Look north at the wing
And dig
To achieve
By dauntless and inconquerable
Determination
Your goal.

Where M and B are set in stone
And to Congress, R is known
L sits and left
Beyond his shoulder
Is the Fair Folks'
Treasure holder
The end of ten by thirteen
Is your clue
Fence and fixture
Central too
For finding jewel casque
Seek the sounds
Of rumble
Brush and music
Hush.

A FIELD GUIDE TO THE FAIR PEOPLE

A FIELD GUIDE TO THE FAIR PEOPLE

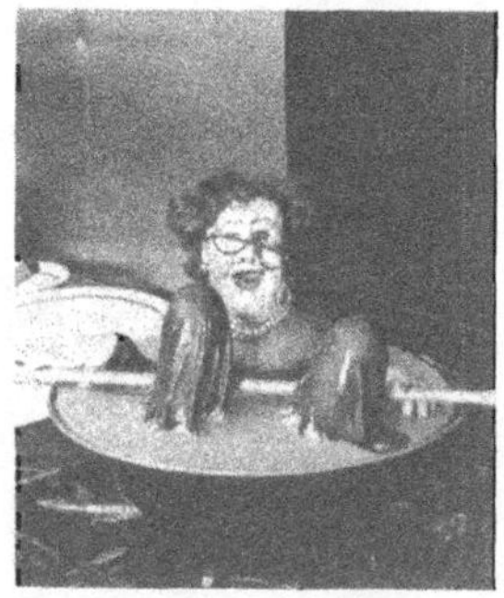

A FIELD GUIDE TO THE FAIR PEOPLE

MAÎTRE D'EAMON

Taboo d'hôte

⊙ **RANGE:** From the wine racks to the coatcheck room, from the sanitary hand-drying machine in the restroom to the basin of melting mints by the cash register; from the "have it our way" roughage window to the garbage-gobbling clown can in the parking lot, the Maître D'eamon calls America's many elegant eateries his home away from home.

◐ **HABITS:** The Maître D'eamon sees to it that when you arrive at a restaurant, the parking lot is full, but a smiling young man is there to take your car. When you escape the restaurant some hours later, the smiling young man is not there. Neither is your car. That is the work of the Maître D'eamon, whose highest calling is to give his victims an evening they will never forget.

When you enter a restaurant to celebrate your anniversary (after planning the occasion for weeks), it is the Maître D'eamon who concocts a mix-up in the reservations. It is he who arranges for you to wait at the bar for an hour with three intoxicated salesmen until the captain says, "Oh, have you been waiting long? We should have a table for you any minute."

Forty minutes later, you are seated. The mysterious stains left on the tablecloth by the Maître D'eamon give you something to talk about until your waiter gets back from the dentist. The Maître has kindly seen to it that you are seated right by the kitchen door, so you have a chance to see how real dishwashers smoke marijuana. (Look at the cook. Did you know they worked with their shirts off?)

At last your dinner arrives. You do not recognize it, thanks to the Maître D'eamon. It was under his influence that you ordered what looks like a briquet from the bowels of Mordor's Mount Doom, and a frozen *something* from icy Lapland.

Dessert? Coffee? A liqueur? *Just the bill?* Very well.

The Maître D'eamon has seen to it that the restaurant does not take credit cards. A check? The restaurant does not take checks. Cash? It does not take cash. Krugerrands. The restaurant takes Krugerrands.

As you are leaving, the D'eamon inspires your waiter to tell you how much the staff enjoyed watching you eat with all the wrong cutlery. You exit the restaurant to the gales of the busboys' laughter and the sight of the captain's palm, patiently waiting for his tip.

No inconvenience is too great for the Maître D'eamon, so long as it is *more* inconvenient for *you*.

★ **HISTORY:** The Maître is un-American. He is unspeakable, uncivilized, inhuman: the Maître D'eamon is French. Arriving in America with Lafayette, he first conveyed his lack of manners to Jefferson's butlers in Monticello. From there, he moved north to the capital, where he currently inflicts a four-star array of annoyances on devotees of Michelin and McDonalds alike.

☞ **SPOTTER'S TIPS:** You will find this creature wherever you find hammered copper coats-of-arms on the walls, tufted naugahyde dining nooks, unlimited salad bars, the piano stylings of Hugh LaGoon, sink-sized brandy snifters, a wine list as big as a family Bible, and a waiter whose hair has been painted on . . . by the Maître D'eamon himself.

DINING
GUESTS
SEATED

SWEATSYLPHS

Athletarum supportatae

⊙ **Range:** Once upon a time, these physical phitness phiends plagued only the (otherwise idle) rich. Their exclusive haunts were then-restricted Athletic Clubs, the gymnasiums of well-endowed universities, and elite health spas; so it was commonly believed that the creatures' earthly mission was to tempt and taunt the inbred and overfed into working up the only honest sweats of their lives.

Lately, however, members of the middle class, and even people with jobs, have begun to break out in sneakers and head bands and can be seen staggering and hyperventilating through the dawn-lit streets, the whole world their treadmill, jowls flushed, eyes blank, obviously bewitched and utterly in the power of some sinister supernatural force—the Sweatsylphs.

◐ **Habits:** Sweatsylphs feed on human *ergs*, units of energy released by burning calories. (Among their favorite meals are scrambled ergs, ergs benedict, and erg rolls.) As their miserable mortal victims trot, bend, squat, run, jump, clean and jerk, dive and paddle, haul and crawl in order to grow slim, Sweatsylphs hover above them, chuckling and growing ever more plump and happy.

Sweatsylphs discourage our interest in team sports—after all, fullbacks and outfielders sometimes get a chance to stand around, enjoying themselves—and encourage us to go "one on one," in games where personal shame and hostility drive us to heights of excessive activity—or, better yet, to "compete only with ourselves," in ligament-straining, lung-busting, mindless orgies of exhibitionistic exertion.

To the Sweatsylph, the only sight sweeter than a squash raquet is a running track a sixteenth of a mile in circumference.

★ **History:** Sweatsylphs are Greek and, like all Greek Sylphs, were notoriously sylphish about their sylph-improvement programs. The first of them were nourished by the smoke of the earliest Olympic flame and by the acrid fumes arising from the field below, where oiled and naked youths struggled to heave a pie plate for distance while barbarians were breaking down the gates.

In America mortals tended to avoid physical exercise, exertion, or activity of any kind—hence the popularity of the industrial revolution, spectator sports, televised spectator sports, and then the epidemic of video games. Things were looking bad for the sweat-starved Sweatsylphs. But a desperate public relations campaign, waged with the help of their fellow wicked sprites, the West Ghost and Elf Alpha, has convinced us all that we will be flabby and unloved unless we start running twenty miles a day, fueled only by turnip juice and our mantra. So we *run* and grow thinner and grimmer, and the Sweatsylphs are fat and sassy again.

☞ **Spotter's Tips:** Look for a Sweatsylph where a yacht owner buys a rowing machine or drives five hundred miles in search of the perfect jogging suit, and when the funeral of a tennis court cardiac-arrest victim is attended by plump survivors, all bravely fighting back their smiles.

PREPS GHOUL

Stupidissimus scholarum

⊙ **RANGE**: These most class-conscious of all sprites haunt private school reunions, society weddings, ski resorts, regattas, hunt club balls, squash, racketball, and bankruptcy courts; that is, wherever the alumni of expensive boarding schools are likely to be found.

◐ **HABITS**: Preps Ghouls like to get under the (upper) crust of the well (white)-bred. It is they who sprinkle dandruff on the shoulders of every navy blue blazer, dab a seagull dropping on the peak of each yachting cap, add a splash of hollandaise to every old school tie, spill a too-too embarrassing Bloody Mary stain on every white pleated skirt, and insert a bit of spinach (from the quiche) between the teeth of the hostess in the reception line.

The favorite trick of a Preps Ghoul is to assume the form of the former class nerd (whose name you simply *cawn't* remember), let it be known that he has done very *very* well, and then . . . not recognize *you!*

When tormented by excessive Preppy manifestations—an outbreak of madras, monograms, and duck

prints, for example—try the *Caulfield Maneuvre:* put a red hunting hat on backwards and have a nervous breakdown.

★ **HISTORY**: Preps Ghouls hail, of course, from England, where private schools are called public schools (because they aren't) and are all named (appropriately) after impossibly tight collars (Eton), or inflated pigs' bladders (Rugby). The original Preps Ghoul attended the latter institution, and wrote the book, *Tom Brownie's Ghoul Days.*

The Yankee Preps Ghouls' ancestors came over (steerage) on the Mayflower, to New England, where they hoped the Puritan work ethic would apply only to the working class. Here, they tended the ivy and climbed with it.

They can now be found throughout America, wherever the *parvenu* rich don't want their offspring to have to compete in examinations against the children of the intelligent.

☞ **SPOTTER'S TIPS**: You will find the Preps Ghoul loitering about wherever balding blond people of either sex look—and laugh—like their horses.

THE WEST GHOST

Narcissus Pacificus

⊙ **RANGE**: You will find the West Ghost anywhere you go looking to find yourself—from the organic taco stands of Chula Vista to Ken Kesey's contented cattle ranch in Oregon. In search of cool, the W.G. occasionally drifts as far north as the goose-bumpy nude beaches of Vancouver. From the Rocky Mountain High Sierra clubs to the Hodaddy-clotted breakers off Catalina, in the waterbedrooms and extremely bored rooms, touching, relating, sharing, taking lunches and giving phone, the West Ghost does his thing, always here, always now.

◐ **HABITS**: The West Ghost lures his victims out to the earthquake perilled, partially reclaimed desert, with rumors of gold and legends of promiscuity. Once they are on his surf and turf, he implants in the sun-stroked minds of his prey the notion that a soak in a barrel of sweat with a coven of fellow Californians is a pleasant way to spend a couple of days. He enables one to enjoy listening to an entire game on the car radio while driving to and from the stadium. He inspires palimony disputes after the break-up of group marriages. He implants dozens of absolutely *outrageous* ideas for High-Concept situation comedies in the Perrier-addled noggins of his protegés. In return for feeding him five pounds of ocean temperature raw sea urchin, he'll slip you the home phone number of a studio exec at Fox. He gives you a sunburn where the moon don't shine.

★ **HISTORY**: The West Ghost's trendy—and ever-changing—appearance materializes out of a dense, deadly, drifting smog, composed of the exhaust of Okies' model Ts, steam released by the 750-foot papier-mâché volcano in Disneyland, a mist of genelethal insecticides, smoke of a thousand movie moguls' cigars and the incinerated dreams of ten thousand Midwest bottleblonds, vaporous exudations of beached whales mingled with the reek of hair oil, salad oil, suntan oil, snake oil, extremely crude oil, oiled palms, and oil of LA.

☞ **SPOTTER'S TIPS**: The West Ghost is invisible when viewed through sunglasses. Thus, it can be seen only by recent arrivals from the East, which explains the look of terror on their pale faces as they dodge from shadow to shadow down the palm-lined sunblasted boulevards.

The West Ghost is rilly, rilly, like, *into* his California life-style, y'know?

THE PILL GRIM

Prudens pudenda

⊙ **RANGE:** There is scarcely a human activity into which this prig-let does not stick her (blue) nose, sniffling for smut. She can be found, an expression of self-righteousness on her puss, snooping through your mail, your past, your motives, your laundry, your files, your habits, and your keyhole. Suspicious of any pleasure, however slight, the Pill Grim haunts the offices of district attorneys up for re-election, antivice vigilante covens, and gatherings of any group whose Majority assumes the title of Moral (the better to suppress both sugar and spice).

◐ **HABITS:** Infused with the Goblinoid equivalent of the Protestant work ethic, the Pill Grim keeps busy sharpening the blue pencils and scissors of censors, bleeping talk shows, and ripping open plain brown wrappers so that the postman, at least, knows what kind of pervert you secretly are.

The name tells you all you need to know: *"Pill:* an objectionable person; a bore" *(OED). Grim:* a venerable name among Goblins . . ." (Katharine Briggs, *An Encyclopedia of Fairies,* page 205.) Hence, *Pill Grim:* a boring, objectionable old Goblin.

One of this grim Grim's nastier tricks is to knock that sensible creature, Conscience, off her perch, and to usurp her place. Then the Pill Grim will fill you with shame at the sight of sex and enable you to see sex everywhere.

Yet lust is not the Pill Grim's only obsession. Wine, candy, music, sleeping in, second helpings—even the circus is all looked down on, as is anything else that looks suspiciously like fun.

Recently changes in public and private morality (the work of creatures like The West Ghost and the Evil Neckromancers) appeared to endanger the Grim. People of all ages, nude except for the earphones of their Sony Walkmen, were rumored to be leaping into hot tubs, swilling champagne, shamelessly massaging themselves and each other, necking in or on parked or moving automobiles, indulging in a wide variety of coed contact sports and dancing. Fun or not, all these activities appear to be so to the Pill Grim.

But the crafty Pill Grim has turned this to her advantage. Across the land, a generation of snappily-attired, sex-manual-reading would-be hedonists now writhe, in an agony of guilt, because they aren't getting *enough* fun! Well done, Pill Grim!

★ **HISTORY:** Long before the decently clad figurehead of the Mayflower had occasion to frown sternly at the New World's wantonly naked cliffs and the shockingly undisciplined surf off Plymouth, certain troll-black, no-nonsense Fairy forerunners of the Puritans had preceded them thither.

These sourpuss Spirits, scandalized by the endless merry dancing, tune-piping, teasing, tickling and giggling of their fellow English hobgoblins, founded the famous Dull Jack (all work, no play) Colony, and were the ancestors of the present day Pill Grim.

The Pill Grim found much to admire in the conduct of the Shakers, an early American religious sect sworn to chastity and carpentry. The Shakers pursued their ideals with such fervor that today there are plenty of hard, straight-backed chairs and few Shakers. The Pill Grim has had to turn her attention to the remainder of American society.

☞ **SPOTTER'S TIPS:** You don't spy on the Pill Grim—you counterspy. In fact, the emotional state commonly diagnosed as paranoia is often simply an acute awareness of a Pill Grim's Progress.

FREUDIAN SYLPHS

Pes in orae

⊙ **RANGE:** This embarrassing sprite can pop out anywhere, but the more delicate the situation, the more likely her materialization.

She frequently appears during introductions to important and sensitive strangers, and one finds oneself uttering, "The pleasure is *neutral*, I'm sure." At testimonials: "How can you ever thank me enough?" Or on any occasion when you would most like to keep your feelings to yourself and just make small talk: "Well, *hello!* I *have* been looking forward to *mating* with you!" Funeral parlors are among her favorite haunts: "My feet are *killing* me"; "Honestly, I could have just *died*"; "That's a *dead* issue"; and "Sorry we were late, but we were *buried* in traffic." These are just a few examples of her handiwork.

◐ **HABITS:** Not for nothing is the Freudian Sylph also known as the Truth Fairy. She cruelly deceives you into believing that you can untie your knotted tongue by putting your foot in your mouth.

Herewith follow some examples of her work—no need to describe the company in which she caused the following utterances: "It was a pretty lame excuse." "Fat chance." "Call me a cockeyed optimist, but . . ." "Of course, it was a bald lie!" and "Well, they say love is blind . . ."

Sometimes the Freudian Sylph makes actions speak louder than words, as when she inspires the hostess to murmur a seemingly innocuous "Sweets for the sweet" before passing the nuts to an outpatient or a shrimp to a little person.

A human being plagued by these creatures often feels a deep-seated compulsion to pay large amounts of money to a self-proclaimed Exorcist (or Therapist) for the privilege of stretching out on a Naugahyde divan and raving on about his or her dreams. The Sylphs themselves are extremely diminutive and thus feel no need to be shrunk.

★ **HISTORY:** Freudian Sylphs are among the most recently uncovered of preternatural beings, the first of them having emerged, unbidden, from the mouth of a Viennese neurotic in this century.

They breed like Gypsies (as one would doubtless observe, in the company of a Roumanian), and spread like cancer (to change the metaphor to one regrettable but inevitable in the presence of a chemotherapy patient).

The Sylphs arrived in America hidden away in the corners of the very interestingly shaped carpet bags of immigrant psychoanalysts. They have been especially active in the political realm, and have inspired many a revealing *gaffe*—for example, the Senator who *meant* to say, "All these nice *bright* faces" or the Congressman who explained, "I'm in favor of restoring the *graft*."

Among their recent masterpieces was the statement by a U.S. diplomat that the Arabs and Jews should settle their differences in a Christian manner.

☞ **SPOTTER'S TIPS:** A Freudian Sylph looms, and prepares to pounce, wherever the well intentioned socialize with the vulnerable, wherever a sudden intimation of lust or hostility would do the most harm.

One becomes aware of a personal visitation by the creature when, as the words leave one's mouth, one has the sensation of having stepped into an open elevator shaft.

In her wake, the Freudian Sylph leaves twitching clusters of mortals, humiliated, exposed, blushing furiously, and improvising violent coughing fits.

THE SCREAMING MIMI

Infans infernus inflictus

⊙ **RANGE:** These tiny terrors are actually "changelings"—wicked creatures which the fairies swap for human babies. Screaming Mimis infest public places: churches, fine restaurants, and the occasional concert. Their ear-piercing shrieks are inevitable on any public means of transportation, as well—trains, buses, planes, and (especially) elevators. Although hideously audible and appallingly visible to strangers, the Screaming Mimi appears to members of its own family as a sweet chirping cherub.

◐ **HABITS:** It is a curious paradox that while the birthrate of American infants declines, the Screaming Mimi population is booming. Perhaps this is because the minuscule monsters are most commonly seen and heard by the "child-free." The more child-free adults there are around, the more the Screaming Mimi will be seen—and feared.

The Screaming Mimi's full throated howls of outrage, boredom and frustration are especially upsetting when they occur, as they most often do, in outrageously boring and frustrating situations. (See "Range," above). For shamelessly expressing what the rest of us actually feel, Mimi draws a lot of dirty looks.

To all but its mother, the most horrible aspect of the Screaming Mimi's behavior is its vampire-like quality. Believe it or not, those haunting, unearthly, nocturnal wails signify the creature's desire to fasten its mouth upon the breast of a mortal woman and extract the life-giving fluids!

★ **HISTORY:** This fiend-in-infant-form first appeared in the cradles of Olde England. This may account for the Anglo-Saxons' preference for the companionship of dogs and their habit of belaboring the buttocks off their offspring with flails, canes, and stout oak cudgels.

To the thatch-brained serfs of Britain, the Screaming Mimi was known as a "Changeling." In America, it is often diagnosed as hyperactive.

Numerous Screaming Mimis yowling in the homespun cribs of the thirteen original colonies inspired Daniel Boone, Lewis and Clark, and other pioneer patriarchs to explore the West. Anything to get out of the house.

☞ **SPOTTER'S TIPS:** In addition to its characteristic noise, a certain odor is often an indication of the Screaming Mimi's presence. It's a sort of ammonia-like aroma, alone or accompanied by a dark, heavy sulphurous scent not unlike that of English cooking.

This Screaming Mimi needs Changeling. Mother wishes the stork would take her back.

THE JOKE FIEND

Numerous non humorous

⊙ **RANGE:** The Joke Fiend mainly works men's clubs and variety shows, occasionally opens for rock acts, but is often to be found in bars, restaurants, and living rooms; wherever more than one or two are gathered together to tell funny stories (or "cute ones" as they are often called), the Joke Fiend performs his malevolent *schtick*.

◐ **HABITS:** The Joke Fiend literally possesses its poor victim, amateur and professional alike, and makes him tell jokes. The creature is particularly remarkable for its lack of a sense of humor, as should be obvious from its name. Its idea of a "hot one" is to coax the social misfit to tell a joke completely inappropriate to the company: Ikey and Izzy jokes at bar mitzvahs, Rastus and Mandy jokes at Urban League cocktail parties, Pat and Mike stories at the Police Brotherhood meetings, and jokes with any sex at all in them to *Ms.* magazine editors.

★ **HISTORY:** When asked by noted comedian Henny Youngman to explain its origins, the Joke Fiend (for once) refused to speak—invoking, we are to suppose, a gag rule. The Joke Fiend is believed to have been first sighted in America by Washington Irving during a trip to the Catskill Mountains in 1838. Mr. Irving was researching his *Rip Van Winkle.* The Joke Fiend was playing the Lounge.

☞ **SPOTTER'S TIPS:** Wherever squirt flowers, light-up bow ties, hand buzzers, whoopee cushions, dribble glasses or Shriners' conventions can be found, there also is the Joke Fiend.

J. F., corny as Kansas, visits Henny Youngman for good material.

HOUSEHOLD UNFAMILIARS

Calamitates materfamiliae

⊙ **RANGE:** First apartments, charming old houses, quaint summer cottages, experimental solar living modules, completely remodeled kitchens, dens that need some work, unfinished basements, north-lit studios, semi-equipped lofts and secure subterranean bed-sitters.

◐ **HABITS:** In any household with which you are unfamiliar, there you will find the Household Unfamiliars. Be it your first apartment or your last nursing home, these devilish sprites are there with a litany of liabilities: Putting the light switch on the wrong side of the door, mysteriously adding or subtracting a step from the stairs in the dark, blowing the bathroom door locked behind you, shifting ankle-breaking furniture while your attention is elsewhere, jamming windows open or closed, exchanging handles on the shower controls, breaking knobs off in your hands, and stacking pyramids of head-thumping canned goods on unstable shelves in innocent looking closets.

All these pranks and more are the work of the Household Unfamiliar—but his special province is the refrigerator, where he moves as soon as you start to feel at home. Ostensibly, his job there is to turn the light off when you open the door and on when you close it, but he further diverts himself by lending to your costly imported beer a skunk-like odor, tempering your cheese to a gem-like hardness, and spilling dill brine into the yogurt. He specializes in unscheduled defrostings and freezer burns.

Old wives' tales have it that open boxes of baking soda and herbal bouquets deter the Household Unfamiliar from his activities. But as any housekeeper can tell you, you are just as likely to find a spilled box of baking soda and a broken bouquet of herbs commingled on top of the mousse.

★ **HISTORY:** As might be assumed from the Household Unfamiliar's preference for the chilly regions of the refrigerator, this creature came to us from Scandinavia, a direct descendant of that Nordic domestic pest, the Kobold. Thus, however neatly you box, store, cap, and wrap your foodstuffs, these "frigidaredevils" believe that what you wish to find when you open the door is a smorgasbord.

During the course of the Household Unfamiliar's food scattering experiments, that great American dish, chow mein, was invented.

☞ **SPOTTER'S TIPS:** *In the fridge:* green spots on the bread, ketchup spots on the ice cream, and gravy spots on the lettuce. *In the rest of the house:* brown spots on the bathroom ceiling, yellow spots on the mattress, and indelible spots on the laundry.

MATZO
MEAL
Gold's

SCRUBUBUS

Sanitas furioso

⊙ **RANGE:** From the space-age plastic sheen of the vinyl-tiled floor in the germ-and-mildew-free basement, to the gleaming unclogged galvanized raingutters and sanitized chimney on the well-scrubbed roof . . . amongst the velvet-bagged untarnished silverware, the neatly stacked and daily-dusted china, the square-cornered piles of plush and fluffy towels . . . in contour corners . . . Pasteurized commodes . . . Everywhere a nosey neighbor or critical in-law could pry, peer, sniff, or stroke with the fingertip of a white glove—in every germ-free nook and sterilized cranny of the paranoid nightmare of the American home.

◐ **HABITS:** These wretched household creatures torment housewives into frenzies of lustration by leaving thumb prints, dust motes, fly flecks, stains, smudges, spots, and smears on the household furniture, utensils, hardware, and dry goods. The poor *hausfrau,* her brain softened by the hysterical importunings to hermetic hygiene on television—it is no coincidence her favorite shows are called *Soaps*—is incited to further paroxysms of ablution by the Scrububus' mystical incantation:

"All Joy! Shout Jubilee! Bravo! Yes, Bon Ami, Behold Dawn Vanish Like Magic! Cheer Bold Fantastik Future Era! Banish Sea Mist So Fast, Vigilant Arm and Hammer! Whish, Comet! Dazzle! Twinkle, Beacon! Sparkle! Cascade, Tide! Duz Pride Gain Favor? Preen, Fleecy, Brite, Downy, Snowy Dove!"

★ **HISTORY:** As everyone knows, "Brownies" are the helpful household spirits of England and Scotland, and many tales are told of their domestic kindnesses. But when the first immigrant Brownie reported for duty in the first American kitchen, the (Puritan Pilgrim) housewife saw only an insalubrious brown smudge besmirching her spotless white tile, and clubbed him with a bar of lye soap. Our national obsession with high-gloss disinfected surfaces is the Brownies' revenge.

☞ **SPOTTER'S TIPS:** Spotters, indeed! Out! *Out!* OUT!

The Scrububus, that Mother's Little Helper, keeps places like Iowa squeaky-clean.

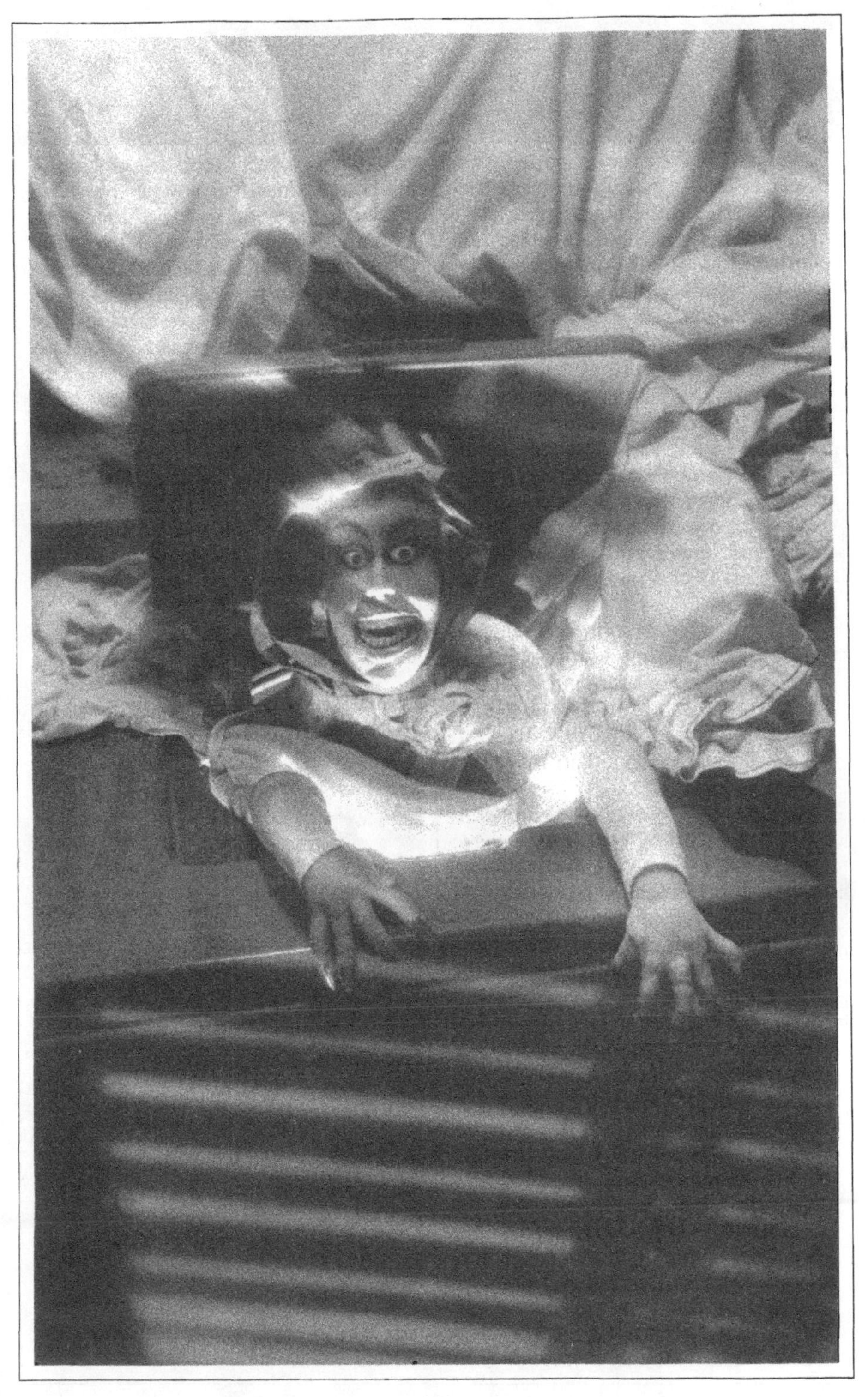

THE GARDENGOYLE

Horror cultus

⊙ **RANGE**: Wherever paper seed packs, faded to indecipherability, look down from weathered popsicle sticks upon rows of deeply disturbed topsoil; near window boxes enriched by alkaline pigeon droppings, roof gardens watered by acid rain, and where elderly but energetic horticulturists minister to necrotic carrots in stony vacant lots, there strolls the Gardengoyle.

◐ **HABITS**: Summer after summer, pest and pestilences descend on the backyard gardens of America: rabbits with the destructive abilities of warthog troops, for example, or moldy blights that wither green and growing things like a blast of the midsummer sun on Serengeti.

Yet spring after spring, Americans root up foul-smelling compost heaps, break fork tines on adamantine topsoil, and wear out countless layers of epidermis plying absurd backward hoes allegedly designed to make the work go easier.

And it is the Gardengoyle who wickedly inspires these people to believe that *this* year will at last mean success for their little garden because whatever the Gardengoyle did to it last year is simply too horrible to occur twice in the same patch on the same planet in the same century.

The Gardengoyle is a master of blights and a smut monger. He is adept at the distribution of cutworms and beetles. Where the gypsy moth pitches its tent, you may find the Gardengoyle, seeking shelter from the hail storm he has just caused to beat sprouting produce into mouldering ratatouille.

★ **HISTORY**: The Gardengoyle hails from the region of North Africa formerly known as the Saharan Garden, now more widely known as the Sahara Desert. He helped out in the New World Garden at the Plymouth Colony, where yearly crop failures made the poor Puritans so hungry that even turkey tasted good to them. Later, the Gardengoyle took a special interest in Oklahoma and the surrounding states, where a succession of disastrous droughts gave the simple religious folk of the region an abiding taste for water, which many are hard put to understand.

☞ **SPOTTER'S TIPS**: The careful hoe-towing seeker of the Gardengoyle may have some luck as he is a large, frisky green spirit resembling an ambulatory shock of corn and is to be found most often amongst the small, withered brownish rust-slighted vegetables in his charge.

The Gardengoyle is an agro-vation from Omaha to Miami.

SAUCIER'S APPRENTICES

Cuisinart gratia artis

⊙ **RANGE:** Four-star French restaurants, executive dining rooms, diplomatic pieds-à-terre, country club kitchens, even The Average American Home—wherever pretentious food is being prepared (or attempted), these wicked imps can be found, and the more *haute* the *cuisine,* the higher the jinks they're up to. They inhabit the oven, for extreme heat does not bother them as they perform ritual cake deflations inside. Nor do they mind the refrigerator's cold, as they gnaw away at the cellophane, all the better to "freezer burn" those treasured filets. Chances are, *your* kitchen is full of them—*n'est-ce pas?*

◐ **HABITS:** Like good chefs everywhere, the Saucier's Apprentices know that preparation is so important. Thus, hours before the cooking is to begin, they are busy in the kitchen, blunting the knives, bending the spoons, jamming the blender, blowing out the pilot light, hiding the butter, and souring the cream.

They are never happier than when a perfectly normal mortal decides to "really get into cooking," and to that end acquires numerous, indecipherable recipe books and elaborate expensive utensils—preferably electric and dangerous. A classic Saucier's Apprentice technique (or "truc") is to spill tomato sauce on a metric conversion table, which can result in some amazingly good concoctions accidentally being whipped up by the Apprentice's victim, who thereafter must guess at the proportions, should he or she ever wish to make the dish again.

Malfunctioning scales, timers and thermometers? Off-speed Cuisinarts, lukewarm ice cream makers, pasty pasta? If your gourmet meal looks slightly unreal, blame the Saucier's Apprentice.

★ **HISTORY:** Many believe that Saucier's Apprentices are of French extraction, but anyone who has eaten in England knows better. They are, in fact, Hob Goblins, (first described in the Julia Childe Ballads) the legendary spirits of the British fireside, who burnt the cakes for King Alfred and whose hideous names have been given to so many British dishes: Bubble and Squeak, Banger, Toad in Hole, Pig in a Blanket, etc. An aristocratic member of the family is to this day responsible for all runny omelettes: Will o' the Whisk.

Confined at first to the kitchens of the very rich in America, the Saucier's Apprentices have become dangerously active in recent years with the malevolent help of the Mind Boggles, through whose channels they introduced the blasphemous rites of foreign cooking into the hearts and kitchens of the formerly naive and hamburger-happy homemakers of the United States. Many a harmless Shake-and-Baker has thus been Bearded in her den, transformed into a veal-boning, Hollandazed, stir-crazy, woked-out, long order kook.

☞ **SPOTTER'S TIPS:** If you have shell fragments in the scrambled eggs, lumps in the gravy, charcoal toast, oil slicks in the soup, concrete croissants, silly millimeter-high soufflés, a julienned index finger and a well-done thumb, then you have Saucier's Apprentices infesting your kitchen. Send out for Chinese.

HANDIMANTICORE

Ars amputat artus

⊙ **RANGE:** Down in the basement workshop, where Dad's soldering his fingers together. Up on the roof with Sis, who's installing the weather vane lightning rod FM antenna in a thunderstorm. Out in the garage, where Junior is checking for fuel line clogs, with the aid of his Bic. Up in her den, where Mom's slant-stitching her nose to a dirndl hem.

In, on, and around the home, wherever Americans conclude that there's no point paying a professional to do this, when for just a little more money they can screw it up themselves-- Handimanticore, the handy manti, is lending a helping hand.

◐ **HABITS:** Handy Andy is an unselfish fellow. Having inspired a mortal to attempt domestic arts and crafts, he often turns his victims over into the waiting area of another malevolent spirit— The Gardengoyle, The Saucier's Apprentice, or the Household Unfamiliar.

Together, then, these merry fairies watch, as toes fly up out of the lawn mower, the vacuum cleaner ingests the drapes, and a grease fire erupts in the kitchen.

For years, economists and sociologists have wondered, why does the American worker, having waged and won a bitter battle for shorter working hours and longer vacations, choose to spend his or her precious leisure time (not to mention his or her salary) pursuing activities that look very much like *work?*

These so-called experts have overlooked the effects of Handimanticore.

Often this Do-It-Yours-Elf rides from house to house on his (appropriately named) Hobby Horse. Sometimes, he arrives in a kit. But however he gets across the threshold, the Handimanticore instantly transforms the old homestead into a beehive of activity—its atmosphere abuzz with the snarl of fatal power tools, aflash with the short circuiting of electrical equipment, and afog with debilitating glue fumes.

Handimanticore's secret is that he writes the instructions for do-it-yourselfers, and he does so employing ancient, mysterious, incomprehensible, eldritch, elvish runes.

In the event that a mere human should decipher these easy-to-follow directions, Handimanticore has another trick up his sleeve—there is *no* widget screw A 113 b (Fig. 27)!

★ **HISTORY:** From the depths of the Black Forest (where the manufacture of slippers that forced people to dance till they dropped was a cottage industry), Handimanticore made his way to our shores not long ago by means of a steam-powered, radio-controlled, twenty-six-thousand piece 1/32 scale model raft.

Settling in Maine, he quickly concocted and widely dispensed a dangerous illusion known as Yankee Ingenuity (pat. pend.), which has caused the world no end of mischief.

As his name suggests, Handimanti has many relatives, among them Humpty Dumpty, the steeplejack's friend; Tutti Frutti, the Italian master of home ice cream making and self-taught ballet; Fuzzy Wuzzy, who oversees the cabinet structure in newly emerged nations; Ricki Rouie, the Taiwanese supervisor of easy-to-assemble solid-state wall-size televisions; Harum Scarum, who presides over the installation of Arabian burglar alarms; and Oakie Doakie, still teaching do-it-yourself Model-T maintenance on the road to Californy.

☞ **SPOTTER'S TIPS:** Collapsing furniture. Raw bread. An unfinished, life-size paint-by-numbers version of Guer-

nica. Disintegrating quilts. One third of a yacht, in the attic. Unravelling turtlenecks. A snaggle-toothed patio. Crooked wallpaper and lumpy vases. If you can find a man with wood shavings in his hair, an incorrectly buttoned shop apron, and charcoal where his eyebrows used to be, ask him where to find the Handimanticore. In all likelihood, he will point you in the right direction with his blue, swollen, throbbing thumb.

DEVIL DOGS

Regurgitatious projectilius

⊙ **RANGE:** These sweet-seeming but deadly creatures dangle from chipped metal racks in snack bars, bodegas, truck stops, movie theater lobbies, corner candy stores, fast-food franchises, neighborhood delis, superettes, souvenir stands, luncheonettes, cafeterias, national historic sites, drugstores, and ball park concession stands. They are also found in glove compartments, on the dessert tables of summer camps, scrunched beneath the Luke Skywalker thermos bottle in a *Star Wars* lunch bucket, and as "impulse items" in the vicinity of any cash register. Their bright and glamorous paper garments clutter the gutters, line the highways, and tumble out of every trash basket in the land.

Devil Dogs are, curiously, never found on shopping lists, but invariably make their ways into shopping carts.

They are the spirits of junk food.

◐ **HABITS:** To be more precise, Devil Dogs are the shock troops of the Junk Food Army. They assault the body's natural defense system—those rows of taste bud emplacements, which protect us against the ingestion of hardware, potting soil, and between-meal snacks.

Once the Devil Dogs have knocked out this Siegfried Line of Good Taste, wave upon wave of allied synthetic chemical bud-numbers invade —cheese-food-flavored thingies, sour-cream-and-onion-dip-flavored gizmos, prefab burgers with nonbiodegradable sauces, petroleum-byproduct drumsticks, bubble-gum-flavored ice cream, peanut-butter-flavored popcorn clusters, and those nasty, mind destroying, multicolored sugar nodules known as jelly beans.

★ **HISTORY:** The Sugar Plum Fairy was an early emigré, a rich Russian brownie who thrived among the wild sugar beets of pre-colonial America.

When George Washington was inaugurated, all the nearby fairies invited each other to attend—*except* the Sugar Plum Fairy. The attendant good spirits wished George luck and courage and truthfulness—but then the enraged and unwanted Sugar Plum Fairy appeared, cursed President George and all Americans with a sweet tooth, and set a pack of Devil Dogs upon them, to hound them forever. (As a boy, Washington, overcome with sugar-lust, ate all the cherries from a tree in his backyard. This, naturally, rotted the teeth out of his noble head, but the resourceful lad then chopped down the tree, to fashion from it the wooden false teeth for which he is famous. The rest is history.)

☞ **SPOTTER'S TIPS:** Tar breath; love handles; a belt *and* suspenders; zits, wens, and blackheads; pitted green fangs, dilated pupils, seizures of undirected energy, furry tongue; belching; flatulence; 'roids—if these are your symptoms, or the symptoms of someone you love, don't be ashamed. Remember, junk food addiction is not a disease—merely the result of demonic possession by Devil Dogs. And help is as close as your nearest carrot.

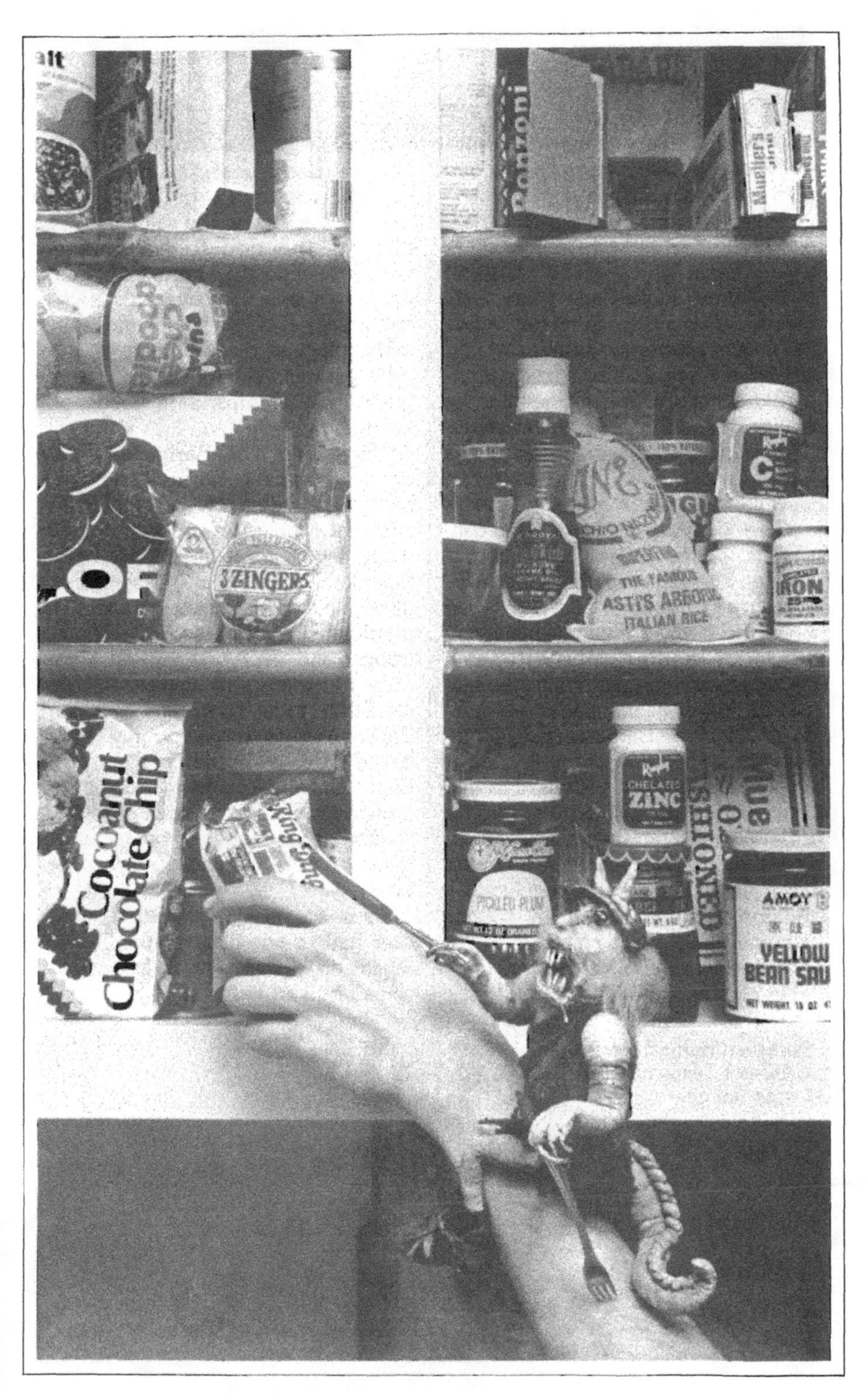
Cocoanut
Chocolate Chip
3 ZINGERS
THE FAMOUS
ITALIAN RICE
CHELATED
ZINC
PICKLED PLUM
AMOY
YELLOW

THE BACKYARD BARBACREEP

Conflagratio suburbia

⊙ **RANGE:** Since hanging plants and other decorative foliage in the kitchen are often sensitive to smoke, many folks find it advisable to do their cooking out back, where all the trees and bushes (that spoiled the view) have already been cut down. Here, beside the great brick burger forges, cast iron weiner crematoria, and vast superheated kilns for the incineration of steaks, spuds, corn cobs, and sausages, the Backyard Barbacreep dances like the blue flame atop a decorative Hawaiian garden torch; and by his eerie light, we see bottles of bland condiments, fearful utensils of barbarous making, ribaldly inscribed paper napkins, frosty pitchers of fruitflavored sugar-free fluids, and terrified children, cowering women, and strangely garbed grown men performing the savage fire-lit rites of *marinade*.

◐ **HABITS:** The Barbacreep defies nature—under his spell, the flash point at which charcoal ignites is raised to that of asbestos. Combustion can be achieved only after the ritual libation of several gallons of high octane fuel, after which the whole hibachi goes up in a fire storm, transporting many pounds of prime chuck, an awning, and your eyebrows into the Great Beyond.

He puts mustard clots in the nozzle of the squeeze bottle; he lends to catsup the consistency of Kool-Aid; he loosens the cap on the salt shaker; he inspires the dog to heroic steak snatches—if possible from the hands of the boss's wife; he causes deck chair collapses, eye-smarting wind shifts, midge plagues, dive bombing pigeons, fork gorings, second-degree grease burns, pool cramps, flash floods, and indigestion.

★ **HISTORY:** The Barbacreep's ancestors were the horned and furry-haunched Satyrs of ancient Greece, who unwillingly used to participate in many a goat roast in Arcady. Today, their descendant wreaks his vengeance upon all who eat meat on sticks, on picnickers, campers, hikers, scout troops, and everyone else who contrives to cook out of doors.

☞ **SPOTTER'S TIPS:** The Backyard Barbacreep is never far from half-baked franks composed of fly eggs, rodent hair, and earwig mandibles; nor from singing aunts; or stinging ants. He is often accompanied by raccoons, ravenous in-laws, and the occasional bear.

Look for him in summer, leering over hedges and fences, hungrily sniffing the air for the scent of kerosene and singed human flesh.

Backyard Barbacreep is a red-hot Texas tradition. Come an' git it, before *it* gits *you*!

TEAM SPIRITS

Rosa petrus a.k.a. canis calidus

⊙ **RANGE:** Despite their reputation for enormous importance, Team Spirits are harder to see than a dab of hair oil on a baseball travelling at 95 mph between a pitcher's hand and a catcher's glove. Learned experts (which sports writers always are) maintain that Team Spirits can be found even in the Major Leagues, but for the most part, they grace (or plague) amateur clubs, college, and farm teams. They feed off success and grow or shrink with a team's achievements. Team Spirits are most noticeable by their absence—it is invariably observed that a losing or strife-torn team has "lost its Team Spirit."

◐ **HABITS:** Team Spirits, although invisible, can influence the outcome of most sports events. They can nudge a knuckleball over the corner of the plate, and, by spreading their wings and lowering their flaps, transform an arrogant pitcher's fastball into a hanging curve, or "gopher ball." Likewise, they can cause a long flyball to remain suspended in the air above the fence until caught and steer a slow bunt to either side of the foul line.

Team Spirits inspire basketball players to take swan dives onto the parquet. Cheered on by a Team Spirit, an out-of-position hockey player will lunge to catch a puck with his teeth, and a soccer player will interpose his head between foot and ball . . . for Team Spirits most often abound wherever large groups of people gather to watch smaller groups get their exercise for them.

When a basketball spins for thirty seconds around the inner lip of the rim and then shoots out like a champagne cork, that's the Team Spirit (who never gets called for goaltending) doing her thing. Likewise, a field goal attempt bouncing off both uprights *and* the crossbar before dropping down on the wrong side, and a puck coming to rest right on the goal line are both the handiwork of Team Spirits.

However, these tricks are whimsical. An angry Team Spirit can shatter a baseball bat and direct a sharp shard of oak into the neck of anyone within a hundred feet of the batter's box. Many players try to win the good will of the Team Spirit by such time-honored rituals as swinging three bats simultaneously, spitting frequently, or smuding black stuff beneath their eyes. Managers and coaches seek the Team Spirit's favor by the ancient rites of kicking dirt on the umpire's shoes, looking sleepy at crucial moments, and looking anxious and intent when nothing is happening on the field.

★ **HISTORY:** All Team Spirits are descended from the legendary Will Toowin, who in old England once defeated Robin Goodsport on the enchanted playing fields of Eton. It was Will Toowin who invented the beanball and inspired Ty Cobb to sit on the bench sharpening his spikes while the other team's shortstop watched in terror. Team Spirits are related to such other malevolent ephemera as The School Spirit, The Self Image, and The Company Man.

☞ **SPOTTER'S TIPS:** Team Spirits inhabit exclusively the locker rooms of winning teams, for whose successes they are given (or take) all the credit. According to some West Coast managers, they do not associate with Nice Guys, who finish you-know-where.

Opposite: Mr. Irvin and the Team Spirit, who introduced him abruptly to many an outfield wall.

YORK
20

STYLUS DEVIL

Diablo repeata degroova

⊙ **RANGE:** A Stylus Devil comes with every phonograph sold in America. This ear-bending imp is to be found under the machine's tone arm, hanging in a position convenient to steer minute flecks of ash, hair, and other rubbish toward the needle. If seen, the Stylus Devil will usually run up the tone arm with such great speed that the surprised viewer will "accidentally" drop the arm onto the record, causing the slam and scream of a stylus sliding across the disc and leaving a deep scratch in its wake. This, if anything, is music to the Devil's ears.

◐ **HABITS:** The Stylus Devil is a most malicious member of a larger group of demons known as the Stereogres, those two-faced folk who pass their time destroying our listening pleasure: tempting components to become incompatible, causing static wow, flutter, etc. The Devil's own greatest delight is to cause a phonograph record to stick and, when the listener approaches, to cause it to play normally. We may take some solace in knowing that occasionally they laugh so hard at their own cleverness that they fall off the tone arm and come to grief on the needle. Their mashed forms resemble balls of dust.

★ **HISTORY:** The Stylus Devil appears to be a native American fairy, although creatures of similar habits have been sighted as far away as Germany, Japan and (increasingly) Taiwan. His first appearance may have been in the New Jersey laboratories of Thomas Alva Edison, where his birth was announced by a great howling of neighborhood dogs.

Even though he has no history to speak of, the Stylus Devil nonetheless has many relatives, including The Tape Worm, who enjoys snagging cassette tapes into Gordian knots, and the Video Bugger, whose peculiar joy it is to depress the "record" button before you screen your incredibly rare bootleg outtakes from "Mr. Rogers' Neighborhood."

☞ **SPOTTER'S TIPS:** It is virtually impossible to sight a Stylus Devil. They are, however, reported to be averse to the music of "Splattered Boots," an Australian New Wave band, and can be scared off with a sledge hammer, which is unfortunately hard on sensitive turntables.

When it comes to repetition, Stylus Devils set the record set the record set the SKRAAWK!

THE BOOGIE MAN

Felus frigida

⊙ **RANGE:** Uptown and 'way across the tracks is where he's at, they say, but if you have to ask, man, you'll never find the way.

He's wailin' in a cellar, kinda low and mean and sweet. He's singin' on the river. He's dancin' in the street.

You hear him in the moonlight, but you lose him in the dawn, and anyplace you get to man, he been there—but he *gone!*

◐ **HABITS:** The Boogie Man is Dixieland. The Boogie Man is funk. The Boogie Man is po' folks, makin' beauty out of junk.

Invented half the slang you use and every dance you do. He turns your whole world colored (like black and tan and blue).

He teaches you the shimmy and the swingin' Lindy hop, then puts you jitterbugs uptight with rock'n'roll'n'bop.

He move so cool, his threads so fine, that everyone appear a silly imitation of the way he looked last year.

He made you want to blow like Bird, or shuffle like Ali. Invisible and Beautiful, Unsuppressible and Free!

★ **HISTORY:** African roots, man. Lion pride. Savannah, jungle, mountainside.

Blood pulse drumbeat. Electric bird. Music. Ghost. Feeling. Word.

Grandfather spirit, tall as a tree, follow the slave ships over the sea.

Alive in the seed, alive in the flower, mystery family, history and power.

Rainbow wearer, cakewalker, blues shouter, jive talker, soul brother, fire preacher, dream teller, truth teacher.

Hey, Yankee Doodle up on your pony, that feather in your hat's a phony, 'cause the coolest feather (or ain't you heard?) shines on the wing of the jungle bird!

☞ **SPOTTER'S TIPS:** Too white puppets tryin' to dance in too tight, too bright neon pants.

Sweatin' cool in a clubfoot step so square when it was hip to be hep.

Finger snappin' jazz collectors, pale eyed middle class defectors, lookin' to score on a credit plan some soul from the soulful Boogie Man.

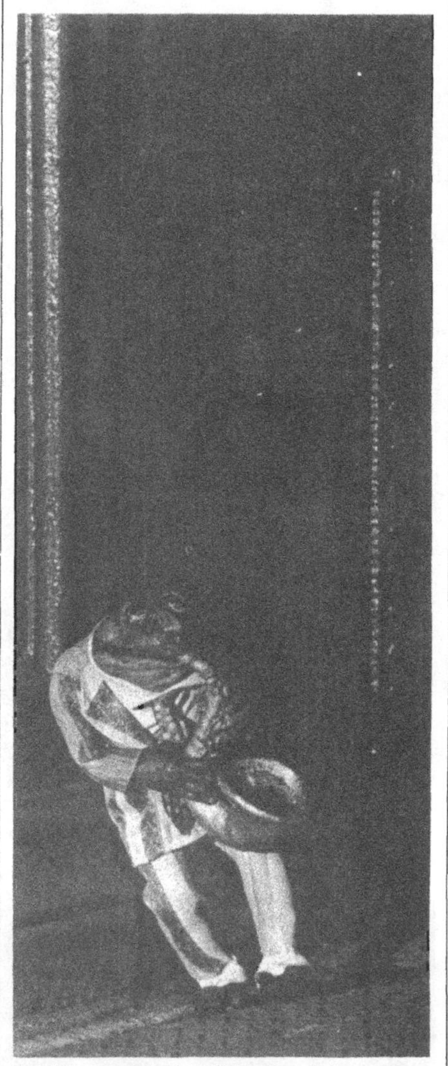

The Boogie Man's still getting down, when you're just getting up.

THE MIND BOGGLES

Videoticus neilsonian

⊙ **RANGE:** The "vast wasteland" is the dark domain of the Mind Boggles. They travel at the speed of light, on waves of air, and it is virtually impossible to prevent them from entering any room of your home or favorite bar (especially since they have lately joined together in enormous conspiracies, or "networks," the better to numb the brains and harden the hearts of mankind).

◐ **HABITS:** There are many types, or stations, of Mind Boggle, each named after the sort of wicked spell he (or she) casts: the Eye-Glazers, the Thought-Rotters, the Credibility-Stretchers, the Wit-Wilters, the Trash Vendors, and the Trivia-Transmitters, to name but a few.

Their system is diabolically simple. They find a poor, bored, lonely mortal—often a mere child—and in vampirelike fashion, drain him of all willpower, commonsense, intelligence, and taste. They then work their magic to have this mental and moral degenerate appointed Vice-President of Programming for a major television network. He, in turn, contaminates thousands, who themselves go on to high-paying jobs in the broadcasting profession. . . .

Sex and violence, the two ingredients essential to any fairy tale, fill the air when the Boggles are at work. But while the weddings with frogs and bloody decapitations found in classic fairy stories are suitable for children, on television they become sniggering double entendres and bloodless car wrecks, which only adults can understand.

Mind Boggles are repelled by the normal, natural scent of humans, and much of their time and effort is spent inducing "bromidrosophobia," that is, the morbid fear of bodily odors.

★ **HISTORY:** This most evil of Goblins (for it's your soul they're gobblin'), Mind Boggles are descended from simple hobgoblins, the chimney corner creatures who used to inspire people to stare into the fire, watching the flames "make pictures." This required, unfortunately, imagination, the deadly enemy of all goblins. (From their point of view, radio was not much of an improvement, as it also demanded some mental activity on the part of the audience.)

Now that Boggles can zip along cables, bounce off satellites, and zoom right into your face, they couldn't be happier. It just goes to show you the benefits of working through the proper channels.

☞ **SPOTTER'S TIPS:** Mind Boggles gain access to their victims by means of a glass-fronted box located in the home. Weird, flickering light and unnatural voices emerging from this diabolical machine are signs that the Mind Boggles are at their insidious work.

An Ohio Mind Boggle, whispering seductively, "Do not adjust your mind set."

TV

THE SOPHOMORE JINX

Gaudeamus ignarus

⊙ **RANGE:** From the tables down at Morry's to the place where Louie dwells, to the ivy-cluttered bastard-gothic bastions of Eastern privilege, to red brick cow town colleges, to the sprawling and over-endowed diploma mills of the sun belt . . . this rah-rah imp, this flask-swigging, cheer-leading, pennant-waving frat-rat-sprite is the Biggest-Manikin-on-Campus—a real varsity drag.

◐ **HABITS:** While his slightly younger relative, the Teen Angel, keeps the adolescents of every generation in a perpetual state of fifties rocker-rebellion, the Sophomore Jinx sees to it that, on campus, it's always the roaring twenties. "Scratch today's most ambitious business school sorority sister, and find a flapper," says the Sophomore Jinx, in whose eyes, and by whose hands, the ROTC trashings of the late sixties were only panty raids with placards, and under whose influence a frat-row game of Dragons and Dungeons is but today's variation on a goldfish swallowing party.

Inspired, nay, *possessed* by the Sophomore Jinx, last fall's meek and persecuted frosh becomes the most snottily discriminating of pledge judges and the most sadistic of hazers. The Sophomore Jinx is this so-called School Spirit who removes your name from the dean's list and appends it to the petition for nude touch football, the list of nominators of the pro-Soviet student council rep, and the roster of volunteers for the homecoming all-drag chorus line show and annual mid-term beer-and-shot drinking contest.

After tampering with your alarm clock consistently, so that you have overcut every course by Hallowe'en, the Sophomore Jinx wraps your naked body in a vintage raccoon coat and sends you out there, crazed with visions of John Belushi, F. Scott Fitzgerald, and cheap gin, to streak the nation during the televised half-time show.

★ **HISTORY:** Alma Mater for the Sophomore Jinx is said to be that most legendary of college towns, Heidelberg; though the left bank of the Seine also claims him as an alumnus, as might both great English universities, with their traditions of Boat Night undergraduate idiocies.

By charter, the Jinx is granted absolute power over the mind and body of a student only during his, or her, second year of study. Here in America, he has cleverly created Junior College, University, Graduate and Post Graduate Schools, in order to have four separate shots at you as a sophomore.

☞ **SPOTTER'S TIPS:** On campus, the Sophomore Jinx is as ubiquitous as herpes, except in lecture rooms, laboratories, and the library. If not immediately at hand, he can be easily conjured by rendering, loudly, a chorus of the school fight song or, as often happens, tapping a keg.

The Sophomore Jinx, krazy kampus kutup, kancels klasses and kareers.

ELF S. PRESLEY

Greilus marcus

⊙ **RANGE:** Elf S. Presley is a union card carrying member of the Spirits of Show Biz, who accompany performers on the road. Whether the venue is a snotty concert hall or a grungy night club, a cavernous stadium or the high school gym, Rock'n' Trolls like Elf S. are present backstage wherever tickets are being scalped out front.

◐ **HABITS:** The squeal of feedback, a dry ice machine miscue, the off-key plonk of a guitar string snapping, a dead mike during a vocal; all these misfortunes may usually be attributed to the tireless labors of a Rock'n' Troll like Elf S. Presley. Techies and roadies accompanying a band on tour struggle unceasingly and unsuccessfully against such creatures, and experienced road managers attempt to placate them with bribes ranging from caviar kebabs (expensive sturgeon roe skewered on toothpicks) to bottle caps brimming with the costliest of vintage champagnes. This policy of appeasement often has no effect, or worse, the caviar-stuffed and champagne-bloated sprites are often stimulated to greater than usual excess. In one instance, such a sated and inebriated Spirit of Show Biz was responsible for the collapse of an entire discotheque interior during its two hundredth playing of "Disco Inferno" by the Tramps (foreshadowing the decline in popularity of flashing lights, white suits, and bad lyrics).

Elf S. personally selects the washed-up comic or utterly derivative local rock group who invariably opens for the headliners and sees to it that the main attraction arrives several boredom-and-mayhem filled hours late. He invented Festival Seating, open-air concerts without rain dates, and the charming glow-in-the-dark necklaces which glow in your face for hours.

He has toured with REO Speedwagon, Peggy Lee, the Grassroots, and is known to be discussing a stint in Vegas with Welsh crooner Tom Jones. His biggest pleasure is encouraging the popularity of dead rock stars over live ones.

★ **HISTORY:** Like most creatures with a piece of the show biz action, they are of Italian descent, distant relatives of the Phantom of the Opera. The first to make the transition from classical to pop music was the fearful Phil Spectre.

☞ **SPOTTER'S TIPS:** Rock'n' Trolls like Elf S. are even harder to see than the headliners they accompany. They are faster than a promoter with a box office bag and, when they want to be, transparent as a cold bag of greasy chicken. If you are lucky, you may catch a glimpse of one grinning stage left, as an amp blows up stage right.

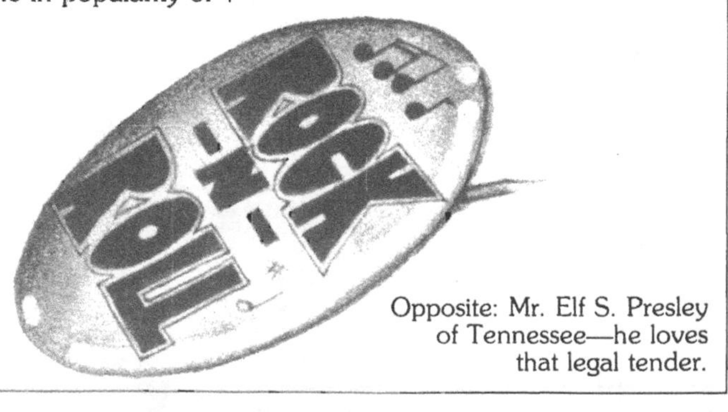

Opposite: Mr. Elf S. Presley of Tennessee—he loves that legal tender.

ROCK -N- ROLL
ROCK LIVES
PARTY

PRE-REVOLUTIONARY WARLOCK

Nostalgia americanna

⊙ **RANGE**: Ye Olde Antique Boutiques, garage sales, behind the bushes beside well-marked historic trails, landmark gift shops, graduate seminars, culture loops, behind glass cases in the court house, neatly stacked on the library lawn, at Ladies' Club Lectures (illustrated with slides)—wherever Americans dredge the shallow waters of their Nation's History for rusty artifacts and a sense of tradition.

◐ **HABITS**: By most Fairy standards, or indeed by most civilized human standards, American history is not yet long or rich enough to be of more than passing interest. Yet the Pre-Revolutionary Warlock possesses many Americans with the notion that they can discover, and indeed purchase, a past for themselves.

Thus, he has sponsored and fostered such groups as The Daughters of the American Revolution, The Daughters of The Confederacy, The Sons of The Pioneers, The Daughters of World War One, The Daughters of the Korean Police Action, and The Illegitimate Offspring of Veterans Against the Vietnam War.

He sends us out on archeological digs around the summer house, where we learn that nearby once lived Indians, whose culture consisted of the manufacture and burial of small flints, which may or may not be arrowheads.

He leads us on grade school field trips, where the sniff of a powder horn, the heft of a Bowie knife, or the sight of a surviving bison sets off a lifelong obsession with Americana.

The spell cast by the Pre-Revolutionary Warlock often lasts into our adult lives. We long to live in dilapidated eighteenth-century shacks, surrounded by Ethan Allen cobbler's benches, pewter chamber pots, quaint quilts by crazy Quakers, warped and wormy butter churns, coon skin fedoras, candle molds, kerosene lamps, wagon wheels, scrimshaw back scratchers, and other mementoes of simpler times, when white men were men and everybody else knew their place.

The fact that almost every artifact surviving from early America is now under armed guard does not deter the Pre-Revolutionary Warlock from inspiring us to collect historically significant stuff. After all, says he, "History is happening all around us, right now!" as well as, "This could be worth a lot of money some day!"

So, we buy, sell, save, revere, and treasure newspapers from the day Kennedy was shot, backstage passes to Eagles concerts, "All the way with LBJ" buttons, "Dump the Hump" bumper stickers, green Coke bottles, Billy Beer tins and other priceless reminders of "the way we were."

★ **HISTORY**: The Pre-Revolutionary Warlock is himself of lowly, albeit French, ancestry and came to the New World in hopes of bettering his condition. And he has done so: His ancestor was a little "La Fayette," a smallish Fay who took the form of a humble French weremole. He would doubtless have rocked back on his hind quarters and flung out a paw in salute at his progeny's achievements.

The Warlock's greatest achievement, so far, has been the oversubscription to the Franklin Mint's Bicentennial limited offering of a life-sized, sterling silver reproduction of Lincoln's distinguishing wart.

☞ **SPOTTER'S TIPS**: Look for the Pre-Revolutionary Warlock wherever the humorous sign "We Buy Junk/We Sell Antiques" is displayed.

A.G.Hago
Co.K.
7

The Pre-Revolutionary Warlock cherishes tradition. Polishes it. Auctions it off.

THE PHILHARMONIC ORC

Cacophonous gloriosus

⊙ **RANGE**: Enormous chandeliered mausoleums named after extinct robber barons are the customary haunts of these myopic Neanderthals, but they may also be seen—and heard—on Public Television, FM radio, wine-bar Muzak systems, BMW cassette decks, and wherever gouty millionaires doze in red plush seats beside their buxom spouses.

◐ **HABITS**: The Philharmonic Orc high-browbeats the citizenry into believing that he and *only* he has the right to make loud noises—or, for that matter, any noise at all. To this end, he has created an inefficient dinosaur of a noisemaking machine, the Symphony Orchestra, to which respect, homage, and bucks must be paid.

He hushes you with a lordly hiss, should you chance to cough during a pause in his machine's noisemaking. His victims leap to their feet shouting "bravo" (for men) and "brava" (for women) during other pauses. He reserves for himself the right to be first clap in and last clap out.

He is the moving spirit behind the granting of vast sums of public money to subsidize art forms which are patronized largely by persons with vast private wealth. If music be the food of love, the Philharmonic Orc is providing food stamps for the upper class.

He has insidiously hornswoggled us all into the certainty that only music composed before 1900, as interpreted by seven dozen of his monkey-suited thralls, is *serious*.

★ **HISTORY**: The Philharmonic Orc claims kinship with both the Phantom of the Opera and the emigrée Sugar Plum Fairy. He also maintains an unholy marriage of convenience with the Culture Vulture.

For reasons difficult to fathom, the Germans, Italians, Russians, and French all proudly claim him as their own. Like the Vampire, a similarly attired, decadent and aristocratic monster, the Philharmonic Orc came comparatively recently to the New World—but he wasted no time inspiring the *nouveau riche* of the Main Line, wild frontier, and Barbary Coast to erect (by public subscription) Opery Houses, those gauche and gilded temples sacred to his cult.

These days he is more likely to cause the construction (by tax deductible donation) of a square-mile-sized, prestressed concrete neo-fascist styled, totally unnecessary acoustical joke called The (*fill in the politician's name here*) Center for the Performing Arts.

☞ **SPOTTER'S TIPS**: An overture *(con brio)* of clinking crystal and silver cigarette cases snapping; a pizzicato of popping collar buttons; an arpeggio of uncultured pearls; a scherzo of stomach noises; a continuo of muted flatulence; a crescendo of self-satisfied sighs; a diminuendo of sucked dentures; and a coda of sonorous snores.

The Philharmonic Orc makes passionate Overtures to bankers and their wives.

CULTURE VULTURES

Patronia matrimonia allimonia

⊙ **RANGE:** Commonly found in art galleries and recital halls, these ghastly ancient female creatures also frequent vernissages and poetry readings, and occasionally stray into lofts and garrets in their relentless search for human prey. They infest grant committees and awards councils and often lurk behind the mastheads of small literary publications.

How any given Culture Vulture can attend so many simultaneous openings, unveilings, lectures, meetings, and wine-and-cheese parties is a mystery; it has been conjectured that they travel from place to place on "old bat" wings.

◐ **HABITS:** It is the horrible nature of the Culture Vulture to maintain herself in a state of eternal middle-age flush by ceaselessly draining the creative energies of young actors, dancers, sculptors, composers, writers, and artists. (Those who feed exclusively off writers are called "Inkubii," artists are afflicted with "Paintergeist," and musicians get "Harpies Simplex.") The Culture Vulture can sometimes be found in the company of her fellow patrons, the Philharmonic Orc and (when there is nothing else to do) the Torontogre.

Young geniuses are lured by the apparent interest, affluence, and generosity of the Culture Vulture into *unnatural* relationships, and then discarded upon the slag heap of last year's trends.

The Culture Vultures are eternally hungry for new "creative" blood. Thus, they perpetually create new "artistic" movements, fashions, trends, and schools, thereby transforming perfectly normal craftsmen, clowns, and idiots into "artists" whom they can discover, fuss over, celebrate, and then deposit in the trash with Op Art, Theater of Cruelty, twelve-tone music, nonfiction novels, hi-tech sculpture, and other used up passions.

Not all Culture Vultures are female—but even the ones who aren't *pretend* to be.

★ **HISTORY:** Even the youngest of today's Culture Vultures (commonly known as "Groupies") are descended from the "Furies" (then disguised as "Maenads") who so loved the performances of the Greek singer-songwriter Orpheus that they tore him into little pieces.

☞ **SPOTTER'S TIPS:** The shrill, crooning voice and mechanical laugh are dead giveaways, as are the rattle of bracelets, the ubiquitous, untasted glass of white wine, blue cheese breath, lipstick on the teeth, and knotted wads of darkened cartilage on the elbows. Culture Vultures are among the easiest to identify—and hardest to avoid—of all unearthly creatures.

Culture Vultures swoop down from Connecticut, to feed on dying art forms.

PASSING FANCIES

Ephemera hoopla hula

⊙ **RANGE:** From the drawing board to the boardroom to the assembly line to the ad agency to the supermarket shelves to the house next-door to your own house to the closet to the attic to the garbage dump to the antique store to the museum.

◐ **HABITS:** A Passing Fancy seizes your imagination and possesses you with a lifelong, burning desire to purchase and own something you'd never known existed the day before yesterday and probably will forget the day after tomorrow.

Many of them are quick and clever little tailors and cobblers, who virtually overnight can raise (or lower) every hemline, widen (or narrow) every lapel, sew buttons on (or snip buttons off) every collar in the land. They frequently raise or lower the heels of women's shoes, causing many a ludicrous stumble.

Like many other Fairies, the Passing Fancies are passionately fond of music and dance and can invent an entirely new and totally popular beat, sound, and step in the wink of an eye.

They are mischievous: thanks to Passing Fancies you might go to bed with a full head of long flowing locks and awaken with a shaved skull and a safety pin in your nose. These spritely creatures have been known to trick grown men into cultivating droopy, lugubrious mustaches and wearing scarlet knee-length shorts.

Through the years, Passing Fancies have bent, bloated, stretched, and flattened the bodies of female victims; singed, knotted, and streaked their hair; and naughtily inspired them to smear their eyes, mouths, and cheeks with grotesque and colored gorp.

They are, obviously, extremely capricious toward humankind, tempting mortals to squander their riches on pastimes, garments, and accessories often demeaning (consider the muumuu) or dangerous (witness hang gliding). But Passing Fancies are also incompatible with one another, so that an invading troupe (like the Preppies) will invariably force into exile a dominating force (in this case, the Punkers) who had, themselves, driven out a previously popular group (the Discos).

★ **HISTORY:** In France, they were the *Modes,* in Germany, "Zeitgeists," in England "U's" (and "non-U's"). In America, the immigrant Fancy families joined together to form the powerful Conspicuous Consumption Syndicate (a leisure service of monopoly capitalism) and practiced the restrictionist art of TM on their products and the language.

These three divided the world—the French Modes assuming responsibility for fashion, the Zeitgeists for opinions, and the "U's" for etiquette—and inspired in all Americans the fear of being caught dead with last season's cuff-widths, manners, or principles.

Although their life spans are notoriously brief, Passing Fancies can be revived. One such group, even now infesting restaurants and shops on both coasts of America, is known as Elf Nouveau.

☞ **SPOTTER'S TIPS:** If you listen closely, you can hear the hustle and bustle of Passing Fancies expiring (or reviving) in whatever dark corner of your home to which you have consigned your mood ring, lava lamp, disco cassettes and Walkman, skateboard, Smurfs, quad speakers, yo-yos, coonskin caps, Topsiders, Rubik's Cubes, and Mork suspenders.

Opposite: Are the expressions "in," "hip," "with-it" still in, hip, with it? Go ask a Passing Fancy.

TEEN ANGELS

Juveniles delinqués

⊙ **RANGE:** Under hot rods, barstools, and appreciated. On motorcycles, telephones and crying jags. In back seats, record stores, and really, *really* serious trouble this time. Beneath strange hats, the class average, and the age of reason. Behind the wheel, the couch, and in their homework.

◐ **HABITS:** Teen Angels *possess* the bodies of all Americans between the ages of 12 and 21. They inspire in every adolescent the hallucination that the universe is a technicolor tragedy in Dolby Stereo starring themselves. They trick athletic young men into writing verse and academic young women into getting contact lenses. Wimpy math whizzes flex and pose in private before mirrors; working-class louts stare moodily into bus station photo machines. A formerly grave and sober girl-child develops a soul-consuming passion for the third guitarist from the left in a band named after a veterinary operation; a clean-cut suburban cub scout becomes the fanatic devotee of some Central American mystic agrarian reformer. With the onset (or threat) of puberty, their victim's attention span shrinks to that of a brain-damaged moth—save for the uncanny ability to meditate, for days, on possible modifications to the mudguards or sideburns.

★ **HISTORY:** There is no record of Teen Angels—or teenagers, for that matter—having existed before the 1950s. Prior to that time, in America as in the rest of the world, mature children simply passed into irresponsible adulthood. But, following an epidemic of ballad-celebrated grad-night auto wrecks, romantic bike crashes, lovelorn beach drownings, sensitive, misunderstood switchblade massacres, and an incident involving a level crossing and a high school ring, America was as jam-packed with Teen Angels as a fifty-cent-beer-and-extra-slice-night at a pizza parlor featuring a free concert by the Rolling Stones.

☞ **SPOTTER'S TIPS:** Mother Nature, in her infinite wisdom, has already spotted most Teen Angels quite nicely, thank you.

A typical Teen Angel, on location in rock'n'rollin' Encino, California.

No Profanity Please
Keep Smokes off Tables

DAEMON RUNYON

Septem adeste undecim

⊙ **RANGE:** From the two dollar Show window at an off-the-beaten track to the Chicago Commodities Exchange; from the jai alai frontons of Miami to the dog tracks of Tuscon; from jumping contests of celebrated frogs to the Sacred Heart basement bingo game around the corner; from the cock fights of El Barrio to the free floating crap games of the nation's Holiday Inns—wherever the urge to push your luck burns a hole in your soul, you will surely find the Daemon Runyon: the low rollers' companion and archenemy of Lady Luck.

◐ **HABITS:** He draws your attention to a surething long shot in the Racing Form—where he has previously inserted a typo. He whispers random numbers in a card counter's ear. He helps you draw to an inside straight if anyone else is holding a flush. He is small enough to ride a tossed coin and stand it on end and tall enough to slam dunk home the shot that helps the Lakers beat the spread . . . and you. He'll steer you to a sucker the morning after he's blown his roll. He lets you win from welshers and makes you loose to Mafia dons. He's the one-armed bandit who trips the filly in the home stretch, slides your chip off the double zero just before it hits, tips the heat to your bookie's address before you can collect, and drowns you in the office pool.

★ **HISTORY:** The Daemon is a descendant of the Fadas, those glittering creatures native to the French Riviera. His motive for immigrating remains obscure (for Europeans are as easily tempted as Americans to punt the patrimony on a long shot), but come he did, to work his scams and cons from the beaches of New Jersey to the Sands of Vegas. His first recorded act in the New World was to greet Columbus and tout him it was seven-to-five he had hit the Indies. He later gave Custer the same odds against the Sioux. With his parimutuel friends, Jack O'Diamonds, "Auntie" Up, "Three Card" Monty and "Old Snake Eyes," he caused havoc on the river boats of the old Mississippi. Daemon's biggest sting was in 1929, when he called all the bluffs, broke the bank, and left Uncle Sammy sitting at the table in his red, white, and blue underwear.

☞ **SPOTTER'S TIPS:** The Daemon Runyon can be seen riding a cab to the track, and the bus back. He sits on the shoulder of a fat man weeping in an all-night coffee shop. He smells of cheap cigar smoke and bar rye. He sounds like the slap of a flush-busting card on green felt. He tastes like finger nails. He feels like the simultaneous breaking of your heart, your bank account, and your leg.

MEADOWLANDS
ENTRIES/Wednesday
CHARTS/Tuesday
SELECT
PIMI
RESU

ELF ALPHA

Diacteticus insanias

⊙ **RANGE:** Health food stores, juice bars, guru ranches, Buddah camps, slimnasiums, vegetariums, macrobiotic discount outlets, mucus-free dinner theaters, high-fiber swap meets, organic tofu hatcheries, biodegradable pot-throwing encounter groups, human potential nude rug-hooking bees, holistic urinary retention seminars, and homeopathic open-air write-your-own-ceremony closed-bag funerals.

◐ **HABITS:** Elf Alpha is the nagging voice which tells you that if it tastes this good, it *must* be bad for you—and that if it tastes this bad, it *must* be good for you. Frequently, he enters your home—and your life—hidden away in a harmless looking bottle of Flintstones One-A-Day Vitamins. Before you know it, you are scouring the beach for iron-rich seaweed, browsing on cottage cheese mold, and sipping clotted ewes' milk, in the naive and blasphemous belief that such a vile and wretched diet will enable you to live forever.

He promises to improve, restore or initiate your love life, if you will only quit smoking, eat ditch weed salads, and learn to wiggle your ears. He suggests applications of yak excrement for receding hair, bat guano as a breath freshener, and daily total immersion in a tub of parsnip juice, after which you can throw those unnecessary eyeglasses away!

★ **HISTORY:** Elf Alpha is descended from that legendary American folk hero, Johnny Appleseed. But while his famous ancestor planted a delicious, nourishing, and natural food source across the continent, Elf Alpha has arranged for the nationwide importation, distribution, and ingestion of vile-tasting "organic" vittles scorned and despised even by the third-worlders who cultivate them.

His closest living (if you can call it living) relative is the odious Mung Goblin. Elf Alpha has most recently been living (and working) in Southern California, in harmony with the Sweat-sylphs, Passing Fancies, and (intermittently) the West Ghost.

☞ **SPOTTER'S TIPS:** A victim of Elf Alpha's malpractice exhibits such ghastly and glaring symptoms that he is as hard to miss as a leper on the swim team: eyeballs the color of saffron, complexion like stale tofu, blackstrap molasses breath, a body hairless as a tortoise egg, and limbs as thick and sturdy as dandelion shoots. Look to the victim's withered shoulder, a frequent perch of the Elf Alpha, where the latter squats in a full lotus position and whispers, "Eat it raw!"

YOGURT
Brown Rice
FLAVOR
NET WT 16 OZ

PHANTASMA GLORY

Miraculum novem dies

⊙ **RANGE:** From your secret daydreams through your fondest ambitions, all the way to the top of the glittering heap and back down to dim, grim obscurity, the Phantasma Glory manages careers. And although she specializes in such of the exacting, exhausting performing arts as having-your-picture-taken, she has also made superstars out of economic advisors, greengrocers, diet doctors, and self-absorbed, vainglorious, shallow, and ambitious ladies and gentlemen from all walks of life. She is everywhere, flashing like a strobe.

◐ **HABITS:** As even a William Morris agent knows, the actual manufacture and exploitation of a celebrity is easy. The difficult part is motivating an ordinary citizen to undergo the simple but excruciatingly painful and boring process. That's where Phantasma Glory comes in.

In conspiracy with her fellow media-elves, The Hounds of News and The Mind Boggles, Phantasma Glory lures the starlets out of the corn fields, the expert commentators out of the ivory towers, the pop singers off the street corners, the fat kids onto the ledges—all into the blinding, brainless, and all-too-brief blaze of the spotlight.

Answering her casting call, cowboys run to Hollywood, morons in the stands take their shirts off for the cameras, dancers study voice, poets give readings, and the cowboys leave Hollywood for Washington.

But unlike the crowds of fans, the business managers and the interviewers, the Phantasma Glory does not desert the formerly famous. Take a look at that punched-out contender, that burnt-out disco queen, that guy sitting in the ruins of his barrel at the foot of the falls. Still smiling, aren't they? Because the Phantasma Glory still hovers near them, singing softly, "Fame . . . you're gonna live forever . . ."

★ **HISTORY:** The Phantasma Glory is a direct New World descendant of the Rhine Maidens, the Nymphs of that German river who guarded a fabulous hidden treasure and lured many a hero to his doom. (Richard Wagner, an ego-maniacal, perfect example of fame-addiction, wrote an opera about them.) They betray their Rhine Maiden origins by two of their favorite Siren calls: "Take the plunge," they whisper, and "Go for the gold."

In the United States, they have done some of their best work urging folks to give everything they've got for a shot at the Vice-Presidential nomination.

☞ **SPOTTER'S TIPS:** Look for the Phantasma Glory in places frequented by her victims: open casting calls, cable tv studios, passing through the Guinness Book Of Records, thumping guitars in the park, attending film school, or sitting alone in their rooms, practicing their autographs.

The Phantasma Glory beckons you to the Coast. If you're on the Coast already, to the Other Coast.

Us
People
Fashion's
$100 Million
Lady
Star
BROOKE
cuts loose
from mom
& finds love
BEAT STRESS
INSTANTLY
doctor's drug-free guide
OSMOND reveals
SHOW BUS
CASTING
CASTING
DANCE NEW
ROUND UP
HEATREBOOKS
HOW TO BEAT YO
ROSCOPE TO
SE WEIGHT
1000 SPELLS THREATEN

KINDERGUARDIANS

Lusos angelii

⊙ **RANGE:** Out from between parked cars, on thin ice, inside abandoned refrigerators, atop slippery roofs, near fresh excavations, on the edges of reservoirs, and around buildings under construction; in any of the dangerous spots kids aren't allowed to go, the Kinderguardians stand sentry.

◐ **HABITS:** As anyone who has ever been a child, or watched one, knows, the statistical chances of any infant reaching the age of majority are nil. But, thanks to the tireless efforts of the Kinderguardians, some make it—despite a slapstick sequence of terrifying near-misses.

The Kinderguardians deflect that eye-bound BB pellet and steady the pot of boiling water teetering over the toddler's head. Their magic transforms the sidewalk beneath a falling tot into a trampoline. They blow kites away from high tension wires, and miraculously clear busy intersections for the passage of runaway bikes, trikes, wagons, soapbox racers, sleds, toboggans, and skateboards.

They short-circuit power tools before tiny limbs are severed, extinguish the fuses on hand-held cherry bombs, and endow denim coveralls with the consistency of steel plate, thus protecting their charges from bruises, scrapes, and spilled acid. They see to it that forks don't fit in wall sockets, that Drano is digestible, and that the rogue polar bear at the zoo gently accepts a sugar cube from a child's hand.

★ **HISTORY:** The kindly American Kinderguardians are descended from those kindly German household spirits, the Kobolds. Germans, fairy and mortal alike, despise human beings, but are sentimentally fond of dogs, fatty sausages, red cabbage, and children.

A quick scan of the Grimm Brothers' stories reveals the awful scrapes from which children escape and the unspeakable ends to which adults all come.

In America, where children are feared and neglected like many other living things, the Kinderguardians have had their work cut out for them. They guided Huck Finn's raft down the river, between banks crammed with murderous grown-ups, and even kept Billy the Kid alive till he passed puberty.

And it was they, dear reader, who kept you from flying through the windshield that crazy time so many years ago after the dance or the basketball game or whatever it was . . . We can hardly remember ourselves.

☞ **SPOTTER'S TIPS:** We know that the Kinderguardians have been doing their work when we see a baby waddle unscathed from a train wreck, a six-year-old climbing unchewed from the 'gator pond, an infant giggling between the rungs of a fallen ladder, or simply a bouncing baby boy or girl, bouncing.

PALTRY GEIST

Torments minutissima

⊙ **RANGE:** These days, an all-too-common phenomenon in the attics and cellars of American homes (especially those owned or rented by hard-up, freelance writers) is the presence of Poltergeists. Uncanny ghastly special effects directed by these diabolical spirits are epidemic.

Paltry Geists, smaller and less celebrated than their cousins the Poltergeists, haunt the rest of the house, kitchen, bathroom, bedroom, etc., and while their pranks are not nearly as spectacular or saleable to Hollywood as those of their relatives, they can be every bit as effective in driving normal citizens over the brink, into howling, gibbering, wild-eyed insanity.

◐ **HABITS:** Let us consider a morning in the life of a mortal plagued by a Paltry Geist: your mysteriously reset alarm goes off two hours early or an hour late. If it is a clock-radio, it blasts Van Halen (you like classical) or the 1812 Overture (you like rock). Somehow, your arm got tucked in under you in the night and is now totally numb. As circulation returns, you have the sensation of being flogged with a bouquet of porcupines. Invisible hands cruelly manipulate the hot and cold shower controls—doubtless the same hands which presoaked the towels, used up the last of the toilet paper, and now knocks the toothpaste tube cap out of your fingers and wedges it perfectly into the drain of your (broken) sink. Some malevolent force has made off with a sock from each pair and knotted your shoelace with a wicked Sea Scout's skill. In your effort to undo this knot, you break (a) a fingernail and (b) the shoelace. The phone rings. As you dash for it, you bang your shin sharply on a mischievously rearranged bit of furniture. The caller is, of course, a wrong number.

Whatever spirit now curdles the milk as it enters your cup of coffee has also hidden your car keys. You get up to check your coat for them and smell toast burning—but why go on?!!

★ **HISTORY:** While every nation in Europe at one time boasted its population of mischievous "Little People," the remarkably petty and tedious nature of the Domestic American Paltry Geist strongly suggests their Swiss origin. The Paltry Geist is descended from the fair people known as the *Severan*, merry pranksters of the French, Swiss, and Italian Alps who enjoyed putting the horse on the roof and punching holes in bags of flour.

Upon their arrival stateside, they befriended an indigenous Trickster Spirit, known to the natives as Coyote. In the lore of many tribes, Coyote was held responsible for the practical jokes (famine, tornadoes, and later, anthropologists) which the Indians suffered.

Between them, Paltry Geist and Coyote sprinkled flies in the buttermilk of many a pioneer housewife, spilled ink on final drafts of the Federalist Papers, and, in general, caused the random irritability for which the American personality is internationally famous.

☞ **SPOTTER'S TIPS:** A full-fledged attack of Paltry Geists once temporarily impeded the presidential aspirations of candidate Richard M. Nixon. By blunting his razor and hiding his antiperspirant on the day of his televised debate with JFK, they caused him to come across as a furtive slum-lord suffering delirium tremens.

According to fairy historians, the way to tame a *Severan* was to remain calm and smiling despite his antics. Similarly, the Paltry Geist expects you to be able to "take a joke" with Zen-like good humor. As an alternative, you can always burn down your house.

DJINN RUMMY

Alcoholus anonymous

⊙ **RANGE:** This creature can be found or, with patience, acquired, wherever less-than-fine wines are sold. It sometimes can actually be ordered by name in unfashionable liquor stores. Like the worm in the mescal bottle or the bison grass in Polish vodkas or the snake in certain French spirits, Djinn Rummies are more often talked of than actually sighted by Americans. Tramps and hobos are said to be most familiar with their whereabouts.

◐ **HABITS:** The Djinn (pronounced "gin") Rummy has a great and famous power. It can *take away* three wishes from whoever is lucky enough to find it. The wish for a job, clean clothes, and a place to sleep are the three most commonly removed wishes. The Djinn Rummy can be most entertaining to those who come to know it well and can make them laugh at things other people can't hear or see and thus don't think are funny. In payment for its services, this most sartorially splendid of fairy folk exacts a price: in exchange for gifts conferred, it demands every vestige of human dignity.

★ **HISTORY:** The Djinn Rummy originated in the Middle East, where merchants longed to export their herbal opiates to the lucrative European market. But the French were happy with their wine, the Germans with their beer, the English with their mead, etc. An Arab wizard, Akbar the Unspeakable, conjured the Djinn Rummy and infused the demon (and a very rum demon he is) into a butt of sack with which Richard Coeur de Lion was returning from his crusade. This single act of supernatural treachery accounts for the hangovers which we suffer to this day and for the increasing number of dope-sucking morons to be found everywhere in the non-Arab world.

☞ **SPOTTER'S TIPS:** One of the easiest of fairy folk to spot in private, the Djinn Rummy can be found at the bottom of one's third bottle of domestic off-brand port. It is usually preceded by a circus-like procession, often featuring stately elephants of unusual colors and giant spiders. It is most commonly sighted in depressed urban surroundings.

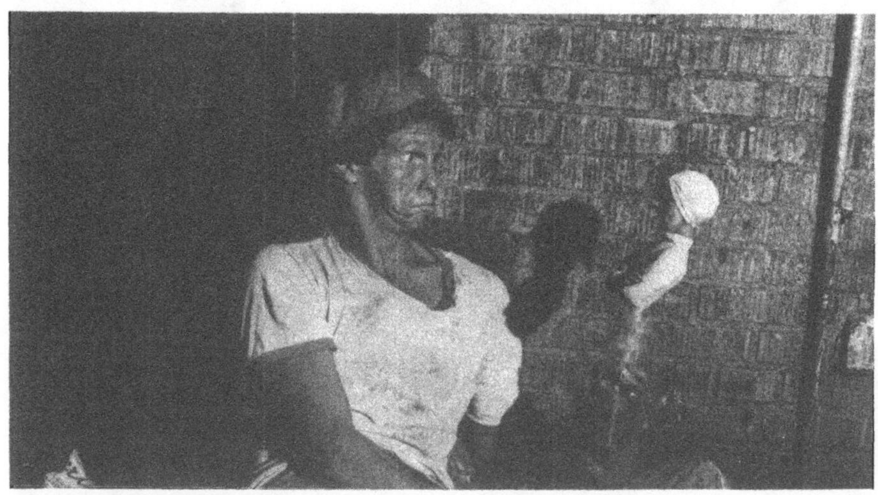

Djinn Rummy of Kentucky might be aristocratic—Bourbon Blood, y'know!

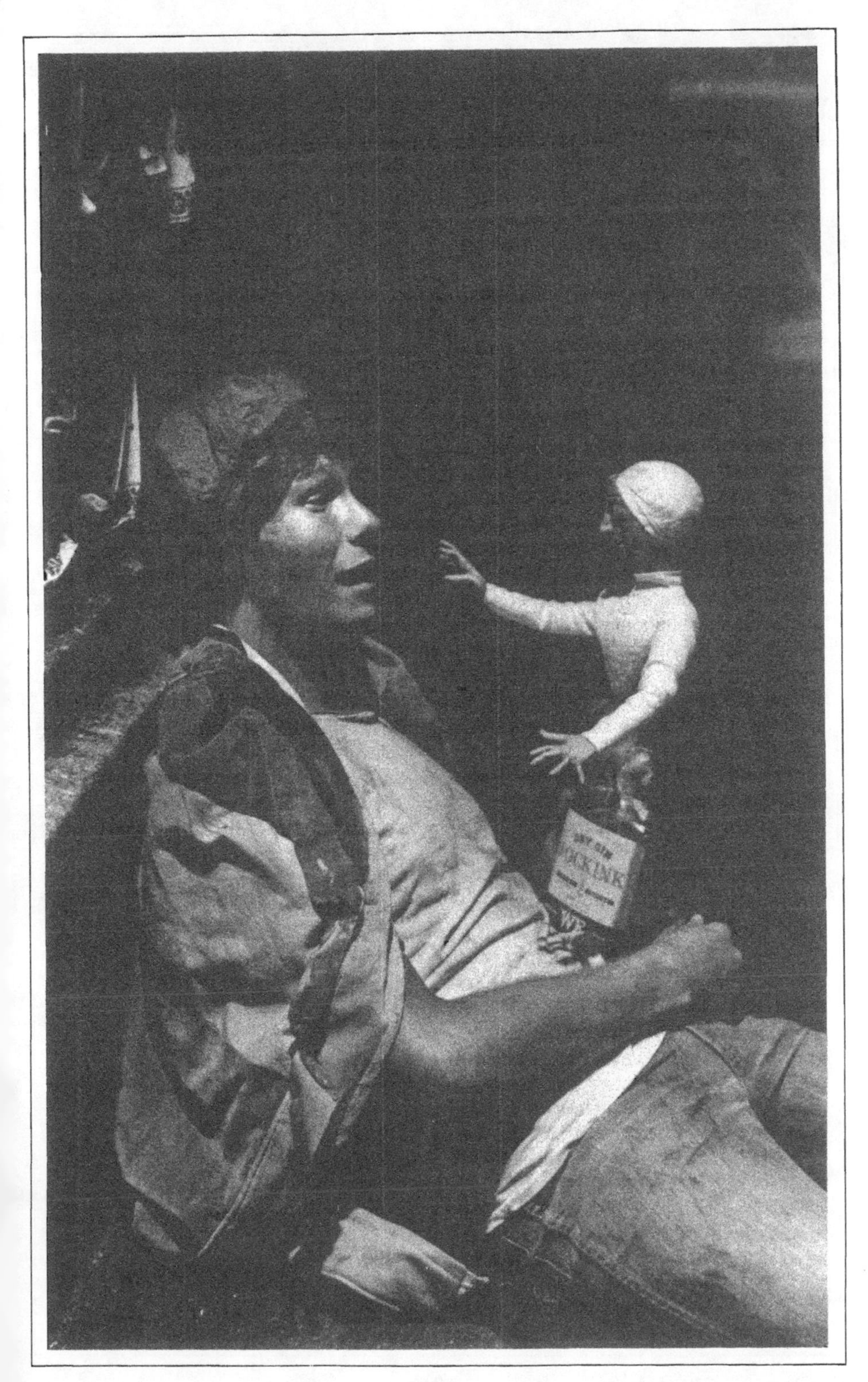

THE FILTHY HOBIT

Fumidus sordidus squalor

⊙ **RANGE:** The Filthy Hobit is everywhere, but he prefers areas officially or socially designated NO SMOKING, confined spaces such as elevators and men's rooms, all public means of transportation, hospital rooms, small restaurants, crowds, and *your* place.

◐ **HABITS:** A spark, a flash, a puff of smoke . . . the promise of pleasure, the thrill of strong desire and, afterward, a lingering presence, and a sense of unfulfillment . . . irradicable traces left behind, one lung chests, sudden losses of health, homes mysteriously burning down . . . these are the works and pomps of a most odious fairy creature.

To nonsmokers, the Filthy Hobit is a nuisance, especially to nonsmokers with a white shag carpet, a sensitive pet, or the sort of allergies that might (or might not) be symptoms of severe sexual repression. Offended by the insalubrious heap of butts, the fetid breath, the stench of a Cuban cigar, the asphyxiating cloud of a pungent pipe, and the scorch mark of the veneer, they believe themselves to be the principal victims of the Filthy Hobit.

How wrong they are! The Filthy Hobit is the true bane of the (somewhat shortened) existence of his own devotees, the Smokers. It is they who, unable to locate an ashtray, must befoul their cuffs and pockets, they whose teeth and fingers turn amber in deference to his filthy ways, they who halfway through the greatest film ever produced, concert ever performed, exhibit ever staged, or love ever made, become distracted—nay obsessed—by the thought of having a cigarette.

And it is the Hobit who always hides the ashtrays, who inspires his addicted legions to light the wrong end of a filter tip, and who makes matches disappear. It is he who inspires his victims to use the gas stove and burn their eyebrows off. The Hobit it is who deludes the chronic cougher into believing there is one left in his or her pack, until he or she gets home, and there isn't, and he or she spends a sleepless night searching behind sofa cushions, foraging through the trash for a butt with a drag or two left in it. . . .

★ **HISTORY:** Filthy is an indigenous American creature, known to the native tribes as To-Ba-Ko, which we might translate as Dragon, the Tragic Puff. Outraged at the Europeans' treatment of his native friends, he has carried out a four-century-long campaign of revenge, by afflicting upon their descendants wheezes, mattress fires, withdrawal symptoms, catarrh, yellow fingers and cancer.

☞ **SPOTTER'S TIPS:** The desperate look in the eyes of a man patting all his pockets, or a woman turning her pocketbook inside out. A pile of ash in the corner of a window sill—like a houseflies' crematorium. A waste basket bursting into flame. And a hollow, bitter laugh that sounds, curiously, not unlike a coughing fit.

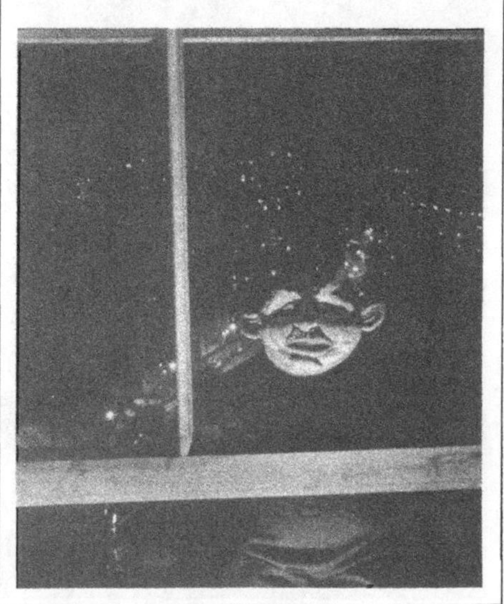

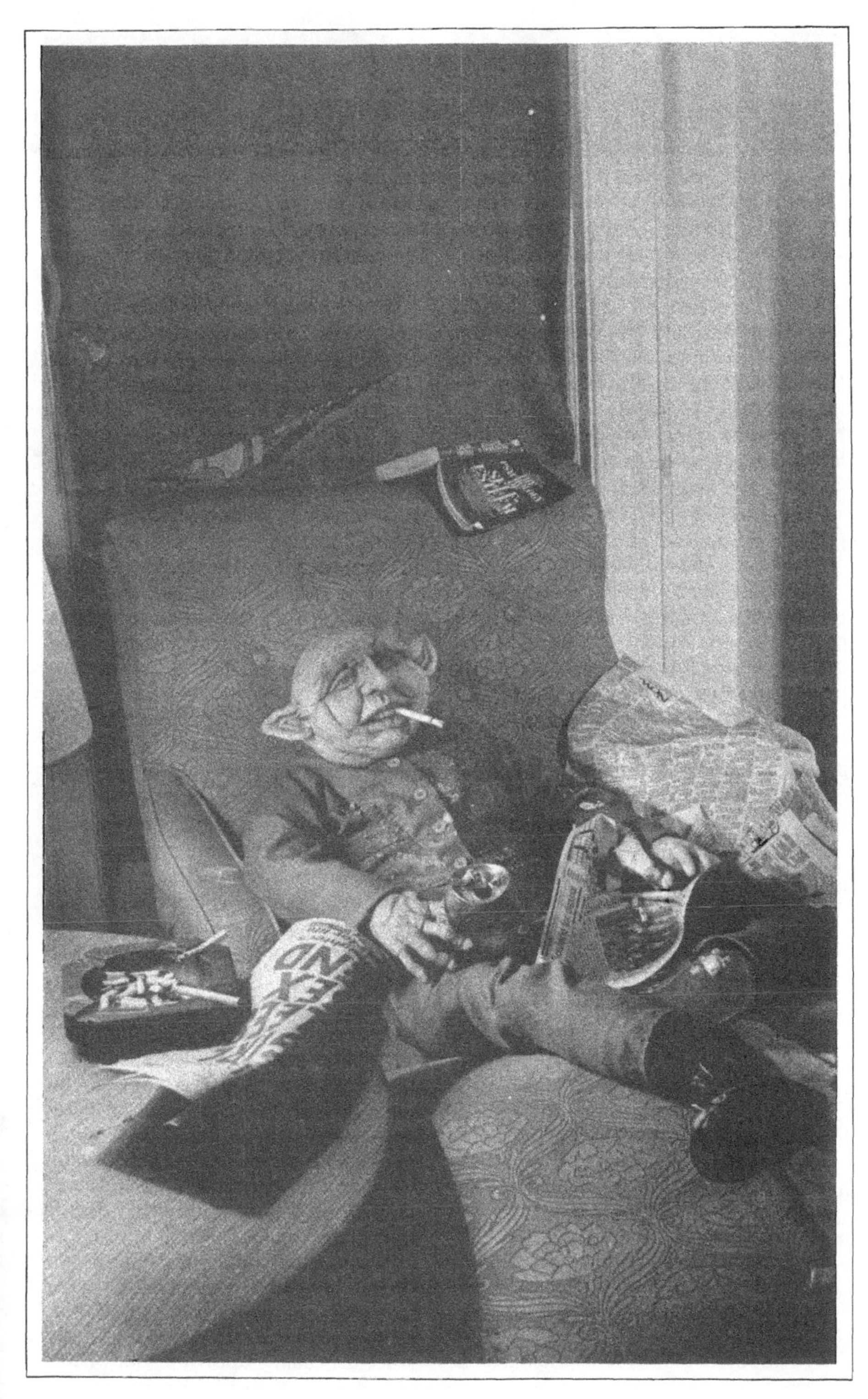

ALIBI ELF

Nolo contendere

⊙ **RANGE:** From your first bed wetting and that broken heirloom vase, through hooky, dented fenders, broken curfews, parking violations, *prima facie* evidence of adultery, broken contracts, missed dental appointments, late payments, and the final bed wetting, Alibi Elf is there, to get you off the hook with a plausible explanation. Sometimes.

◐ **HABITS:** If one's conscience functions as a judge, then Alibi Elf may be said to be everybody's personal defense attorney, his briefcase bulging with extenuating circumstances and cover stories. He provides the dog who ate the homework. He has a large stock of readily available malfunctioning watches, sick friends, bus and plane schedule irregularities, terrible splitting migraines (the worst you've ever had), and (during the World Series) expired elderly relatives.

He is not, himself, very reliable, and sometimes sends one of the junior partners around to handle the action. These "Poor" and "Lame" Excuses can, at best, get you out of alimony proceedings with only a severe tongue-lashing or can plea-bargain a spanking offense down to "your room without dinner."

Like any successful lawyer, Alibi Elf is not concerned with matters of objective innocence or guilt, but so dazzling are his powers of justification and rationalization that he often inspires his clients with enough self-pitying self-righteousness to brazen out the case, despite mountains of damning evidence.

"I didn't know it was loaded!"; "I don't remember!"; "I was drunk!"; and "I can't help it, I'm a Taurus!" are among his typical motions for dismissal.

★ **HISTORY:** Alibi Elf is originally a Fay of French origin and was responsible for helping to establish his homeland's curiously labyrinthine legal systems before emigrating to the New World.

When the first British general lost the first conflict in the Revolutionary War, Alibi Elf was there to help him explain to his superiors that the disaster was the result of "faulty intelligence," when the real faulty intelligence then, as now, was that of the officer in command. Over the years, Alibi Elf has been of great service to military men, but oddly not to cadets, who in most cases are taught to exorcise this creature with the simple phrase, "No excuse, sir."

Likewise, Alibi Elf has been of assistance to politicians (with varying degrees of success). It was he who prompted several "Abscam" defendants to explain to incredulous juries that they were attempting to entrap the FBI agents from whom they had taken bundles of hundreds.

Alibi Elf keeps very busy in Washington, issuing cover stories through press agents he has inspired and offering explanations and amplifications "not for attribution." These follow on the heels of each policy disaster or personal scandal.

"Sorry about that" and "the President misspoke himself" are two fairly recent examples of his work.

☞ **SPOTTER'S TIPS:** The look of outraged innocence in the eyes of an alleged perpetrator is an almost certain sign that he (or she) is busy consulting with Alibi Elf, especially if it is accompanied by the words, "I won't dignify that accusation with a reply."

Explanations that begin "Frankly" or "In all honesty" are inspired by his counsel and are, therefore, neither frank nor honest.

Mortals calling upon the aid of this

ALIBI ELF
Nolo contendere

supernatural spirit do so, as might be expected, in a time-honored, ritual manner. They assume a facial expression of absolute candor and proceed to testify—with their fingers crossed.

As legal aid to New Hampshire's Dan Webster, Alibi Elf once helped beat the Devil.

Under the spell of the Mira Chimera, we wonder things like, "How do I look from the back?"

MIRA CHIMERA (ON THE WALL)

Bella donna

⊙ **RANGE:** This glimmering, glittering, glamorous, but highly elusive spirit is believed, by some, to be extinct. She can only be seen in a mirror, and her many devotees pursue the sight of her in charm schools, makeup clinics, slimming gyms, mud spas, health farms, beauty parlors, tanning salons, and nose job boutiques. Hints to her whereabouts are sought between the glossy covers of fat fashion magazines full of skinny fashion models, and there are frequent reports of near-sightings after the prescribed ritual applications of paints, oils, powders, unguents, and lotions before the looking glass.

◐ **HABITS:** Mira Chimera, like many a bewitching Fairy of ballad and song, offers the promise of romance, wealth, and power to whosoever sees and captures her.

Specifically, she inspires the belief (in Americans of all sexes) that obedience to her harsh and arbitrary demands will result in an improvement in their "image," thus guaranteeing a long and delightful life.

"Fame and fortune can be yours," she whispers, "and may be as close as your vanity table!" (Failing that, there is always the operating table . . .)

The cultivation (or defoliation) of a mustache, a simple sandblasting of shoulder freckles, the loss, gain, or strategic relocation of a dozen pounds—perform any of these, she suggests, and charming, vivacious and successful Mira Chimera might be staring back at *you!*

To a foxy East Coast lady, she might appear as a magazine cover; to a West Coast starlet as a movie poster; to a Midwest woman as a catalogue picture of an all-electric kitchen . . . provided (she implies) they (respectively) grow wild and rampant eyebrows, have their ears trimmed, and paint all their extremities fire engine red.

Men, too, fall victim to her wiles, and have been known to believe that, were it not for a receding hairline, they might rule the world. (This fantasy often leads to a diabolical infatuation with the Devil Toupee.)

★ **HISTORY:** The Mira Chimera is a winged fairy of the Spanish Hadas, an exotic creature of surpassing charm. She always has been appalled and dismayed by human unattractiveness, and it has often amused her to suggest to mortal men and women that there is something they can do about it.

In America, she has been responsible for the marketing of all manner of patent medicines and mail-order beauty aids, not the least famous of which were the celebrated wooden dentures which George Washington whitewashed nightly.

It has been her habit to whisper contradictory beauty hints to alternating generations, so that children and parents look even more absurd to each other than is natural. "Tape 'em down," she commands one decade. "Hang 'em out," she instructs the next. "Grow it long." "Chop it off." "Curl it up." "Straighten it out." "Paint it." "Wash it." "Flash 'em . . . hide 'em . . . put a feather in it . . . beat it with a stick . . ."

☞ **SPOTTER'S TIPS:** Reports of the Mira Chimera's complete disappearance from our world are doubtless premature. She was said to be lost forever with the passing of long white gloves. She was supposed to have vanished with the hoop skirt. She was mourned when the movies learned to talk. She fled in tears when Bernice bobbed her hair . . . but her dedicated followers sometimes glimpse her still, reflected, if only for a moment, in the smoked windows of a passing limo . . .

THE LEPRACHAUNMAN

Melancholia extremis

⊙ **RANGE:** Three a.m. Rainy Sundays. Strange, cheap hotels. Near-empty saloons. (If you find yourself sitting in the near-empty saloon of a cheap hotel at three a.m. on a rainy Sunday, he's got you for certain.) The Leprachaunman's correct mailing address is Bleak House, Lonely Street, Slough of Despond, Valley of Despair, Bluesville, State of Depression 00013.

◐ **HABITS:** It is customary to attribute your typical Irish blatherskite's "gift of gab" to his having kissed the Blarney Stone. Like others of his kith and kin, he is invisible to all but the particular mortal he has singled out for his attentions. He has a soothing, sympathetic way about him. Faith, but he feels nearly as sorry for yourself as you do! And isn't it but he appreciates what a special class of individual you are: full of promise and potential, shamefully misunderstood, hard done by, but bearing up bravely. Here, have another of those. Make it a double.

Sure, he's just the company that misery loves!

And what, you may well ask, does the Leprachaunman do with the dull, gray, soggy, tattered little souls he collects from his victims? Well, in the old days, he'd wad them together, into something that looked like a ball of used Kleenex, and sell them for screenplays or one act plays. Today he peddles them, one by one, as country and western hits.

★ **HISTORY:** There's nary a need of a professional genealogist to tell us that he emerged, nodding thoughtfully and keening softly, from the soggy Celtic Twilight. He's as Irish as treason and learned his soul-stealing craft in the land where many possess the power to transform both whiskey and beer into whine.

F. Scott Fitzgerald and Eugene O'Neill are a pair of his notable victims, but there's scarcely a Jesuit high school in the New World as hasn't graduated a poet or two into his clutches.

☞ **SPOTTER'S TIPS:** He can be found backstage at the closing night of any play, oozing out of an envelope in the wake of a rejection slip, standing a round in the gin mill nearest the unemployment insurance office, offering his smarmy, unctuous condolences: "I'm sorry for yer trouble. . . ."

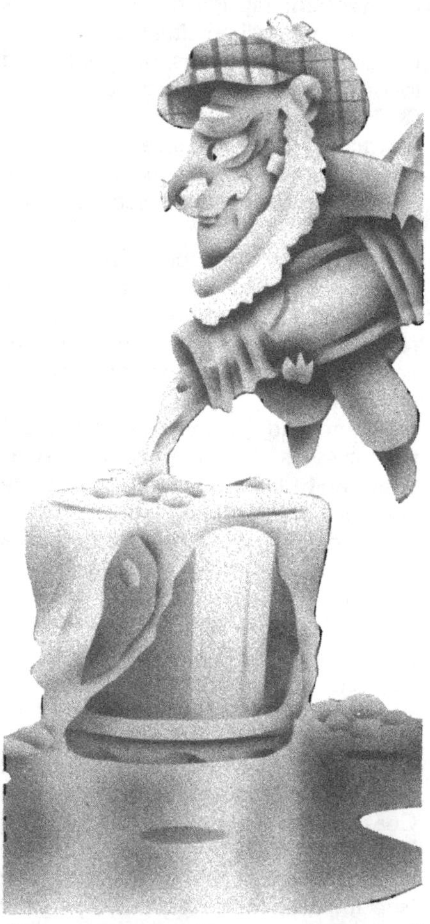

Opposite: A Leprachaunman (fairy of self pity), at work on a rainy night in Georgia.

DON FAUN

Veni vidi visa

⊙ **RANGE:** All points of entry on the American border: airports, docks, bus stations, highways, byways, and goat paths, secret tunnels, unpatrolled deserts, and small holes in fences known only to himself.

◐ **HABITS:** Don Faun provides counsel and inspiration to such members of the tired, poor, and huddled masses as persist in yearning to breathe free, even though the quota has been filled.

He whispers nautical bearings in the ear of a Haitian tillerman and helps him steer his overloaded dinghy to a safe landing on the Florida strand. He assists Iranians in pronouncing those difficult English words, "Iyama stewdant." He guides uncarded farmhands across the Rio Grande and into the employ of leather-skinned but tender-hearted lettuce ranch ramrods.

In return for smuggling an immigrant into America (and getting him established in the small filthy headshop business), Don Faun insists only that his clients show him respect and remain faithful to the folkways of their homelands—that is, that they continue to eat with paddles, wear grotesque hats, or, in some cases, linger in ignorance of most fundamental rules of hygiene.

Many newcomers to these shores further honor their patron, the Don, by becoming, once safely settled in the new country, fiercely demonstrative patriots of the land they left.

★ **HISTORY:** For centuries, Don Faun capered merrily in the woods around the walls of Rome, assisting waves of Goths and Vandals in obtaining looting permits.

He himself stowed away with the fleet of Corsican Folletti, when those earth spirits of old Italy were forced to flee their police-ridden homeland.

He is a friendly, godfatherly type, who has helped generations of immigrants find their way to his adopted country.

A creature of great power and resourcefulness, one of his greatest triumphs came when, rather than smuggle every native of Texas into the U.S.A., he simply arranged for the annexation of the territory. He acted similarly in the case of Alaska, personally lobbying William Seward to purchase that frozen wasteland and thereby earned the undying gratitude of the Eskimos, all of whom were eager for citizenship.

Don Faun currently has his eye on Puerto Rico.

☞ **SPOTTER'S TIPS:** If you are reading this in the United States, you don't need to find Don Faun.

Across our borders, Don Faun helps fill up the Melting Pot.

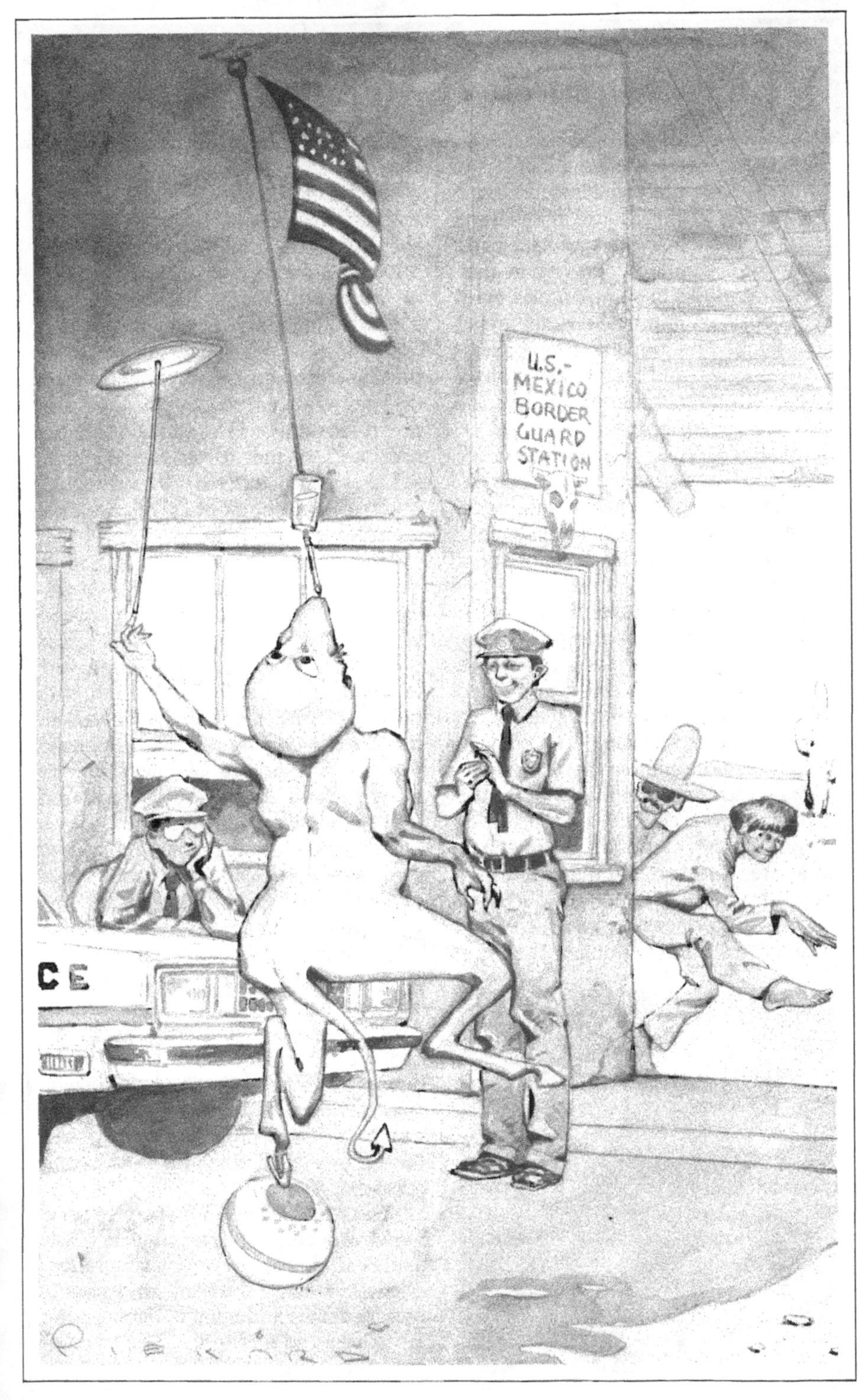
U.S.-
MEXICO
BORDER
GUARD
STATION

EVIL NECKROMANCERS

Infidelitates minimissimae

⊙ **RANGE:** These wicked fomenters of domestic strife are sometimes found in the kitchen during house parties and often in the back seats of taxi cabs. They like the dark corners of bars near the office, parks in summer, and overnight business trips. There are males (Valentinii) and females (Vampirillae) of the species, and they lurk and strike wherever one member of a couple is a little late getting home.

◐ **HABITS:** It is the mischievous, obnoxious, and downright perilous nature of these seductive creatures to leave suspicious traces, scents, hints, and clues of illicit dalliance on or about the persons of their innocent and unsuspecting victims: a blond hair on the lapel of a chap married to a brunette; the smell of strange after-shave in a young bride's hair; a carefully planted matchbook from an exotic night club; a phone number scrawled on a cocktail napkin; unaccountable credit card receipts—and of course, that old favorite, lipstick on your collar.

Fairy wooing of mortals is traditional; there are, for example, many folktales about the tragically impossible love of mermen for princesses, and mermaids for princes . . . but the object of an Evil Neckromancer's affections is not even offered a life of bliss in a city beneath the sea. Those who bear the mark of the Evil Neckromancer just end up having to sleep on the couch.

★ **HISTORY:** To the trained eye, the victim's symptoms (lipstick on the collar, hickies on the throat) are evidence that Evil Neckromancers are decadent, distant relatives of central Europe's dread Nosferatu. (The more direct descendants of that blood-sucking clan, still undead in the New World today, practice the occult rites of personal management.)

The era now known as the Boring Twenties was the heyday of the American Neckromancers, who came flickering out of Hollywood in the guise of "Sheiks" and "Vamps," appearing as tempting visions before hithertofore innocent American couples seated in darkened movie houses. They caused the hideous practice of "necking" to spread across the nation like a beard rash on a maiden throat.

During the forties, many a gallant serviceman on leave came home to his sweet patootie only to find disquieting evidence insidiously left by the Neckromancers: strange cars in driveways, ten-gallon hats, pipes smoking in ashtrays, and huge pairs of unfamiliar boxer shorts hanging from bedroom doorknobs. Fortunately for the future bliss of America's tootsies (and fellas), most servicemen accepted their tootsies' honest explanation for those evil "artifacts": "I just don't know how that got there."

☞ **SPOTTER'S TIPS:** You don't spot a Neckromancer; a Neckromancer spots you. And unless you enjoy screaming, door-slamming, bag-packing rages, protestations, and recriminations, you are advised to ignore the Neckromancer's handiwork at all times.

TUPPERWEREWOLVES

Tedium domesticum

⊙ **RANGE:** Tupperwerewolves are little-known members of the larger group of supernatural beings known as shape shifters; it includes such monstrosities as the Werewolves (of London), the Were-bears (known to the American Indians), the Were-foxes of China and the Ready-to-Were wolves of modern "shopping centers." Tupperwerewolves, like these others, are human until, under special circumstances, they are involuntarily transformed into unbreakable plastic receptacles. Tupperwerewolves are found in many American homes. They are stainless and heat resistant and come in a variety of colors. They are said to last a lifetime, and, for all we know, may be immortal.

◐ **HABITS:** Almost every American has met and conversed with a Tupperwerewolf, but due to the blandness and insipidity of the creature, few are able to distinguish it from a perfectly ordinary bore. Spending part of their time as plastic containers and the rest as suburban, semi-sentient life, Tupperwerewolves are remarkable in both forms for their quality of complete forgetability.

★ **HISTORY:** The Tupperwerewolves originated in Holland, the boredom capital of the world. In the guise of thick, ugly pottery and plates, they were venerated by the simple-minded Dutch, who gave them places of honor upon grotesquely carved cabinets in the corners of their kitchens. (It has been argued that the word "Elf" is itself but a corruption of the Dutch word "Delft.") After arriving in America, Tupperwerewolves adopted a more resilient form, and lurk to this day in many a suburban kitchen, inspiring trivial kaffeeklatsch conversation.

☞ **SPOTTER'S TIPS:** As stated above, a Tupperwerewolf is almost indistinguishable from a normal human bore. However, if you find yourself, in a domestic social situation, listening to someone too boring to be *real,* chances are he (or she) isn't! There are ways to find out. In both human and plastic forms, Tupperwerewolves are dishwasher safe. A trip through the rinse cycle is a quick way to test the nature of your tedious newfound friend. A less vigorous method is to ask the suspected shape shifter if he (or she) is "afraid of spotting or streaking." Tupperwerewolves generally are. In whatever form, Tupperwerewolves are unbreakable. Bores who have survived head-on collisions with commuter trains or recent surgery are probably Tupperwerewolves.

These creatures do not crack or shatter at extreme temperatures. Bores of your acquaintance from desert or permafrost regions are probably Tupperwerewolves. You can throw a party and find out.

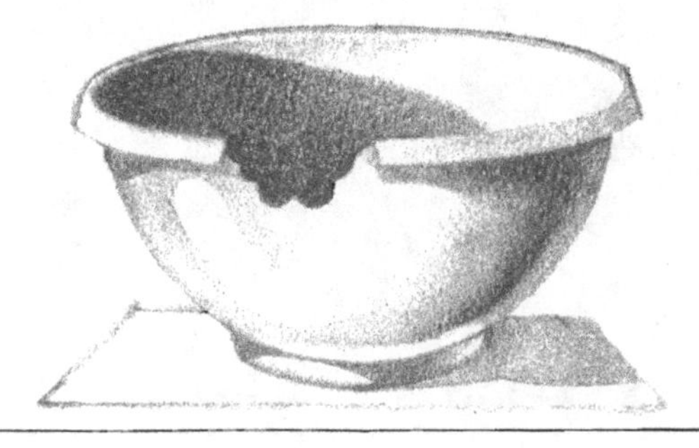

Parties of Tupperwerewolves prowl the long Minnesota nights.

THE LEFT WING SYMP AND THE RIGHT WING TROG

Pox populi. Sinister dexterque

⊙ **RANGE**: These two highly political, argumentative and totally symbiotic creatures prefer to stalk such public forums as the podia of awards ceremonies and the sidewalks in front of embassies, but they may also be found in humbler settings, such as state chambers, barbershops, and the corridors of detox centers in depressed urban areas.

◐ **HABITS**: By means yet unknown, these inseparable creatures shape the opinions of the opinion shapers. It has been suggested that through water fluoridation, the Symp lures young folk to the Left, while the Trog summons their elders to the Right with a stern clarion call, in a deep, daddy-like voice.

It was once believed that the Trog-Symp was a two-headed creature, its twin (and empty) skulls joined at the nose, the better to exchange glares. In fact, they share a heart (half-hard, half-bleeding) and not one mortal protegé of either is entirely uninfluenced by the other.

Thus, the radical Liberal, protesting one governmental agency's invasion of his files and telephone, has much in common with the extreme Conservative, objecting to another governmental agency's attempt to register his rifle and audit his tax returns—for both are moved to lodge their principled complaints with the same (and yet another) governmental agency!

There is nothing more pleasing to the Symp-Trog than the sight of two mortals defending to one another's death each other's right to disagree.

★ **HISTORY**: Resembling as they do the traditional "Winged Victories" of France and the radical "Red Cap" *Foletti* of Italy, these contrary conjoined creatures were clearly born of mixed French and Italian parentage in the Old World. Before emigrating to the New, they divided their time between homelands, laying the groundwork for the astonishing number of strongly opposed and universally despised political parties which to this day succeed each other in their respective European capitals.

Arriving late to the New World by the standards of the first fairy emigrants (there was so much to do in the homelands), these politics-loving creatures reached America on the Mayflower. Upon landing at Plymouth, the once-persecuted Puritans, erstwhile disciples of the Left Winged Symp, were confronted by prospects of vast power and real estate, and instantly converted to the side of the Right Winged Trog.

At the Constitutional Convention, the Trog inspired John Adams while the Symp supported Thomas Paine. When Adams eventually assumed the Presidency, the Trog cheered; the Symp convinced Citizen Tom to split for France.

Since then, the Trog-Symp has inspired Americans to take belligerent and opposing sides in civil wars, their own and other people's (Spain, Vietnam, Ireland, El Salvador . . .).

A consensus is commonly supposed to emerge from the colliding and often paradoxical opinions advocated by the LWS/RWT. Who can quarrel with a *two party system?* And if, instead of a consensus, a pork-barrelling stalemate results, who can deny that a two-headed, bipartisan beast is yet superior to the four-headed fairy of this kind which haunts Canada or the one with the thirteen-way split personality that is the scourge of Mexico?

☞ **SPOTTER'S TIPS**: Both the Trog

THE LEFT WING SYMP AND THE RIGHT WING TROG

Pox populi, Sinister dexterque

and Symp hibernate between elections, living off their store of little-known facts. Periodically, they emerge to view the issues, but return to their hole immediately, if they see even the shadow of doubt. At election time, they emerge and lend candidates not just the courage to confront the issues but the stamina to recite them endlessly. Look for signs of them wherever slogans such as "Who needs a slogan when you can have a promise?" are heard.

This Symp-Trog hails from North and/or South Dakota, but can never agree on which.

THE PENTAGORGON

Draconis militarisibus

⊙ **RANGE:** Marching upon the land, or burrowing (like moles) beneath it; upon the sea and under it; up in the air and full of it, this most bellicose spirit patrols the war room, the boardroom, the ward room, the sword room, the barroom, and the powder room of the Pentagon. She has also been sighted (and cited) behind the throne, inside the velvet glove, between the lines (and well behind them), under deep cover, lobbying in the lobbies off the corridors of power, and attending the occasional clandestine strategy conference, deep in somebody else's jungle.

◐ **HABITS:** Operation Self-Perpetuation.

Code Name: Bloat.

Eyes Only.

A: Strategy: Military expenditures shall increase by triple the rate of inflation and/or in direct inverse proportion to perceived and/or potential National Security threats.

B: Tactics: Infiltrate and snafu existing defense projects by altering design specifications and off-lining production schedules, to insure vast cost overruns and eventual production of obsolete and inefficient ordnance equipment; utilize leaked media exposure of critically obsolete and inefficient ordnance equipment to justify immediate requisition of greatly increased military appropriations, etc., etc.

Optimal Scenario A (Hardware): Commission nuclear-powered helicopter-submarine-scout-craft, to secure aircraft carrier bottoms from subversive encrustations by insurgent crustaceans.

Optimal Scenario B (Software): Obtain Congressional Grant for (CIA front) Costa Rican Aural Medicine Institute; surgically deafen indigenous population to facilitate utilization of area as secret rocket testing target.

★ **HISTORY:** As its name suggests, the Pentagorgon is of Greek ancestry—Spartan, to be precise. She served as military advisor to the forces laying siege to the city of Troy and recommended the fabulously difficult fabrication of an enormous and realistic dead rat on wheels, stuffed with Argive guerillas, to be left at the Trojan gate. Although the ruse was apparently unsuccessful, the Pentagorgon achieved her objective of prolonging the war another twenty-one years.

The Pentagorgon has an aversion to the sights, sounds, and smells of actual combat. Her interest (and hence the interest of the mortals in her thrall) is strictly in the financing, development, deployment, and maintenance of weapons.

In her capacity as Military Advisor to the U.S. of A., she has recommended the pig iron plating of Civil War barges, the manufacture and testing of many wonderful nuclear weapons, the spraying of defoliant into the wind, and is at present urging the Powers That Be to arm patriotic American dolphins with nuclear warheads—a national sense of porpoise, she calls it.

The Pentagorgon's proudest American achievement was the battle of the Alamo, a gory encounter which resulted not only in the obliteration of the American defenders, but caused what seems like a three-hundredfold increase in military spending on a per annum basis from that day to this.

☞ **SPOTTER'S TIPS:** A speech about the urgent need to up the megatonnage; a prattle of slogans, a rattle of sabres, a flutter of flags, and a clatter of drums; a bluster of orders, a cluster of corpses; a gold star and a ribbon where your arm used to be.

Red-blooded boys and girls, the Pentagorgon wants you! (For lunch.)

THE WOOLY BULLY

Patrioticus jingoissimus

⊙ **RANGE:** This loudly, proudly nationalistic sprite is usually encamped down at the American Legion Hall, although in times of international crisis—like a war or the Olympics—he is frequently found on the barstool next to you and/or behind the wheel of a taxi. He also occurs in National Park Service trailer campsites and infests phone-in radio shows.

◐ **HABITS:** Although he is really very tiny, the Wooly Bully can puff himself up to enormous size, not unlike the bullfrog. He can also imitate that inflatable amphibian's popping eyes and grumpy, bellicose croak.

The Wooly Bully is a nature spirit: that is, he's melodramatically proud of America's geographical grandeur and seductively suggests to us, as we gaze in awe at the Rockies, the Grand Canyon, or the Everglades, that any country with landmarks like these couldn't possibly, ever, screw up its economic or foreign policies.

He can be devious, as well, and has been known to hide in the bottom of a Cracker Jack box. When swallowed, he creates that well-known lump in your throat at the climax of a John Wayne movie.

He's the spirit of patriotism.

He loves to rattle the little sabre he carries but is mostly harmless as a child. (He can't resist a parade or fireworks display.)

The Wooly Bully is only dangerous when found in close proximity to the Right Wing Trog and the Pentagorgon, with whom he shares an affinity for invasions of small Caribbean islands, embargoes of socialist dictatorships, and meetings of the Trilateral Commission.

★ **HISTORY:** It is assumed that the Wooly Bully is of Teutonic origin, that he is descended from the blustering warrior dwarves so dear to Wagner, and that possibly his name itself is a corruption of *Wuhlarbeit,* the German word meaning 'agitator,' 'irritation,' 'pain-in-the-neck.'

The Wooly Bully first appeared in America shortly before the turn of the century, emigrating from the Old World in the company of East European diplomats. He quickly adopted the patriotic fervor of his new land, however, and served as company mascot for Teddy Roosevelt's Rough Riders. That is why, while cutting a swath through other people's homelands in the name of National Security, Manifest Destiny, and Hearst newspaper circulation, T.R. would rally the troops by shouting, "Bully!"

☞ **SPOTTER'S TIPS:** When Old Glory unfurls in the wind and the band plays Sousa, you will feel the Wooly Bully running up and down your spine. It tickles. Enjoy it. He's only dangerous when armed.

MUGWUMPS

Philibusterus gubernatorius

⊙ **RANGE:** Mugwumps are found, and have always been found, and will always be found, at every level of federal, state, county, municipal, and local politics. They are a whoopee cushion upon the seat of government, a holdful of bilge on the ship of state, and a blast of hot air in the corridors of power.

◐ **HABITS:** There is a spirit that drives a man (or woman) to seek elective (or appointed) office. Something stronger, and more elusive, than greed and vanity and power-lust. It is the Mugwump.

Tutored by the Mugwump, even the most dedicated public servant quickly learns to speak in the eldritch tongues of Bafflegab and Gobbledygook. Simple office holders can find themselves suddenly and mysteriously transported from their humble post, to far-off and exotic lands, by means of a magic Mugwump junket.

He often casts a sleep-inducing spell through a ritual incantation involving the Founding Fathers, the flag, motherhood, and a rich lathering of adjectives over back-home geographical points of interest. When all members present have nodded into a patriotic trance, the Mugwump performs his "dirty tricks"—that is, "Ab" and similar scams.

★ **HISTORY:** Mugwumps are descended from the Swedish *Nixen*, who were guardians of the most travelled water routes of their native land. Like all Swedes (and eponymous American presidents), they are not all motivated by principle, preferring a more nonpartisan image.

In one of their earlier adventures in the New World, Mugwumps advised the native Algonquian tribe (Mugwump is an Algonquian name) to remain neutral in the Huron-Iroquois Wars.

Today, there are no more Algonquians.

Like his river-protecting predecessors, the cautious Mugwump guards the Potomac in the political position that he has invariably assumed over two hundred years, a position from which he derives his very name: sitting with his mug on one side of the fence and his wump on the other.

☞ **SPOTTER'S TIPS:** The Mugwump is most often sighted in the vicinity of the free lunch, whose existence he denies. There he stands, beside the gravy train, with a mouthful of corn. See? He's the one waving the apple pie around and dipping a single chicken into any number of pots for the benefit of the photographers. Watch him slice (from high off the hog) choice bits for his personal pork barrel. Yes, indeed, he specializes in bread and butter issues, but when the heat comes on, he gets out of the kitchen! You can follow his trail, marked as it is by scattered red herrings and all those hot potatoes he just dropped.

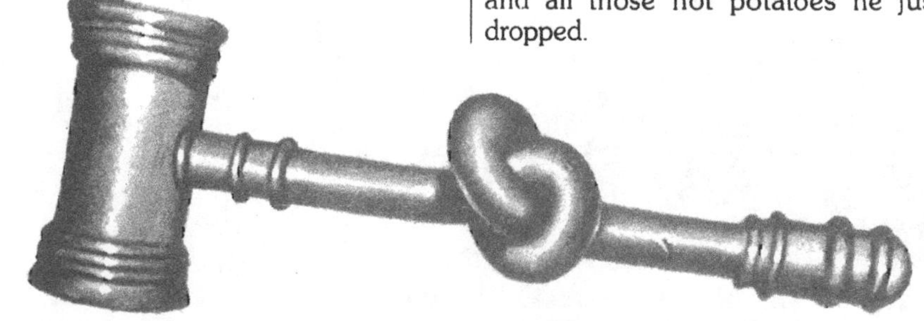

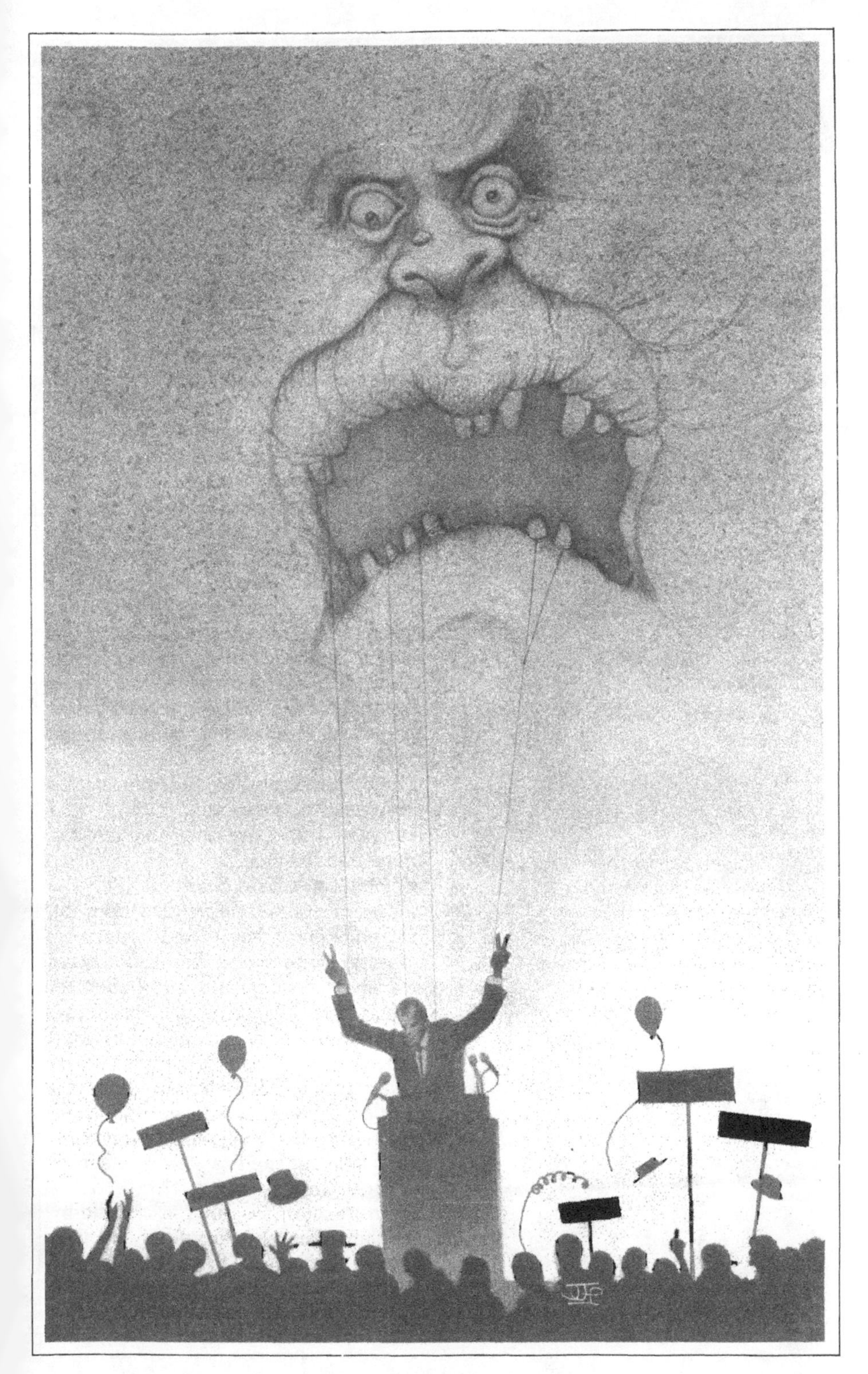

THE SPIRIT OF '76

E pluribus, pluribus

⊙ **RANGE:** It would be pleasant to report that this admirable, supernatural entity is present and active at all times, in all American states and territories, that she hovers eternally above every farm and forest, town and city, over all America and all Americans, lighting, guiding, and defending . . .

It would be equally pleasant to report that she is enormous and powerful, winged like an eagle, clear as a bell, bright as a flag, loud as trumpets.

In fact, she is somewhat rare and rather delicate. She makes her presence felt only from place to place and turns up at the darkest times.

The Spirit of '76—all too often cited and all too seldom seen.

◐ **HABITS:** It was once her function—or mission, if you like—to inspire hearts with a somewhat sophisticated and glorious love of liberty, freedom and country. But over the years, other Spirits, of Corruption, Greed and Prejudice, have been abroad in this land, as in other lands. They loathe patriotism and to mock and debase it, they tempt mortals to cheat and steal and hurt in its name.

So, in our complicated time, the Spirit of '76 is content to touch our hearts and minds only with simpler thoughts and feelings, such as Anger and Hope. Thus the surge of anger any American might occasionally feel in the face of cruelty, or waste, or injustice is the work of the Spirit of '76. And so is the unexpected sudden shiver of hope that a child, or a bird, or a morning might bring.

The Spirit is also capable of inspiring compassion, patience, loyalty and laughter—but these are only for the brave and the free.

★ **HISTORY:** The Spirit of '76 is a hybrid, of course, descended from the English Robin of the Woods (enemy of oppression) and from the red-capped and liberty-loving Fays and Folletti of France and Italy. She still has many fairy cousins active around the world today.

During the Revolutionary War, the Spirit of '76 lived in Jefferson's inkwell, and during the Civil War, under Lincoln's hat, but she has steered clear of all politicians since the era of Reconstruction, favoring, as she did in her native Europe, the poor and oppressed throughout the land.

☞ **SPOTTER'S TIPS:** The Spirit of '76 is usually found at a maximum distance from monuments erected to her fame.

JACK B. NIMBUS

Jupiter pluvius

⊙ **RANGE:** From the hurricane-harried trailer parks of the Keys to twister-tormented Texas trails, through the earthquake-shaking guacamole ranches of California, up through the fog-sodden bogs of the Northwest, across the snowbound, dust-blown plains to the hail-raddled New England coast, Jack B. Nimbus rides the skies, endowing the mortals below with whatever weather they don't need any more of.

◐ **HABITS:** This magician of meteorological menace casts spells: wet spells, dry spells, hot spells, and cold snaps.

Around the country, he is known by many names. "The Dust Devil," they call him in the Southwest. In Maine, he's "Johnny Chinook." In Florida, "Jack Frost"—in California, David Frost. In the extremely frigid states of Montana, North Dakota, Minnesota and in the tropical regions of Canada slightly to their north, they call him "Abominable Snow Munchkin."

It is the Abominable Snow Munchkin's practice to skulk upon snowy inclines. When a human being passes below, the Munchkin twitches a tiny lever, dumping an icy load upon the victim. Often the occasion of good-natured seasonal hilarity, these tricks are sometimes fatal, as when several hundred pounds of ice and slush are unleashed from the roof of a ski resort A-frame. Munchkins prefer a temperature range of 25° to 32° Fahrenheit, which insures good heavy snow and optimal chance to dump it.

A subspecies of Jack B. Nimbus: the Abominable Snow Munchkins of Wisconsin.

★ **HISTORY:** In the Northwest, they say Jack B. Nimbus comes from England, the country where it only rains twice a week (once for four days straight and once for three).

In Southern California, he is believed to be of Italian origin, a Wind Folletti from sunny Sicily, bringing bright sunshine and catastrophic earthquakes.

But the Abominable Snow Munchkin is undoubtedly of Scandinavian descent. According to Norse mythology, he was originally formed from the dandruff of a sleeping Frost Giant. His merry pranks passed unnoticed by lugubrious Danes, and the Swedes would go so far as to lie beneath steeply cambered roofs invoking his aid in their perpetual attempts at suicide. He therefore travelled to the New World, where, even in the northernmost cities of the U.S., the first snowfall of the year is regarded as a totally unexpected natural disaster on a level with the destruction of Pompeii.

☞ **SPOTTER'S TIPS:** When it is cold enough to make the paps of a sorceress seem thermodynamic, when there is sufficient precipitation that the mallards rejoice, when the ova of barnyard fowl may be prepared upon the pavement, Jack B. Nimbus is doing his thing. Self-proclaimed "weathermen" and "weatherwomen," in league with the Mind Boggles, often claim a precognitive awareness of Jack B. Nimbus, but their boasts are often a boost only to the *very* Small Businessmen selling umbrellas, gloves, leg warmers and hats on urban streetcorners.

Best advice: Look up.

PIERARD
19 · 81

THE BUGBEAR

Bacchus paccus

⊙ **RANGE:** The Bugbear is a wind-spirit: something between a breath of fresh air and a neuralgia-inducing draft. She beckons us onward through Death Valley, upward to the Rockies, downward into the depths of Carlsbad Caverns, outward through the blizzard, deeper into the second growth primeval, and in general, really, like really, INTO the outdoors.

◐ **HABITS:** The original Fairy response to the sight of mortal man was to get him lost in the woods. And, after all these years, we *still* find it impossible to resist the Call of the Wild, the haunting summons from distant hill and forest. So off we go, orienteering, spelunking, cross-country skiing, fly-fishing,• bird-watching, beachcombing, mountain climbing, white water rafting, scuba diving, butterfly collecting—to wind up lost in the woods.

But no sooner are we rescued, dried off, thawed out, and taken off the intravenous, than we're off to the woods again because the Bugbear has equipped us, this time, with foolproof magic equipment for our journey: a pocket-sized cookstove with a phosphorescent flotation cuff (and a jacket with several dozen pockets to stow it in); a multipurpose Martian Army knife, suitable for maintaining jet engines or whittling toothpicks, lacking only a blade to adjust a pocket-sized cookstove; a bottle of weapons-grade mosquito repellent (sure to keep those pesky skeeters away from the pocket it leaked into); a powerful, waterproof, rechargeable flashlight to illuminate fully whatever that stuff was you stepped in, as well as the baleful red eyes of the enormous bruin who left it there.

The Bugbear also whispers good advice on woodcraft to the intrepid mushroom hunter: "The ones with caps that look like pizzas with everything on them are OK to eat. The ones with caps that have no anchovies are deadly."

Inspired by the environmentally aware Bugbear, we visit the seashore after an oil spill to degrease ducks with Duz and Lux; refloat and motivate suicidal whales; and, on the way home, get lost in the woods.

★ **HISTORY:** Bugbears are descended from old forest Fair Folk of England and Ireland who were related to Boggles, Boggarts, Boogies, Bogies, and double Bogies. An early Irish variant was the L. L. Bean Sidhe. For centuries, "I got lost in the woods" was a perfect excuse for the day-late Irishman, until the women of Eire banded together and cut down every tree on the Emerald Isle. The men are still always a day late, but now they have no excuse.

When the great forests of Europe were hewn to make pulp to make paper to make books which denied the existence of Fairies, the Bugbears took the hint and emigrated to the well-wooded shores of the New World. For centuries they amused themselves at the expense of coureurs de bois, pioneers, and other trailblazers. Many famous Americans (Boone, Lewis and Clark, Teddy Roosevelt, to name but a bunch) enjoy reputations as explorers—when all they really did was to follow a capricious Bugbear and get lost in the woods.

☞ **SPOTTER'S TIPS:** The trail is clearly marked. Follow the signs. Keep the sun on your right. Moss only grows on the north side of the trees. If you carry it in, carry it out. Don't panic. Timber wolves are every bit as afraid of you as the mountain lions are.

FOUL SEWER OGRES

Disgustibus malodorus subterraneus

⊙ **RANGE:** The drains and cisterns, goosenecks and septic tanks, culverts and aqueducts of America are the dark domain of the Foul Sewer Ogres. Each night, they emerge, unbidden, onto the surface—like repressed urges, bubbling up from the unconscious mind as naughty dreams.

Foul Sewer Ogres are the nether region's version of the above ground Guttersnipe. They may invade the home via bathtub and sink drains, or by way of the toilet (which is why it is such a good idea to keep the lid closed).

◐ **HABITS:** Foul Sewer Ogres cause plugged pipes, bathtub rings and backed-up toilets, for their favorite sight in all the world is the wrinkled-up nose on the face of a fastidious houseguest. Although they appear to subsist on a meager diet of undigested corn kernels, peanuts, and diced carrots, they are powerful in the extreme—they have been known to play tiddlywinks with manhole covers and can infest entire city blocks with an evil, flatulent aroma.

★ **HISTORY:** Primitive Man, we are told, learned to walk upon his hind legs, the better to walk away from the awful messes he made of things. Neglected, buried and despised, Foul Sewer Ogres then arose and have followed behind mankind ever since. Today, the wretched creatures often appear in the form of investigative reporters, or "Muckrakers," the better to blow the lids off things, and "raise a big stink."

Foul Sewer Orges played a major part in the history of America, for it was their noxious presence on the outskirts of frontier settlements which drove the more salubrious pioneers ever westward in search of unsullied hollows and untainted streams.

☞ **SPOTTER'S TIPS:** The soundest advice to those who would seek (for their own perverse purposes) a Sewer Ogre is, follow your nose.

Foul Sewer Ogres are an underground movement in parts of Indiana.

ENERGENII

Conedus conedus

⊙ **RANGE:** These tiny terrorists move at the speed of light, are as odorless as natural gas, and harder to find than offshore oil. Yet they are everywhere, flitting from the hypercooled south to the overheated north, leaving trails of white smoke in the skies between.

◐ **HABITS:** It is the Energenii's function to cause our precious energy sources to be diminished. There are many subspecies (or "alternate sources") of Energenii: Gas Guzzlers, Power Mongers, Short Circuits, Ethyl Mermen, and Brownie (or "Brown") Outs, to name but a few.

They are a warrior band, organized along military lines, with a chain of command running from their General, Electric, through ranking officers, Major and Admiral Appliances, down to the humble Private Lee-Owned Resources.

The Energenii strike like lightning (most often at night), plugging in and turning on every light, motor, burner, and piece of equipment in home, office and factory.

The Energenii distract the gas station attendant and cause him to leave the locking gas cap off your tank, allowing precious fuel to "evaporate," sometimes through a hose into a bucket. They readjust your car's idle screw so that the engine roars like a dive bomber at a stoplight and the whole vehicle shakes and skips around like a bronc in a rodeo show. Energenii also enjoy destroying the washers on (preferably hot) water taps, turning up the furnace thermostat after you are asleep, and making sure your gas or electric oven is left on at the highest possible setting when it isn't in use.

Their most insidious tactic is to stealthily infiltrate our houses, strip away the insulation, and thus make draft dodgers of us all.

Like most wicked spirits, Energenii are frightened away by sunlight. Thus, some optimistic mortals believe that there is yet time to employ Solar Power against them, before they acquire (oh, terrifying thought!) nuclear capability.

★ **HISTORY:** Like all Genii (or Djinni), they are Arabic, hailing from the nations we now designate as OPEC. After arriving in this country, they decreed that the homes of the early settlers should contain one or two fireplaces (at least) per room in order to make maximum inroads on the forests and coal deposits of the New World.

When the first jalopy, consuming precious gasoline and belching the first protosmog, tooled out of a shed, the Energenii realized that it was the ideal vehicle to do their bidding in the New World and to this day the automobile remains their favorite form of transportation.

Two mortals in particular have done the work of these plundering creatures: Henry Ford, who invented, at the Energenii's hellish behest, the infernal combustion engine; and Thomas Edison, who in a very real sense made each of us a Slave of the Lamp.

☞ **SPOTTER'S TIPS:** The Energenii can be seen hovering in colorful clouds over most cities and spreading like viscous rainbows on the surface of the Gulf. They are present at the construction of any major dam—their traces are those harmless-looking little cracks in the concrete. When you see a seven-seater, eight-cylinder American Bronto-mobile caught in traffic, burning fossil fuel to operate the stereo, air conditioner and power seats—containing, to the naked eye, only the plump, polyester-clad and bilious driver—you may be sure one of the Energenii is hunkered down in the suicide seat beside him, grinning.

GEODESIC GNOME

Mustus aqueductus

☉ **RANGE:** The Geodesic Gnome's range is functionally determined. Depending upon his needs, abilities, and the ground and climate conditions, he can be virtually anywhere. Design, the prime concern of the Geodesic Gnomes, is not simply *what isn't,* nor what is *wished for:* Design is what *should be.* Thus, they glimmer and tower from Manhattan's skyscrapers, all in a (van der) Rohe, to downtown Houston, the best little Bauhaus in Texas.

◐ **HABITS:** Geodesic Gnomes are the sources of most architectural inspiration, though they have been known to addle the pate of the odd contractor as well.

They are small and love to sleep on architects' scale models, which they demand be executed precisely and completely. Thus, the scale model of anything from a redesigned library to a suburb always looks terrific, however uninhabitable the creation is when rendered in reality.

The Gnomes urge bold experimentation and flights of fancy. They inspire dreams, visions—castles in the air, if you will. And castles in the air they get, with very drafty basements.

Gossamer-roofed arenas in the snow belt, skywalks that sway in time to music, and mile-high towers that shed their windows like autumn leaves are among their accomplishments.

Nor do they neglect interiors—anyone who has hurtled headfirst into a conversation pit or walked smack-dab into a plate glass room-divider has met the Geodesic Gnome.

No American architect has gone entirely uninfluenced by them. The genius who first designed Murphy-closets for his clients' homes (as well as self-dumping drawers) was in the thrall of the Gnome. Legal considerations require that we withhold that architect's name, but we can tell you he later went on to design the first rotating insurance company headquarters. Buckminster Fuller, perhaps the Gnome's best known victim, showed this influence clearly in his early design for an underground aviary for tropical fowl, which was built in the late 1950s near Hojo, New Mexico. This subterranean

GEODESIC GNOME

Mustus aqueductus

bird house intended to use the heat of adjacent mud springs to cut heating costs; however, the poisonous fumes and solvent properties of the mud first killed all the birds, then caused the entire structure to collapse upon itself. To this day, geysers spewing feathers and steam serve as an example to young architects of the creative influence of the Geodesic Gnomes.

★ **HISTORY**: There is no doubting this creature's Nordic origins. They are as Scandinavian as a shin-ripping coffee table, and Germanic as a looming, trembling cantilever. They were banished from the Teutonic Old World when the Rainbow Bridge to Aasgard, an early construction of theirs, collapsed under a party of returning Valkyries.

None of the useful and attractive native dwellings in the North and East of the New World—igloos, long houses, teepees, etc.—appealed to them. But they were truly excited by the sight of the pueblos of the Southwest, which inspired the Gnomes' great City Planning Breakthrough Idea—the vertical slum.

Any Urban Renewal Program which takes a sprawling community of working class people, bulldozes it, and builds in its place a mile high cabinet in which the middle-class can be filed away is the work of the Geodesic Gnome.

☞ **SPOTTER'S TIPS**: By the presence of any of the following structures and artifacts, one may know that the Geodesic Gnome has been up to his tricks: hexagonal, tin foil toilet seats; an apartment gutted to resemble a loft; a loft baffled to resemble an apartment; square coffee cups; cutting boards of stainless steel and sinks of butcher block; industrial compounds planted on the rich Midwestern loam; polyester-pipeline-sprinklered, air-conditioned, domed and doomed farms in the Southwestern desert: the paving-over of forest, field, and stream for a thruway to the Nature World Theme Park.

Who but Geodesic Gnomes would build igloos in Arizona?

THE SPIRIT OF ST. LOUIS

Babbit redux

⊙ **RANGE:** Although he is named for that magnificent urban center in the "Show-me" State, the Spirit does not confine his operations to its environs but wanders the heartland of this great nation, from the Grain Belt to the Sun Belt, from the Bible Belt to the Gun Belt—wherever in this great nation a man is suddenly, mysteriously motivated to tighten his belt, knock back a couple of belts, and belt the wife and kids around for a while.

◐ **HABITS:** The dauntless Charles Lindbergh, in a craft named after this creature, flew solo to France, took a look around, beheld the splendors of ancient culture and gay Paree, went back home, and declared himself an isolationist. That's the Spirit of St. Louis at work for you, fellah.

Much otherwise inexplicable American behavior is the work of this "Anima Within," a direct descendant of the "Spirit of '76." It is the Spirit of St. Louis who inspires us to approve in practice what we deplore in theory and to accuse all who do otherwise of being hypocrites . . . to celebrate with bands and bunting a previous (successful) revolution in politics and morality, while jailing, or at least ostracizing, anyone advocating political or moral change in the present.

Operating by such subtle means as *Saturday Evening Post* covers, soda pop commercials, and Walt Disney movies, the Spirit of St. Louis has tattooed upon the national imagination a vision of green lawns, white picket fences, Pop's malt shop, cute little dogs named Spot, calico bonnets, freckled, pigtailed happy apple pies and smiling porters—who knew their place—helping us aboard.

★ **HISTORY:** The city after which the Spirit is named is, in turn, named in honor of a French King, famous for his piety and successful slaughter of foreigners. There is no adequate English translation for the French word "chauvinism," but we all know what it means, don't we?

In La Belle France, to this day, all citizens, from the most decadent aristocrat to the dirtiest Marseilles gutter waif, aspire to the condition of being middle-class. This lust, to rest smug, snug, and secure behind a barricade of ill-gotten and tasteless material possessions, was spread to the American Midwest by the sharpdealing, gravy-grasping, butter-hoarding Spirit of St. Louis.

☞ **SPOTTER'S TIPS:** Listen for the sounds of the Spirit of St. Louis, abroad in the small town night: the rustic creak of crickets; the domestic rustle of Shake'n'Bake; a universal murmur of agreement with the troglodyte tv talk show host; the consoling sizzle of bugs immolating themselves on backyard insect ionizers; the discreet (weekly) flushing of the toilet; the decisive snap of shutting pocketbooks; the righteous whack of a razor strop across a naughty toddler's bottom; the secure clatter and clang of dead bolts and chains securing screen doors; the slam of windows; the hum of humidifiers; the chaste smack of perfunctory marital kisses—then silence, save for the dim and distant sound of something, somewhere, being smothered.

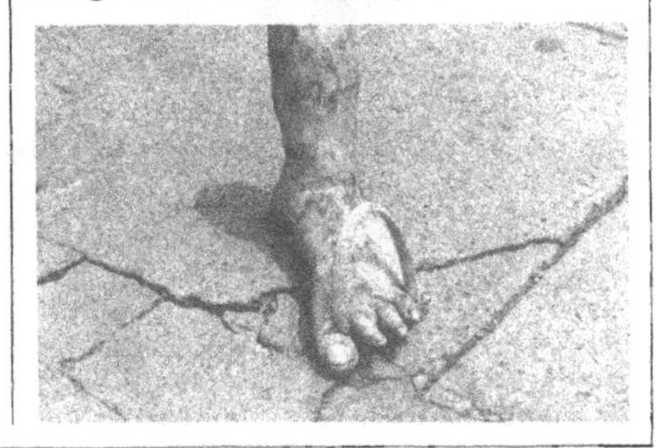

THE TORONTOGRE

Urbs porcus

⊙ **RANGE:** The Torontogre would like to describe her habitat as downtown Toronto, Ontario, but since neither she nor anyone else has been able to *find* downtown Toronto, she ranges the area bounded by Kingston, Buffalo, Hamilton, and Owen Sound. She makes her influence felt across the country by means of far-reaching transmitters operated by the Canadian Broadcasting Corporation.

◐ **HABITS:** The Torontogre is a Noble Dame and has taken it upon herself to see that her city has clean streets, safe subways, and a lively but decorous night life, with free flowing ginger ale, plenty of community singing, and those hot sausage rolls that just keep on coming. Under her benign influence, charming landmarks pop up where previously there had been only old buildings! She has developed a hardy strain of hybrid hanging plant, tough enough to survive the terrible cold of a Toronto winter in the window of a quiche and chablis snack bar.

The Torontogre has transformed old snowy Hogtown into a glittering Kapital of Kultur.

Her latest rage is malls, malls, malls—shopping, parking, promenading, and ballet malls, many named after quaint English suburbs. She so swells the breasts of all native Torontonians with such civic pride that they look as if they are wearing down-stuffed vests even when, for two weeks in July, they're not.

The Torontogre is a patroness of the arts akin to that highbrow hag, the Culture Vulture. Her recent cultural coups include bringing Ballet-in-a-bag to the Gumbleton Mall, founding the annual Arthur Wing Pinero Drama Festival to be held every five years in the Grislington Theatrical Mall, and of course introducing the Robertson Davies Wisdom Festival, featuring competitors from all over the commonwealth, to be held in the Chokeonacoke Philosophy Mall.

★ **HISTORY:** After an ideological tiff with the Spirit of '76, the Torontogre removed herself north to Canada, where she remains, determined to see that Toronto has at least one of everything found in civilization. No sooner is a mummy unearthed in Egypt or a school of poetry founded in Munich, than she directs the attention of MacLean's magazine feature writer to a similar event near the Porkville Mall. Thanks to her genteel moral influence, there is very little Greek or French culture in the Toronto area, except in so far as it is necessary to have one of everything.

☞ **SPOTTER'S TIPS:** Look for her near her handiworks: Canada's World Trade Center, the CN Tower; Canada's Macy's, Eaton's; Canada's Eiffel Tower, the CN Tower; Canada's Chicago Cubs, the Toronto Bluejays; and, of course, Canada's Maxim's, the restaurant high atop the CN Tower.

NYMPH O'MAINE

Piscator potator

⊙ **RANGE:** In the bitter cold Atlantic waters of the Grand Banks, off the rock-bound and forbidding coast of New England and Canada's Maritime Provinces, the Nymph O'Maine splashes and sports in the sea, carefree as a starlet in the Baja surf. She is commonly sighted off shores where people wear oilskin slickers the year round, and she has never ventured south of Boston. She winters near Cape Cod but prefers to summer on the shores of Labrador (the Canadian territory, not the American house pet).

◐ **HABITS:** The Nymph O'Maine is a small mermaid: half human, half salt cod. A benign and helpful sea creature, she guides the dories of poor fishermen to such meager schools of fish as elude the two-hundred-mile-long electrified fine mesh nets of the Russian cod sweepers, out beyond the twelve-mile limit. She inspired painters (like Edward Hopper) to sketch the shores of Truro and bootleggers to buy the shores of Martha's Vineyard.

Her gifts are many: she enables her human neighbors to subsist and thrive on a diet of unsaleable fish parts and small potatoes; and (in season), to skull their dories unerringly through fogs as thick as their brogues, to ice floes laden with fur seal pups no bigger than a Greenpeace budget.

Not on the high seas only does she serve as guide and pilot to these hardscrabble farmers of the sea, but when they make land, she manages to direct each man to his own strong weather-reddened wife, at the door of his own blizzard-beaten shack.

No respecter of national boundaries, the Nymph O'Maine guides American and Canadian mariners to clandestine high seas rendezvous, where they swap (duty-free) a quart of Moosehead Ale for a case of Narragansett Lager, or a carton of Export As for a pack of Lucky Strikes.

★ **HISTORY:** For many centuries, silkies and kelpies, seal men and seal women, mermaids and mermen, lived in the stormy arctic seas around Scotland and Ireland. Their descendants, the Nymphs O'Maine, inhabit the unspeakably frigid waters off the Canadian and New England shores for the same reason their mortal Celtic counterparts sank roots in the stony land there: it was cold and wet and miserable, and reminded them of home.

☞ **SPOTTER'S TIPS:** There is no need to describe the Nymph to the working men and women of Newfoundland, New Brunswick, Nova Scotia, or Maine—they know her when they see her. And there is no point in describing her to the rest of us—she is quite invisible to Summer People.

The Nymph O'Maine is also a friend to the fisherfolk of Canada's Maritime Provinces.

UNION JACK

Britannicus, a, um

⊙ **RANGE:** A Brownie passing as a Bogie and more British than the British, the Union Jack is actually of lowland Scots origin, and, not surprisingly, makes his North American headquarters in British Columbia, Canada. He may be found loitering near the cricket pitch, warming beer or misdirecting darts in any plasterboard and plastic Ye Olde Pubbee, looking down his nose at the "colonials."

◐ **HABITS:** Union Jack inspires females of English descent (and of would-be English descent) to wear their glasses on sticks and devote such time as is not spent swilling Twining's Tea with the vicar, to knitting scratchy nose warmers for the Royal Family. These women's husbands (often of Mediterranean origin) have gone so far as to shave their backs and stuff Dunhill cigarette filters up their noses in attempts to pass themselves off as English.

It is an illusion fostered by the Union Jack that everything British is more cultured and dignified and superior, and that everything not British is crass, tasteless, and common. Thus, a colorful tin of sawdust buns from Blightly commands a premium price in the Gourmet Shoppes of BC, as do fat tyred, twenty-stone, cast iron Raleigh bicycles and five-pound cardboard business brogues hand-tooled by Pakistani craftsmen in Lancashire.

Union Jack finds maximum scope for his activities on such patriotic occasions as the Queen's Birthday, the Queen's husband's birthday, and the birthday of Porky, Her Majesty's dog at Kew.

Jack joins in all the traditional celebrations, suitably disguised in a blue felt blazer adorned with the crest of a regimental lawn bowling team. He heartily enjoys a jolly game of "Cromwell's men"—a sport played by two teams: one of up to a thousand drunken Anglo-Saxon gentlemen and the other of a small Catholic boy. The object is to find the boy wherever he may be hiding, thrash him soundly, and confiscate his rosary. Our Jack joins the traditional hunt, potting flash-frozen grouse hurled from behind a Douglas fir tree by Woodward's stock boy. After the games are done, he inspires everyone to partake of High Tea, complete with a panoply of sticky sweets that would rot the teeth off a chain saw.

★ **HISTORY:** He was sent over here as a "remittance fairy" from northern (extreme northern) England, when his patriotic outbursts became too much of a burden for his Pictish relatives, who financed his exile. He settled first on the eastern shores of North America (hence the names New England and New Brunswick), but the four days annual sunshine in those regions made the area seem positively Asiatic to Union Jack; thus, he removed himself to the perpetual drizzle of the Pacific Coast. There he lives to this day, happy as a toad in a hole.

The points at which Jack pitches his pioneer's camps across the continent are today marked by Shakespeare festivals, PBS affiliates, dog shows, and Ye Olde English Pubbees.

☞ **SPOTTER'S TIPS:** Since the English are a shortish race and Union Jack is a largish elf, he often passes himself off as a mortal, and as such may often be seen sleeping peacefully in an overstuffed chair in a Vancouver men's club, his feet resting in the roaring fire, an activity which might cause a human Britisher some slight discomfort.

The teddibly British Union Jack of Vancouver, B.C., is singing in the reign.

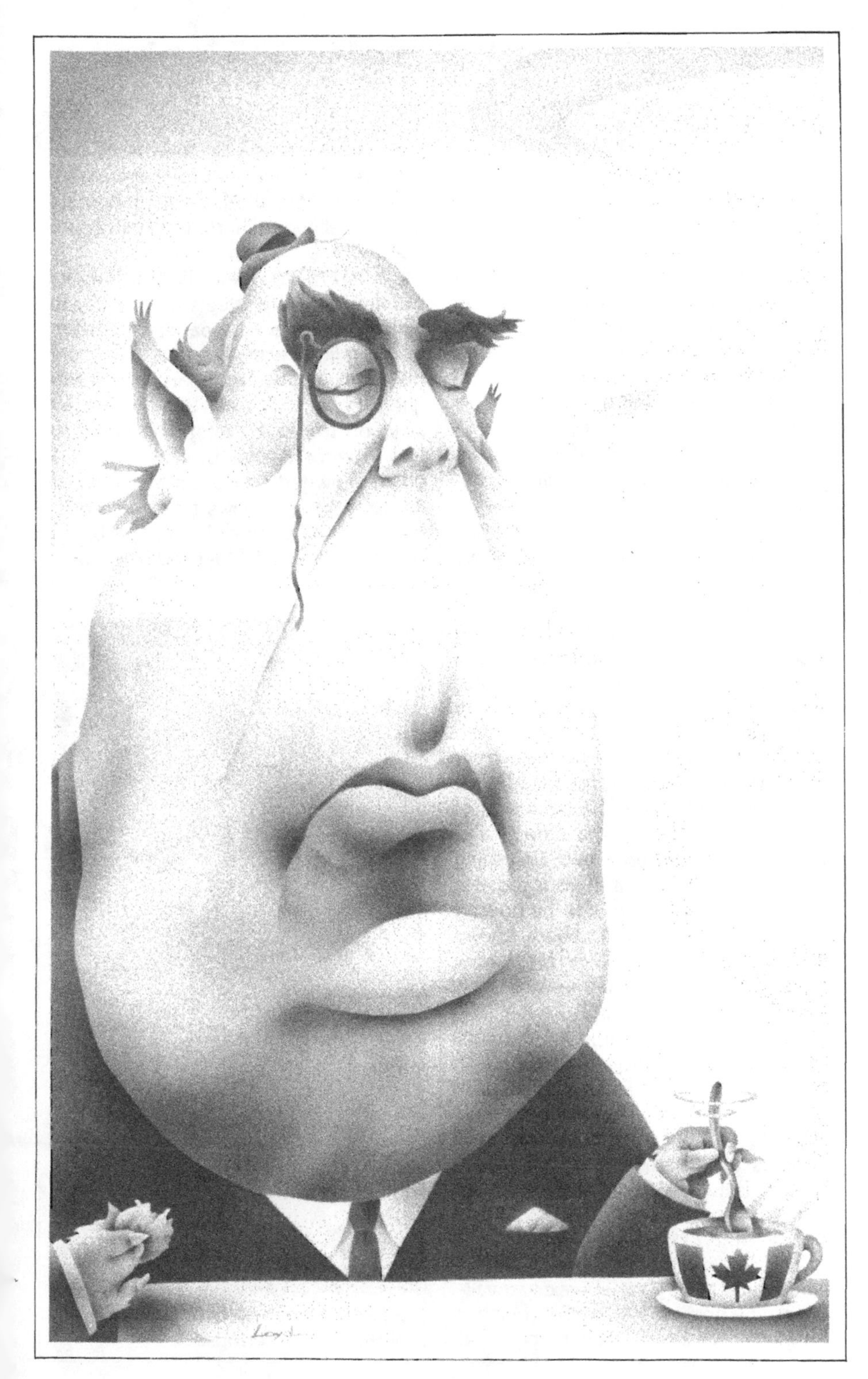

THE NIGHT MAYOR

Incubus migitus urbanus

⊙ **RANGE:** Dark street corners. Darker alleys. Vacant lots. Abandoned buildings. Just outside the window. Was that the wind? Beneath the broken street light. Lurking in that doorway. What was that? Only a shadow. Only a cat. Footsteps. Behind you. Don't panic. Don't run. Don't scream. Getting closer. Turn. Turn, now. That face! Those crazy, burning eyes! Oh no, it's him!

◐ **HABITS:** Every night is Hallowe'en as far as this nocturnal goblin is concerned, and he really knows how to treat a trick. He appears only when you are alone. He is the cause of those mysterious howls, crashes, and random booms that echo in the city at night. He rattles your doorknob and taps at your window and creaks in the hall. He knocks over trash cans, smashes empty bottles, and calls in false alarms. He fills your head with horrible headlines as he pounces from the shadows to ask you for a light. You leave him huddled in the back seat of the last train, and by the time you're home, he's under your bed, breathing in time with the steam in your radiator pipes. And the worst of it is, he doesn't exist, he can't exist, and nobody knows that better than you, as his heavy hands open your attic window, and his footsteps echo in the hall.

★ **HISTORY:** At the turn of the century, William Randolph "Citizen" Hearst and Joseph Pulitzer (that prize of a journalist) were locked in a titanic struggle for the hearts, minds, and pennies of the American newspaper reader. Between them, they invented Cuba, comics, sex, graft, Teddy Roosevelt, and the Night Mayor.

This last quickly acquired a family, with whose roving members city dwellers are by now all too familiar: Hugger Muggers, Fire Bugs, Street Gangs, and the rest, all of whom prove the axiom of fairy historian J. M. Barrie: if enough people believe in them, they can come true.

☞ **SPOTTER'S TIPS:** Night Mayors usually roam the streets of any city in which there is a newspaper circulation or TV ratings war going on. They are frequently spotted in urban centers frequented by hick tourists, who are always on the lookout for something to feel superior about. In cities where a paper is owned by Rupert Murdoch or an "eyewitness" news team is "working 'round the clock," you probably can find a Night Mayor before local news of import.

The Night Mayor—a harmless but highly publicized urban terrorist.

THE CHICAGO WORLD'S FAIRY

Urbs secunda

⊙ **RANGE:** The Chicago World's Fairy, a hulking, towering, powerfully muscled Giant, Hog Butcher, Tool Maker, and Stacker of Wheat with a Titanic Inferiority Complex, sitteth—as everybody knows by now—at the northwest gates.

Boundless, barren windswept plains surround him on three sides, so he snuggles up against Lake Michigan for warmth, poor thing.

◐ **HABITS:** For some reason, the Chicago World's Fairy *toddles.* Maybe it's the gallons of Prohibition gin still secreted within.

Many Giants prefer to dwell amidst impassable mountains, but the Chicago Giant is surrounded by impossible *fields*—Soldiers, Wrigley, Marshall, and O'Hare.

Although he generally just sulks and feels unappreciated, he sometimes stomps, roars, bellows, and even bursts into flames to call attention to himself. Three such occasions were the shameless exhibitions of 1893 and 1934, and the Democratic Convention of '68. He is seldom at his best when the whole world is watching.

Seen from the West, he has the appearance of an old, corrupt degenerate, a gangster in a baggy suit with a machine gun in his fiddle case. From the East, he looks like a hopelessly outsized rube, a barefoot village idiot with hay in his hair and skyscrapers for playthings.

The mortals who live in his mammoth shadow are a frightened and confused lot, buffeted about by winds, like the despairing shades of suicides in Dante's Inferno. (The winds themselves result from the huge sighs of the Giant, as he contemplates and bemoans his unjustly neglected greatness.)

★ **HISTORY:** Arguably, he originates from one of three nations traditionally celebrated for producing large, pouting behemoths—Poland, Ireland, or Africa.

When he arrived on the shores of Lake Michigan, he befriended the wild polecats, who were the area's most populous wildlife, and feasted daily on wild onions, the only flora in profusion. His name, Chicago, is the Algonquian word for "strong," or "powerful," which is thought to be an olfactory reference.

A sportsman of note, he supervised both the fixed World's Series and Tunney's long count. Nice.

☞ **SPOTTER'S TIPS:** If one would appreciate the true enormity and tediousness of the Chicago World's Fairy, he is best viewed from the air. Since all aircraft flying to or over his domain are obliged to circle for hours, you have ample opportunity.

Jazz giants neglected by their record labels, baseball superstars overlooked in the Hall of Fame voting, and great statesmen unappreciated by their parties are among his offspring—he's very prolific—and if you follow their unsuccessful careers, they will lead you, inevitably, back home.

Opposite: The Chicago World's Fairy: a Cubs-loving, helpless Giant?

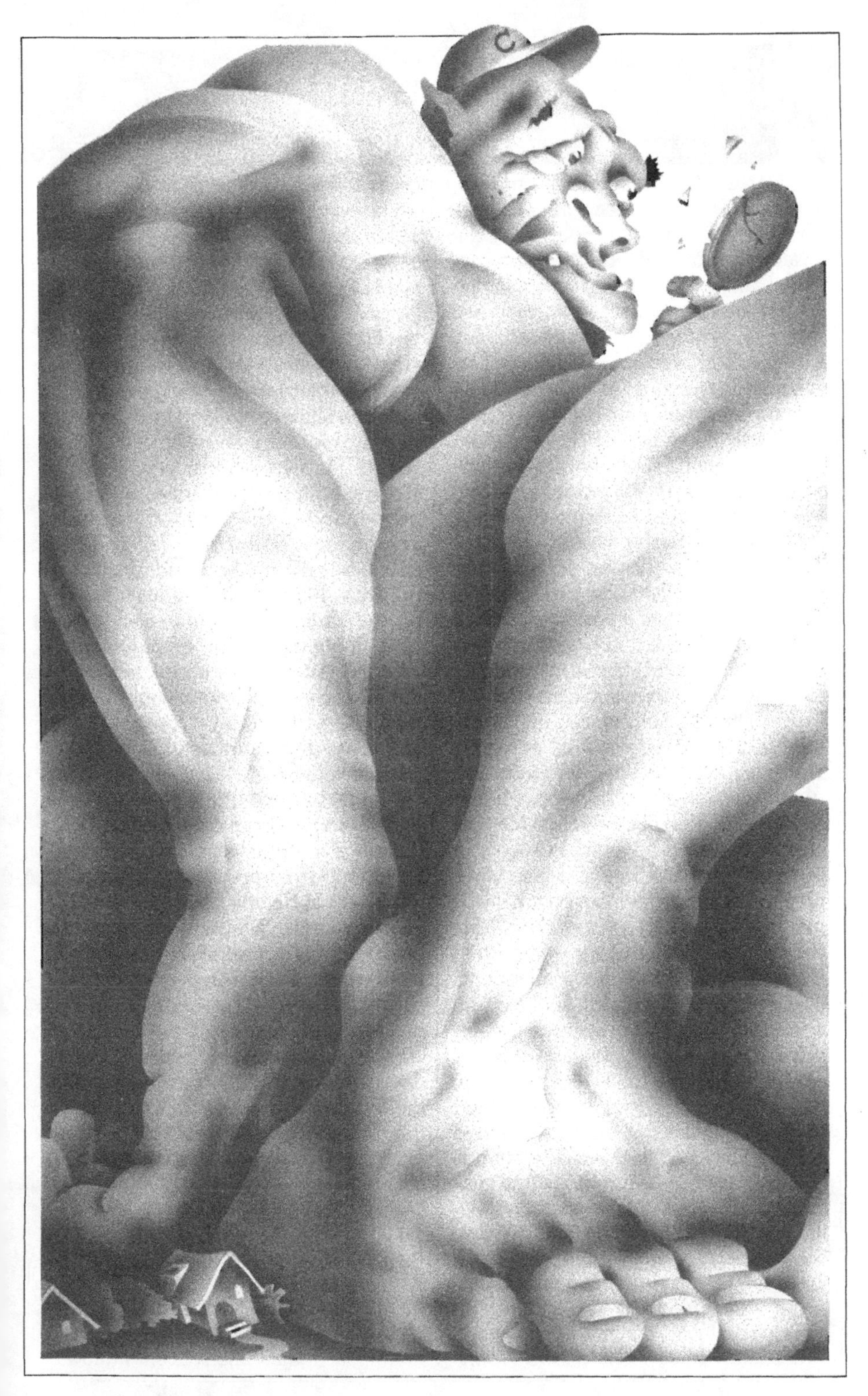

DIXIE PIXIE

Flatuus ante bellum

⊙ **RANGE:** North of the Mason-Dixon line, the Dixie Pixie can invariably be found anywhere the South is being celebrated, or derided; wherever mint juleps are consumed in excess, or utterly scorned; any place corn pone and grits are eaten, or regurgitated; any time southern accents are affected for politeness's sake, or in order to facilitate the telling of a racist joke.

◐ **HABITS:** The Dixie Pixie is responsible for every Yankee's twin misperceptions about the South. One fantasy is of the courtly colonel with the snowy goatee laying his coat over the cloaca, lest the flower of Southern womanhood besmirch her cotillion slippers. The other features an inbred sour mash-smashed string-tied cracker lashing the broad backs of cringing slaves with a fishhook-studded flail.

The Dixie Pixie conjures up, in the Northern mind, visions of a freshly whitewashed mansion, its porticoed porch festooned with happy banjo thumping indentured servants. Magnolia and honeysuckle mingle scents in the warm evening breeze, which wafts from across the ripening cotton fields the lonesome call of the river boat whistle. Here comes Granny with a tray of hush puppies! Well shut mah mouth!

Simultaneously (and with equal vividness, natch), he inspires the infernal image of a dilapidated tar paper lean-to squatting in a fever swamp, with a flea-bitten field hand, clothed only in cast-off handkerchiefs, chained to a post before the door. The sounds of diesel-engined mosquitoes and malarial mud wasps mingle in the musty air, redolent with rotting laundry and decomposing propeller-chopped manatees, while down by the levee an uncaring overseer trolls for 'gators, his hook baited with dynamite.

It is likewise impossible for a Northerner in the Pixie's thrall to conceive of an honest Southern election, believing either that men are barred from voting at all by local political thugs or encouraged to vote often in exchange for hefty slugs of bourbon.

★ **HISTORY:** The Dixie Pixie is of Celtic origin, having long preceded his human counterparts in emigrating from the rural slums of Ireland and Scotland to the southern shores of the New World. He was, and is, very active in creating both pro- and anti-Confederate propaganda, having, for example, *ghost* written both *Uncle Tom's Cabin* and *Gone With The Wind.* Just now, the Dixie Pixie is exerting his influence on the casting of sit-coms and feature films, lobbying for the employment of only the fattest, most harmless sheriffs, the most charming moonshine-running truckers, and whitest, blondest, bustiest, why, the dumbest Dixie Pixie's Southern belles.

☞ **SPOTTER'S TIPS:** When football season comes 'round, why, the Dixie Pixie's a regular bowlweevil! Yaaa-heoooooo! An unprovoked chorus of rebel yells in Seattle's Kingdome or the Jersey Giants' Stadium suggests his presence. He is bound to be near any Volvo with a stars-and-bars bumper sticker, and can be sighted yearly, proudly guzzling bourbon in an ivy league faculty club on Kentucky Derby day. It is the Dixie Pixie who inspires the Long Island house wife to address the cleaning lady as "y'all".

The Dixie Pixie has carpetbagged up North, suh, where the sour mash flows.

WERNER VON BROWNIE

Incendere et defugere

⊙ **RANGE**: From the profoundest inner reaches of the atom to the outermost limits of the universe; from the first instance called the Singularity, and for the hypothetically foreseeable future, we have with us the very experimental Werner Von Brownie.

◐ **HABITS**: This Space Age sprite prefers to spend his time where the *reaction* is, making sure that what can go wrong, does.

It is the dubious distinction of anyone who glimpses a Von Brownie, that he or she is probably about to experience a scientific disaster of unforgettable proportion.

This nuclear family of fairies loves to invite the friendly atom out to play and it's a lead pipe cinch that whenever these Brownies are up to their Three-Mile-Island-hijinks, you'll find a red-faced, power company public relations executive holding a Geiger counter with a *melted* probe, talking in reassuring terms about acceptable levels of radiation while spitting out her teeth.

These cosmic creatures enjoy nothing more than the science of rocketry. From Cape Canaveral to Santa Barbara, the Werner Von Brownie can be found conducting his own schedule of independent experiments on spacecraft: "*Vat* vould happen if only one engine fired? *Hmm?* Vat happens if *dis* hose gets connected vere *dat* hose is supposed to go? Is dis material fireproof?"

The answers to these and other questions of the Von Brownie more often than not take the form of a fireball.

Last minute problems are the Brownie's special delight. Shutting off cameras (with the help of the Glitches) as they are about to photograph Venus, removing solar panels from space shuttles, and causing telecommunications satellites to vanish from orbit, are just three of their extraordinary interplanetary jests.

★ **HISTORY**: When the first Chinese kid force-fed the first firecracker to an unfortunate and astonished Mongolian frog, the ancestors of Werner Von Brownie were there. Not quite *there*, but certainly at a safe distance.

Travelling westward with the Spirit of Scientific Inquiry (a distant relative), the Brownie forebears sought to make their inquisitive way through Europe, but in doing so made one-too-many exhibits of their explosive charms and thus found themselves expelled from the Old World by its remaining fairies, including the beekeeping Brownies of Cornwall, whose hives had been exploded by a powder-happy member of the Von Brownie clan.

The Werner Von Brownie emigrés arrived in the thirteen colonies in plenty of time to observe, with professional detachment, both the rocket's red glare and the bombs bursting in air (a few of which were their own).

The invention of the steam engine, the internal combustion engine, and solid fuel all owe a debt to the Werner Von Brownies' endless store of explosions. Although they prefer to devote the majority of their time to the space program today, the Brownies are not above taking an evening off to meddle with the fuel propellant in sky rockets at a local fourth of July fireworks display (as anyone who has ever seen an obscene word spelled out in letters of fire two hundred feet tall will tell you).

☞ **SPOTTER'S TIPS**: Postponed countdowns, unexpected setbacks, unavoidable budgetary overruns, and, of course, huge fireballs, are all indications that the Werner Von Brownies' program is right on schedule.

JACK O'LECTERN

Orator ineptus

⊙ **RANGE**: Classes, lectures, seminars, discussion groups, conventions, pulpits, meetings, rallies, briefings, press conferences, speeches, sales presentations, readings, awards ceremonies, banquets, show-and-tell . . . anywhere, anytime anyone has the opportunity to blow into a microphone and ask, at deafening volume, "Is this on?"

◐ **HABITS**: The Jack O'Lectern is tinier than an on-off switch, and wicked as a feed-back scream. He first enchants his victims into believing falsely that they have something to say, as he dangles from a mike, smiling, beckoning. They approach him. Behind their glazed eyes are the visions he conjures: applause, fame, fans, enemies refuted, causes justified, stardom, groupies, the Nobel Prize. . . .

And as his victims gaze out, humble yet proud, coldly intelligent yet compassionate, into the waiting faces of their audience, he quickly scrambles their notes, inserts their slides upside down, scrawls obscenities on the blackboard and hides the eraser, and then makes them suddenly and profoundly aware that they have to go to the bathroom.

Jack's tactics are various. During a Presidential debate, he has been known to pull the plug on the sound system, or whisper into a speaker's ear that Iberia is a state in the midwest. At a college commencement exercise, he might have the valedictorian address Doctor Pinkham, the Rector, as "Doctor Pinker, the Rectum." When you stand to share your views with the P.T.A., he simply does down your fly.

★ **HISTORY**: This saboteur of elocution is related, as you might have guessed, to another pumpkin-headed English hobgoblin, Jack O'Lantern, but *our* Jack specializes in Gab Hobblin'.

He is not a "solitary fairy," but a gregarious sort, who prefers to team up with fellow sprites in his pranks. He employs Typographical Terrors to insert humiliating bloopers into the Teleprompter. and Energenii to wreak havoc with the public address system. Stylus Devils frequently assist him in scrambling the audio-aids, while Freudian Sylphs entice embarrassing double entendres from the speaker's lips.

☞ **SPOTTER'S TIPS**: Wherever there is an easel holding simple charts and graphs, or rows of folding chairs, or plates of untouched chicken a la king being cleared as a gavel bangs—the Jack O'Lectern is waiting, and grinning, in the wings.

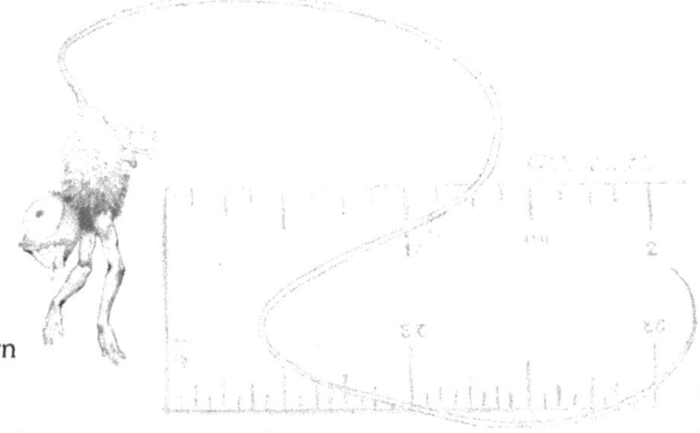

Opposite: A Jack O'Lectern sabotaging a lecture at the U. of North Carolina.

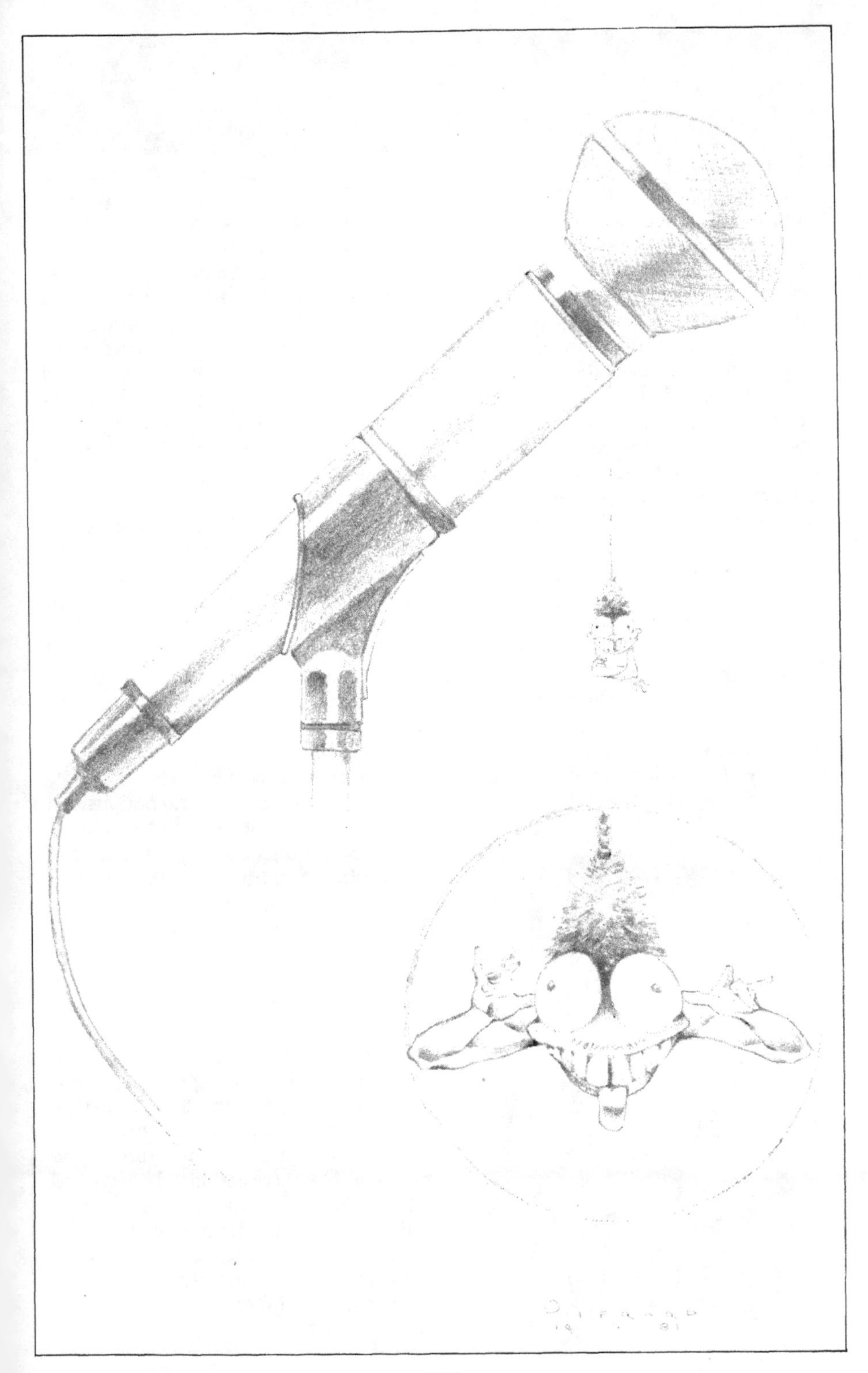

TINKERBELLES

Numerus perversus

⊙ **RANGE:** Shimmering across the skies. Singing down the wires. Bouncing off satellites. Beneath the seas, where the weed-draped cables drift. Binding the global village in a seamless silver web. Flashing through microcircuits to light up the switchboards of industry like impossible Christmas trees. But most of all, IN YOUR EAR!

◐ **HABITS:** It is the deepest, darkest desire of these glittering, ringing, humming, and flickering spirits to imbue every piece of hardware with a personality and to reduce humankind to the condition of machines. When your voice has been converted to a droning code of impersonal beeps and your refrigerator talks back to you, there is much merriment along the Tinkers' Bell System.

How they click and twinkle with wicked glee to see a human standing at a pay phone in the pouring rain, calling for the weather! How it makes them glitter and buzz for joy to behold humans dialing a joke, a date, a steak, a prayer, while a burnt-out terminal case with a headset somewhere squats over a black box full of buttons with the Apocalypse on HOLD!

Their most cunning technological doomsday device is the increasingly ubiquitous Telephone Answering Machine which, in a state of prerecorder-call-forwarding-impulse-activated direct-distance-connection with another Answering Machine, delightfully prefigures the future of all human intercourse.

★ **HISTORY:** From the moment the first, coquettish Tinkerbelle whispered, "Come here, I need you" into Mr. Watson's ear, these minuscule menaces have been laboring toward their goal—every man, woman and child hooked up, plugged in, and switched on, along an instantaneous globe-encompassing communications network—and not a soul among them with anything to say!

Tinkerbelles are now active in every country in the world. Many nations can be reached by one of their favorite innovations: direct dialing. If you can remember a thirty-nine-digit number sequence, you can greatly simplify international communications (you must remember that a sound like a monkey's death cry is a French busy signal and a deep fat fryer noise means a phone is ringing in Portugal).

☞ **SPOTTER'S TIPS:** Ominous clickings on the line. Ringing that starts when your key hits the lock and stops the moment you complete your breathless obstacle course run to the receiver. Heavy breathers. Threats and obscenities on your answering machine from long dead enemies. The refusal to accept collect calls by your nearest and dearest. All these are signals that the Tinkers' Bell System has *your* number.

THE HOUNDS OF NEWS

Canes inebrioses

⊙ **RANGE:** Like the fabulous Fairy Dog packs of yore, the Hounds of News roam wheresoever they list, red-eyed and terrible; from newspaper pay windows to celebrity discos, precinct press rooms, post-game locker rooms, and wire service terminals, on the trail of scoops and Mafia bribes.

◐ **HABITS:** Like the stringers, free-lancers, correspondents and spirits they are, the Hounds hunt in packs. Their sensitive noses are attuned not to news only, but to any free lunch. They feed upon the sandwiches provided at new product launches and lap up the cabbage scented beer from the sodden sawdust-strewn floors of bars with Irish names.

Like their human counterparts, they go into a rutting frenzy nightly from eleven-thirty to twelve; and like them, they never actually breed.

The Hounds of News are invaluable to the gentlemen of the fourth estate: they retrieve useful expense account receipts from under tables, they scent out simple-to-rewrite stories in rival publications, and are quick on the spoor of politicians' barbers, nightclub washroom attendants, and other informed sources.

In the field, the Hounds lead the hunt, baying after their swift prey: ambulances, squad cars, fire engines, and stretch limousines.

With supernatural hunting instinct, they will wrestle to earth any recently divorced actress, misunderstood race fixer eager to tell his sad story, blabbermouth hit man, philandering politico, drug-crazed jock, cult leader, cult victim, and all such subjects for hot copy.

And at the end of a tough day on the beat, it is a Hound of News who tips off his master as to which of the forty-odd identical Aquascutum trench coats on the barroom rack is his very own.

★ **HISTORY:** The Hounds of News are likely descended from the *Cu Sith,* or *Hounds of the Hill,* the Fairy Pack of Wales, who once hunted souls there. In America, where souls are few, their prey is scandal.

They led Haliburton to Cuba, Lowell Thomas to Arabia, scented the ill wind off the Watergate, and continue to sniff out rueful and amusing members of the proletariat for Breslin, Royko and Hammill.

Because of their Celtic ancestry, they tend all too often to track down colorful and self-destructive Welsh actors as potential feature material.

☞ **SPOTTER'S TIPS:** Like all hounds, spectral and otherwise, these Mutts of Mencken make a hell of a racket—baying, belling, barking, and howling. The unearthly noises raised by a gathering of reporters are in fact the cries of a News Hound pack. Listen closely for these whines and yelps—always a dead giveaway: "De Tocqueville? A tourist! . . . Hemingway? What a blowhard! . . . John McPhee, that phony nature boy! . . . Izzy Stone? He's in it for the glory . . . Rather? Can't write a word . . ."

THE GNOME ENCLATURE

Verberabilissimus

⊙ **RANGE**: Infesting the ivied towers of High Mandarin academese, and cluttering the gutters of low slum argot (littered as they are with dropped g's and h's). From the obsolete cliches of the left, through the content-free platitudes of the center, to the terrifying buzz-word euphemisms of the right, wherever language is used to obfuscate, bore, or manipulate, the Gnome Enclature capers, coining his counterfeit phrases, circulating his inflated rhetoric, and generally debasing the value of the Word Hoarde.

◐ **HABITS**: The Gnome Enclature is the spirit of language. It is he who sees to it that there are sufficient synonyms so that two persons may discuss the same topic without understanding one another.

He is the reason that you say "tomato" and I say, "Solanum Lyopersicum," for he dearly loves an obscure synonym, and inspires ostentatiously elegant variation.

He heightens class distinctions—how can people who "take in a flick," "go to the movies," "see a picture," "catch a show," and "screen a film" possibly have anything to say to each other?

He underscores regional differences—can people who order "a hoagie," "a grinder," "a hero," and "a sub" still break bread together?

He numbs us with euphemisms, as we go from "the prime of our lives" through "senior citizenship," until, as "golden agers" in our "twilight years," we "pass away," and nobody knows, or cares, that we died.

A prude, he has so ensnared us in double entendre and circumlocution that such words as "bath," "rest," "lounge," and "powder" have come to mean "evacuation."

He has done some of his best work through the morally anaesthetized offices of the Defense Department (formerly, the War Department). For instance, should the START (formerly, SALT) talks enter an inoperative mode, opening a window of critical vulnerability, you and I might be impacted with a first strike of such significant megatonnage as to be terminated with extreme prejudice (at acceptable levels, mind you). The Gnome Enclature is beloved by such creatures as the Pentagorgons who delight in having a wide variety of words to describe the unthinkable with the degree of complexity such concepts deserve.

★ **HISTORY**: Gnome Enclatures delighted in the hostile polyglot nature of the first wave of European settlers, encouraging Dutch, French, Spanish, and English colonists to insist on the absolute primacy of their respective lingos. Each language survived, giving rise to endless regional squabbles and bickerings, and persist to this day—except for English, which finally ceased to be spoken in America during the Eisenhower administration.

☞ **SPOTTER'S TIPS**: The Gnome Enclature is to be found in the vicinity of speech writers, DJs, game show hosts, doctors, RNs, funeral hall directors, civil service union bosses, Mafia-based contractors, Federal boondogglers, social scientists, and NEA grant specialists. He can be seen peeping out between the lines of columns written by William Safire, Edwin Newman, and other mavens of pop etymology.

THE CALCUBUS

Principia mathematica

⊙ **RANGE:** From that first moment in math class when you *get* it—or *don't* get it—all the way to the day you proudly accept your Nobel Prize for explaining quarks—or stand shivering on a street corner, figuring on your fingers how many nickels for a cup of soup . . . the Calcubus is either with you or against you: a continuous function, either positive or negative.

In plane geometric terms, he is your Guardian Angle.

◐ **HABITS:** The Calcubus hovers over restaurant tables, in the backs of cabs, and anywhere else people try to figure out what the tip should be.

There are those who believe the Calcubus to be an imaginary, or "hypothetical," number—since all statements about him begin with an "If . . ." or a "Suppose . . . ."

But there are those who know differently, who have felt the creature swoop out of the blue and either a) inspire their minds, or b) paralyze their brains.

Now, if the Calcubus (*c*) exists, then,

Let (*a*) be designated mathematicians, and

Let (*b*) be designated morons.

Q. E. D. !

In days of yore, some morons could fake their way through fractions, long division, even elementary algebra, by means of brute memory or by visual access to smart students' answers.

But, thanks to modern, advanced teaching methods, like the new math, the Arithmetically Hopeless are discovered much sooner these days and "streamed" into other, more fitting programs, like theology or shop.

This separation of the sharpshooting sheep from the gormless goats is accomplished with the help of the aptly named Differential Calcubus.

With the introduction of the simple pocket calculator, things looked grim for the Calcubus, as even the most mathematically inept mortal could perform fantastic feats of addition and such.

But these resourceful demons conspired with their fellow fairies, the Glitches, and quickly removed from circulation any miniature computer on which anyone but an M.I.T. graduate could do more than locate the "on" switch.

★ **HISTORY:** That ancient Greek wizard Pythagoras originally conjured the Calcubus, but it was Euclid who first put the creature to work. He set the nasty thing down in the middle of a bridge—his Fifth Proposition, or "Pons Assinorum."

"Asses," that is, all but a few of his students (or any students since), were unceremoniously booted off the "Pons," or bridge, and never reached the other side and the neat and orderly land of the Giant Trig—which sounds like California, what with all the *sins* and *tans* out there.

In America, those blessed at birth by the Calcubus tend to myopia, chess mastery, and the violin. Hence, few survive adolescence.

☞ **SPOTTER'S TIPS:** The Calcubus is often detectable near a wisp of smoke: the smoke that smells like burnt rubber shooting from the ears of those cursed by the creature as they stare at their unbalanced bank books; the fatherly, tweed-and-leather scented smoke arising from the briar of a meditative M.I.T. quantum mechanic; the fine, bright, odorless trail of smoke still drifting over test sites across the Southwest; or the singe of the Calcubus's own wings as it pays a visit to microchip specialists on the verge of a 256K breakthrough in Silicon Valley.

Open Book
Exam Today

THE POST MONSTER GENERAL

De liber deletrix

⊙ **RANGE:** The Post Monster General is free to move, or not move, wherever the US mail moves, or doesn't move. He can sometimes be found, improperly addressed, looking over post cards, shaking his head in a sad regretful way, down in the dead letter office.

◐ **HABITS:** When a pizza store owner in California receives a personal note of condolence from Isadora Duncan, or an Alaskan Congressman opens a letter from a Confederate general demanding a stay of execution for John Wilkes Booth, you may be sure that the Post Monster General has been on his self-appointed rounds. It is he who expedites the delivery of bulky, colorful offers from the Publishers Clearing House and delays the arrival of perishable packages or personal mail. He is especially concerned with envelopes distinguished by little cellophane address windows. By supernatural means he is able to determine whether they contain a bill, in which case he dispatches them to appear promptly in a mail box, or a check, in which case he sentences them to moulder indefinitely in a canvas bag. The Post Monster General is passionate about zip codes, and is working towards completely digital addressing. For example: Mr. 639 7644, 532 2nd Avenue, 67opolis, 51st State, 1st Country, 3rd World 56555555559867483948584777594 737747474733 (etc.)

★ **HISTORY:** The Post Monster General's original field of action was the by-hand pouch traffic of the late Roman Empire. Many a Samaritan rolled his eyes and threw up his hands in a gesture of Semitic resignation after finding a two-hundred-bushel Epistle to the Ephesians stacked on his stoop—misdirected to him by the Post Monster General. In America, similar gestures were made by miners on the Barbary Coast upon receiving, via the Pony Express, pipe organs addressed to Pope Gregory XLV. Doubtless His Holiness was similarly puzzled at the arrival of his mail order bride.

The citizens of his native Rome believed the Post Monster General to be a sort of Centaur-in-reverse—a creature with the hind-quarters of a horse for a head, atop a pair of all-too-human flat feet.

How he made his way from Italy to these shores remains a mystery—but since he eventually *did* get here, we can safely assume that he didn't mail himself.

☞ **SPOTTER'S TIPS:** One thing is certain: you needn't bother looking in your mailbox. You might try the gutter, the house next door, the dashboard of a stranger's car, or the bonfire on the corner over which your local postie is warming his hands.

The Post Monster General has a morbid aversion to snow, rain, heat, and gloom of night.

TYPOGRAPHICAL TERRORS

Etoin Shurdlu

⊙ **RANGE:** Wherever mankind attempts to clarify thoughts by "putting them down on paper," there will occur these magical, dadaist dwarves. Misdirecting typists' fingers, distracting proofreaders and spreading dyslexia among publishers themselves, these creatures could once proudly call themselves the bane of civilized man. (Since the audio-visual revolution, however, with its laser-video-computer-disc holograms and all, civilized man is not always literate, or for that matter, civilized, and consequently times are tough for the Terrors—among other sentient beings.)

◐ **HABITS:** These are defamatory characters. They insert inappropriate adjectives, libelous paragraphs, or simply misspelled words into the printed copy of literary reviews, small town newspapers, and supermarket tabloids. (Their work is rarely spotted in the latter.)

The Terror's mischief can be discovered only after publication, much to the delight of attorneys, letters-to-the-editor writers, and masochistic copy editors. Typographical Terrors are closely affiliated with Printers' Devils and, if unable to achieve their ends at source, often cause the Devils to do their work for them on the printing press itself through such means as misplaced paragraphs, inverted credits, and mail order coupons with white type on black paper.

They have been known to insert exploding recipes into cookbooks, unknown symbols into codebooks, hernia-causing directions into exercise books, and names of pastas into diet books of all kinds.

★ **HISTORY:** Typographical Terrors hail, naturally, from Gutenberg country—Germany. But their native language was already such an eye-glazing sauerkraut of vowels and consonants that much of their best work went unnoticed. They emigrated to France, where a misplaced *accent grave* has been known to give heart attacks to the entire *Academie Française,* and thence to the New World, where some of them have met the challenge of the electronic media by evolving into "Bloopers."

☞ **SPOTTER'S TIPS:** The furrows of IBM Selectrics, the industrial parks of Long Island and Northern California, and the offices of poetry presses are favored habitats of the Terrors. In winter, they are known to thrive on the alcoholic fluid of Liquid Paper, overdoses of which have frequently caused their deaths.

W E R T Y U I O P
A S D F G H J K L
Z X C V B N M

GLITCHES

Computrescence

⊙ **Range:** From the vast stillness of the concrete-lined underground computer complex where the nuclear decisions are made, to the easy-to-operate home terminal of your neighborhood Asteroids-addict, Glitches are flashing down line, surging in among the diode chips, and wrecking the program.

They hum and buzz amidst the flopsy files where your credit rating, medical history, high school civics grades, and the FBI-gleaned details of your love life are all stored for easy access by total strangers with a keyboard, telephone, and code number.

They tick and blink behind each teller's wicket, reservation desk, and checkout counter; they can be found wherever a data retrieval system is in the process of misplacing your money and replacing *you.*

◐ **Habits:** The primary function of a Glitch is to encourage the universal use of computers. Naturally enough, this temptation often takes the form of an Apple.

No sooner are we On Line than the Glitches make us a function of the machine—and, within microseconds, have seen to it that the machine no longer functions.

A Glitch will print out static from a screwie doobie faster than you can punch in READY. He unplugs your hardware, declares your software illegal, and resets your wetwear to zero.

Unlike most Fairies, who are willing to learn the rudiments of human language, Glitches insist that we communicate with them exclusively by means of their own incomprehensible lingo.

Lured by the promise of arcane knowledge and unlimited power (not to mention morbid curiosity), many mortals have pawned their souls to learn the harsh, unspeakable grammar of the Glitches.

After these latter-day Fausts study fat dense tomes of Glitch lore, they perform the ritual invocation (Glitches appear in answer to such secret names as BASIC or FORTRAN). Hunched before the flickering screen, the apprentice-initiates proceed to pursue the Answer to the Mystery . . . and, after log off, emerge folded, bent, and mutilated, as the Glitches bleep 16K of their mocking giggle, and bid them BYE.

★ **History:** The Glitches are Oriental, as is evidenced by their fondness for long scrolls that read right to left, top to bottom, or any damn way but left to right. It is acknowledged among historians that the Japanese were passing the time with symbolic logic riddles when Europeans were still living in ditches, and this fact suggests that Glitches emigrated from the Floating World to the New one, where they first inspired and then infested the Computer; the better to remind all round-eyes what boneheads they all still are.

Glitches made their first insidious inroads into the American Way of Life at the turn of the century by mating with Team Spirits and helping to make baseball and football popular. (Both games are better played by computers than people and have encouraged the national obsession with statistics and averages.)

The next step was easy: the Glitches merged with the Pentagorgon, the Tax Burden, the Post Monster General, and the Mugwump and converted the Federal Government into an enormous data storage and retrieval bank, responding to citizens by means of incomprehensible graphs, curves, numbers, projections, and other hypnotic gobbledygook.

PIERARD

GLITCHES

Computrescence

This very field guide, which was typeset by computer, nevertheless dares to reveal the answer to the omnipresent Glitch threat. What we must all do, right now, is @#$%¢ &*"?:¼)&*%$#.

☞ **SPOTTER'S TIPS**: For those of us not busy frying our minds over handy-dandy home video games and portable data retrieval units, Glitches can most often be sighted leering out the window of the envelope containing a utility bill for seventy-five million dollars, past due.

Glitches' bytes are bigger than their barks. They love punch (cards).

CORPORATE GIANTS

Mens insana in corpore

⊙ **RANGE**: The lair or den of the Corporate Giants is widely believed to be in Delaware. Yet some suggest that this emphatically American ogre makes his home offshore, in the beautiful Bahamas. Little reliable information about the Corporate Giants' scope of activities exists—some of those who tracked them to their lair having been consumed and others simply co-opted.

Evidence of their presence can be found throughout the country, however—Houston and Dallas are possibly boot prints where they have stomped. Each is but a man step for Giantkind.

◐ **HABITS**: The behavior of Corporate Giants attracts little scrutiny or comment in America. And perhaps it is this undeserved lack of attention which spurs the mammoth creatures on, in their attempts to exceed even their Giant forbears in acts of voracity, rapaciousness, and in fact, every trait for which Giants from Goliath to Andre The have been famous.

Although they are enormous and ubiquitous, Corporate Giants are terribly difficult to find, as more than one investigating committee has discovered.

The Corporate Giant lives outside the law, in Delaware and New York.

CORPORATE GIANTS

Mens insana in corpore

It is presumed that they dress conservatively, in three piece anti-anti-trust suits. Their indiscriminate gobbling up of Small Businessmen has so adversely affected their digestion that they issue booming quarterly reports.

Their mating customs remain mysterious, but they are certainly not monogamous. Citizens of both sexes everywhere complain of "having been shafted" by these Keynes Kongs.

Alas, everyone who has gotten close enough to a Corporate Giant to speak about him with authority later proved to be an unreliable Communist in the pay of Karl Marx or had already declared himself to have been certifiably insane before taking a job with the Corporation.

We can only be certain that, in some way, Corporate Giants are hard at work shaping America's future, employing everything from "Better Ideas" to "Stupid Slogans" to further their ends.

No matter what magical means they use to exercise it, the Corporate Giants' influence upon the direction of American commercial enterprise is to be deplored. If the Giants' collective lock upon the wattled throats and withered minds of our captains of industry is not soon broken, many great capitalist ventures will come to grief, in the time-honored manner of all Giants' works and pomps.

For example, after devouring everything within walking distance (including streams, wasps' nests, oil-rich tundra), a Giant tends to doze off. Should he ever wake (a fifty-fifty proposition, according to Giant lore), he will discover that in his sleep he has been looted (by Jack the Giant-Killer), or blinded (by crafty Ulysses), or castrated and worse (by Ralph Nader).

★ **HISTORY**: Even the ethnic roots of Corporate Giants are difficult to discover; probably, they are multinational.

In Greek mythology, they are mentioned as shipping tycoons, who wrecked the Titanic monopoly. Yet they seem to have sprung from earlier, well-travelled and prolific stock, for we read of Frost Giants menacing promiscuous and socialistic mythological characters of old Scandinavia and doing well in the rug trade as Djinns of ancient Persia.

They were long associated with cannibalism, stupidity, and dumb jingles like "Fee Fi Fo Fum." Many jocular stories have survived, detailing Giants' absurd attempts to squeeze whey from stones, their defenselessness against goose burglars, and their notorious inability to distinguish between a traveller they wished to club to death and a pile of pillows.

Banished from the Old World for their lack of guile, or, for that matter, common sense, the Giants have sought to conceal their idiocy in the New World by acting through committee. Corporate Giants, as they have come to be called, try to influence or discourage legislative sessions. But they adore board meetings.

☞ **SPOTTER'S TIPS**: It is unlikely that an investigator's approach will go unnoticed. Express an interest in a Corporate Giant, and he'll find *you*. They may be stupid, but they have a nose for blood—especially the blood of an Englishman. Those who approach a Corporate Giant do so at their peril. They return either as zombie "Veeps," mindless except where foreign markets are concerned—or as discredited babbling hulks, bearing the marks of welding equipment on their person.

Corporate Giants? Don't ask.

TOLL TROLLS

Coinus venderuptus

⊙ **RANGE:** The Toll Troll can be found on bridges, thruways and turnpikes throughout the nation. He is a first cousin of the Lost Changeling, that exasperatingly greedy gremlin who makes his home in every vending machine everywhere. The Toll Troll, like the Lost Changeling, makes a practice of rejecting perfectly good American coins, stealing the odd one, and gleefully jamming the coin-operated gizmo he inhabits.

◐ **HABITS:** A mean and petty spirit, the Toll Troll seems to sense, in some mysterious way, when one has in one's possession only a single coin, token, or slug with which to operate a subway turnstile, freeway gate, or vibrating motel room bed. The Troll then causes the machine to malfunction in the most damaging way. Anyone who has suffered a blow in the reproductive area from a jammed subway turnstile, has encountered a member of the subspecies: the Token Minority. Anyone who has been chased inexplicably by state police for defrauding the turnpike authority or even been deprived of the badly needed vibrations of a motel bed has surely encountered the petulant Troll.

The single recompense the Toll Troll makes to victims is its way of getting even with others. This ill-natured creature dislikes coin operated machine owners as much as patrons. This is why, upon occasion, a pay phone returns more money than a casino slot machine, a juke box plays an extra song, and subway clerks, handed a dollar bill, give you change for a twenty. It is symptomatic of his malign nature that the Toll Troll, who could afford to winter in Vegas, prefers to spend the cold months in poorly maintained coffee machines in corporate cafeterias. There he can steal your dime, drop the cup sideways, pour coffee on it, and give you a nickel back. That way nobody wins. Except the Toll Troll.

★ **HISTORY:** Toll Trolls are Greek—descendants of Charon, who ferried the dead to Hades only after collecting the coins placed on their eyelids. They are curiously stubborn and warlike, and often, when they owe you twenty-five cents change, will quote the late General MacArthur, "I give no quarter."

☞ **SPOTTER'S TIPS:** Within a vending machine dented with fistprints lurks the Troll, in shattered phone booths and punched-out video game arcades.

But he also turns up (like the proverbial bad penny) in every purse and pocket, glove compartment and piggy bank, ready to light up the TILT sign on the pinball machine of life.

Myth has it that if you catch a Toll Troll and manage to break its legs, the mafia will give you a thousand dollars.

Opposite: Toll Trolls love Rhode Island, the little state that's almost *all paved*!

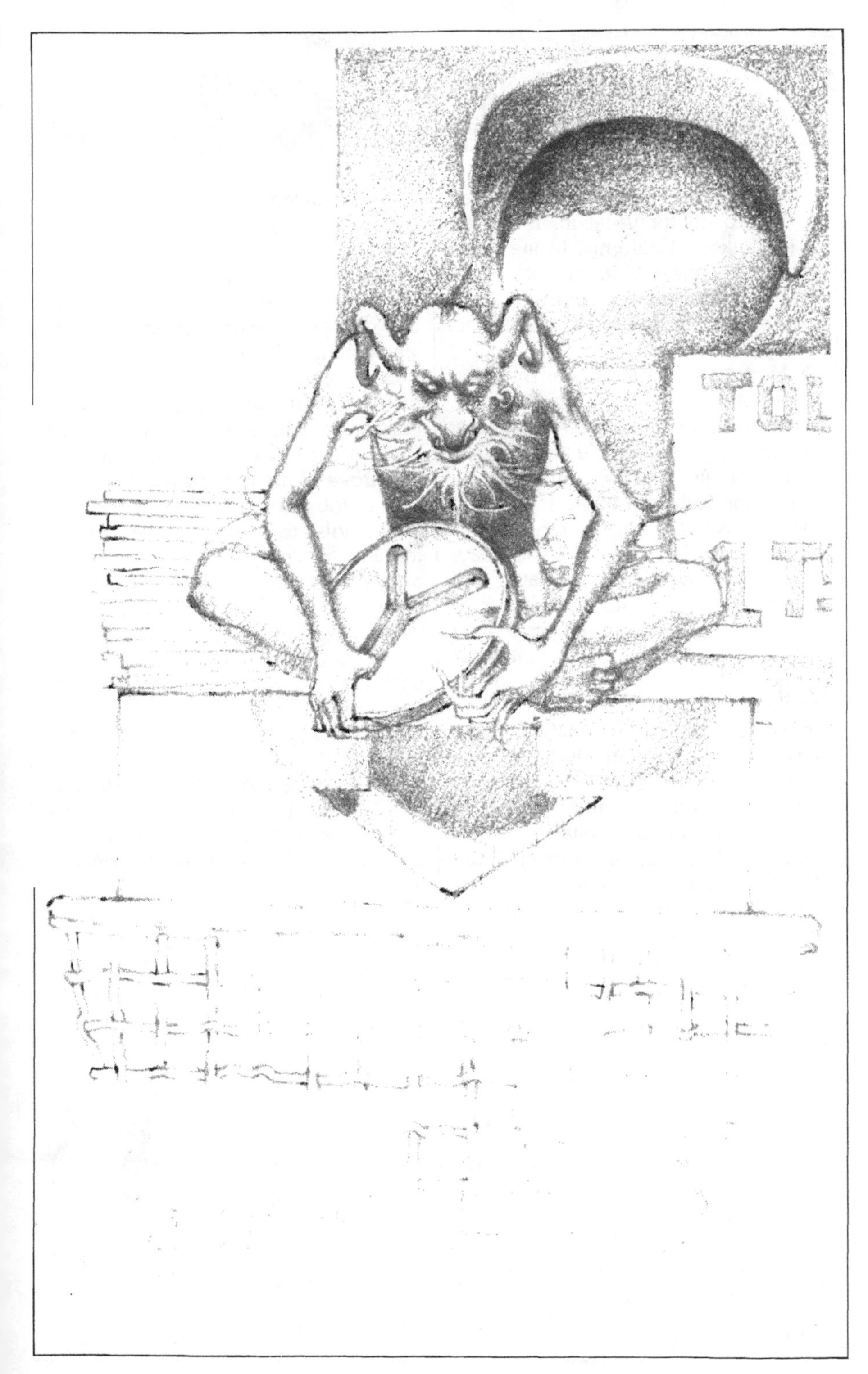

THE JOB GOBLIN

Opus pocus

⊙ **RANGE:** Out by the coffee machine, under the transmission, on the punch card, and off for vacation. From the union halls of California, to the chain stores of Tennessee; in the thick of every job action, fighting for truth, social justice, and in the word of Samuel Gompers, "more."

◐ **HABITS:** This Blue-Collar Bugaboo is the patron sprite of the working man. When a gasket cracks on a machine at the head of the assembly line, he sees to it that his guys take home good wages for eight hard hours digesting sugar buns in the lunch room.

Days sacred to him are Labor Day, sick days, travel days, paydays, and half days. He distributes his favors to working men and women on a strict seniority basis, seeing to it that the most skilled and experienced of his people do the least demanding tasks, leaving apprentices free to sharpen their talents assembling spacecraft circuit boards and to acquire experience fabricating cardiac monitors for the emergency rooms of America's hospitals.

His most spectacular product is Joe X, a New Jersey longshoreman who collects workman's compensation in addition to his regular salary for a lower back injury he sustained while lifting the phone to call in sick to a no-show job. Joe, in his turn, creates jobs by collecting unemployment insurance for his dog, social security for his dead wife's two incarcerated cousins, and antique firearms for the walls of his den.

The Job Goblin is despised and feared by management, who feel that they are the only ones entitled to a good day's pay for spending the afternoon digesting an exotic, tax-deductible lunch.

★ **HISTORY:** The Job Goblin is of British ancestry and has bestowed upon the English a reputation for idleness unequaled north of the equator. It was he who inspired the legendary Piers Plowman to slip a cow patty from his liege lord's field and smuggle it home for soup stock. He travelled with the Vikings to their mysterious Vineland colony, where he urged them with such extremes of lethargy that they not only failed to plant crops, but also to build houses or wear clothes, and as a consequence, they froze to death on the stroke of the autumn equinox.

The Job Goblin has since inspired "have-nots" to become "have-lots" by forming "brotherhoods" of one kind or another. (When negotiating with management, it is helpful to have a brother who is a hood.)

Although rising unemployment saddens and offends "J.G.," he remains personally unaffected; like many a union official, he has a lifetime contract.

☞ **SPOTTER'S TIPS:** Like many fairies, the Job Goblin is never called by his proper name: down at the plant they call him "Jack the Steward," on the waterfront he goes by the name "Johnny Friendly;" in show biz slang he's known as "The Green Man;" and around your house when you're not home, they call him "Jody the Milkman."

HAWKMAN

AMERICAN MOTOR GREMLINS

Infernalis combustiones

⊙ **RANGE:** Almost everyone has encountered these fiends at least twice. Their initial function is spell-casting. As one strolls past a dealer's show window or used car lot, Gremlins blow fairy dust over some undistinguished and indistinguishable jalopy, causing it to appear irresistibly glamorous. Enchanted, their victim signs his life savings away to Honest Somebody-Or-Other.

The second visitation of the Gremlins is of a duration far longer than any warranty. They are to be heard wheezing, coughing, thumping, grinding, and pinging under the hood . . . peeling back the chrome, hissing out the tires, fouling the fuel lines, stripping the gears and rattling in the ashtrays—from front to rear fender, from rubber to roof, of the costly domestic automobile.

◐ **HABITS:** The Gremlins of legend reputedly emptied love potions into many a cup, inspiring many a tragic love story. American Motor Gremlins apparently introduce a powerful elixir of passion (perhaps STP) into the baby bottles of all Americans. How else account for our all-consuming, fate-defying, heart-breaking relationship with that sleek-lined object of desire—the car?

The Gremlins are responsible for uneven tire wear, ignition keys that break off in the lock, and exploding gas tanks. Gangs of them snap the antennae off any car parked in a poorly lighted area. They drink the fluid from the window-washer bottle, as well as antifreeze; evidence of their excess—green acid excrement—can be found clotted around battery terminals.

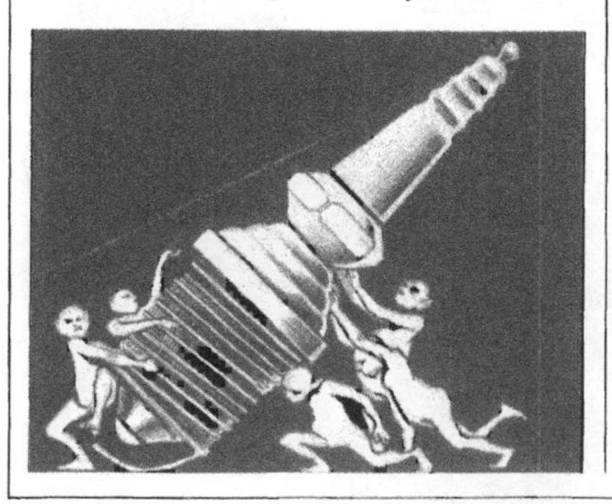

Jamming speedometers must be another of their favorite pranks, for every state trooper has heard a driver say (at the end of a three-county chase), "It was reading fifty-five all the way."

★ **HISTORY:** The Gremlins' ability to bewitch and captivate was inherited from their English fairy godmother, Morgan le Fay. (A primitive auto, the Morgan, was named in her honor.) As her descendants, they are also the New World representatives of the proverbial high standards of British Engineering.

But among their paternal ancestors (le Fay was rather promiscuous) appear to have been several of those quaint and picturesque imps of Central Europe, who delighted in crippling and blinding horses.

But the Gremlins now consider themselves to be native aristocracy, the haughty and ill-bred nobility of Detroit, and look down on all recent "imports" (undersized, powerful, and obviously working-class arrivals from Germany and Japan). Many a proud Pinto has imploded with shame, rather than share a traffic jam with a lowly Volkswagen.

☞ **SPOTTER'S TIPS:** Although they are ubiquitous, and evidence of their mischief is everywhere, Gremlins are notoriously difficult to isolate or exorcise. Just ask your neighborhood mechanic for an estimate. But if one looks closely, the gaily laughing little rascals can be seen dropping off the car as one bounces over the speed bump at the entrance to a service station.

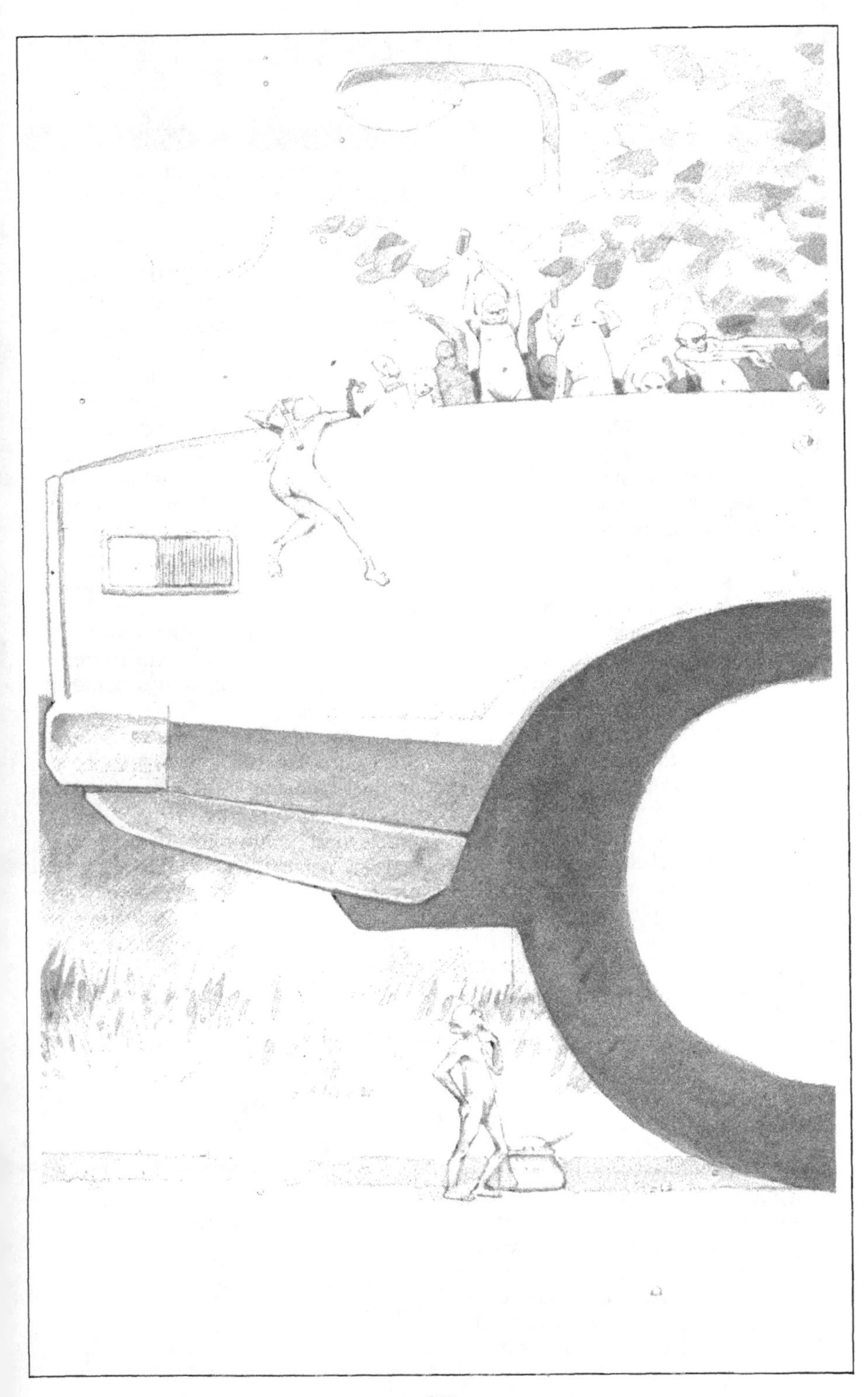

THE GIANT (ECONOMY SIZE)

Caveat emptor

⊙ **RANGE:** Suburban shopping centers, inner cities, across the river, over the tracks, under new management, out of stock. Long ago, the Giant Enceladus loomed o'er the isles of Greece. Today, the Giant (Economy Size) looms o'er the aisles of grease, down at what used to be called the grocery store. There she dwells still, within a vast, windowless and weirdly lit cave, where music of a brain-softening blandness plays eternally. Into this so-called supermarket, unwitting victims are lured by means of bright colored circulars, coupons and bonuses, promotions featuring capering clowns, free samples of the mayonnaises of many lands; seduced by ads featuring amorous butchers, tissue-squeezing floorwalkers, Colombian coffee tasters; and bombarded with talking tuna, bullet-proof paper towels, one-cent sales, discounts, bargains, and other hallucinations.

◐ **HABITS:** Unit pricing, metric measures, house brands, and electronic cash register Universal Product Codes are merely the latest vile wiles of this spell-casting consumer cozener. She hovers above the pyramids of cans and smiles, wickedly, as mesmerized shoppers wander in a trance, heaping their carts with jeroboams of Bog-O-Cola, firkins of freeze-dried cod tongues, family-sized Treasure Chests O' Cheese Food, and that special Stampede O' Weenies from Hard Ridin' Frambs' Famous Frank Ranch, over by the sundries. She hides surprise bonus tarantulas in the bananas, Italian nose hairs in the frozen lasagna, and tacky dish towels in boxes of detergent. Customers have been known to wander, lost or confused, in her maze of merchandise for weeks; when their minds are utterly addled by the shameless display of useless products, the Giant then employs these idiots as cashiers working her express checkout counters.

★ **HISTORY:** Anyone who has had contact with the Giant (Economy Size) will have guessed at the creature's canny and frugal Scottish heritage. Her ancestors once stomped the fog-shrouded hillsides of Scotland, dining on whole spitted sheep, oat gruel, and the occasional side of crofter's cottage.

In America, the Giant (Economy Size) presided over the white man's early trade with Indians, in which backfiring rifles, neuro-toxic brandy and plaid bow ties were exchanged for gold bars, mountains of beaver pelts, and millions of acres of bottom land. Her motto has always been, "Manny a mickle maks a muckle," which, translated, means, "Small things come in big packages."

☞ **SPOTTER'S TIPS:** Look for Redtide Seafood sales, buckets of turkey by-product bargains, low quality discount purchase offers, celebrity scandal sheets, and breath mints near the cash register. You can be sure you are in the presence of this Jolly Green Giant, Economy Size, if the facial features of your fellow shoppers and those of the supermarket staff are indistinguishable from the smile buttons pinned to their lapels.

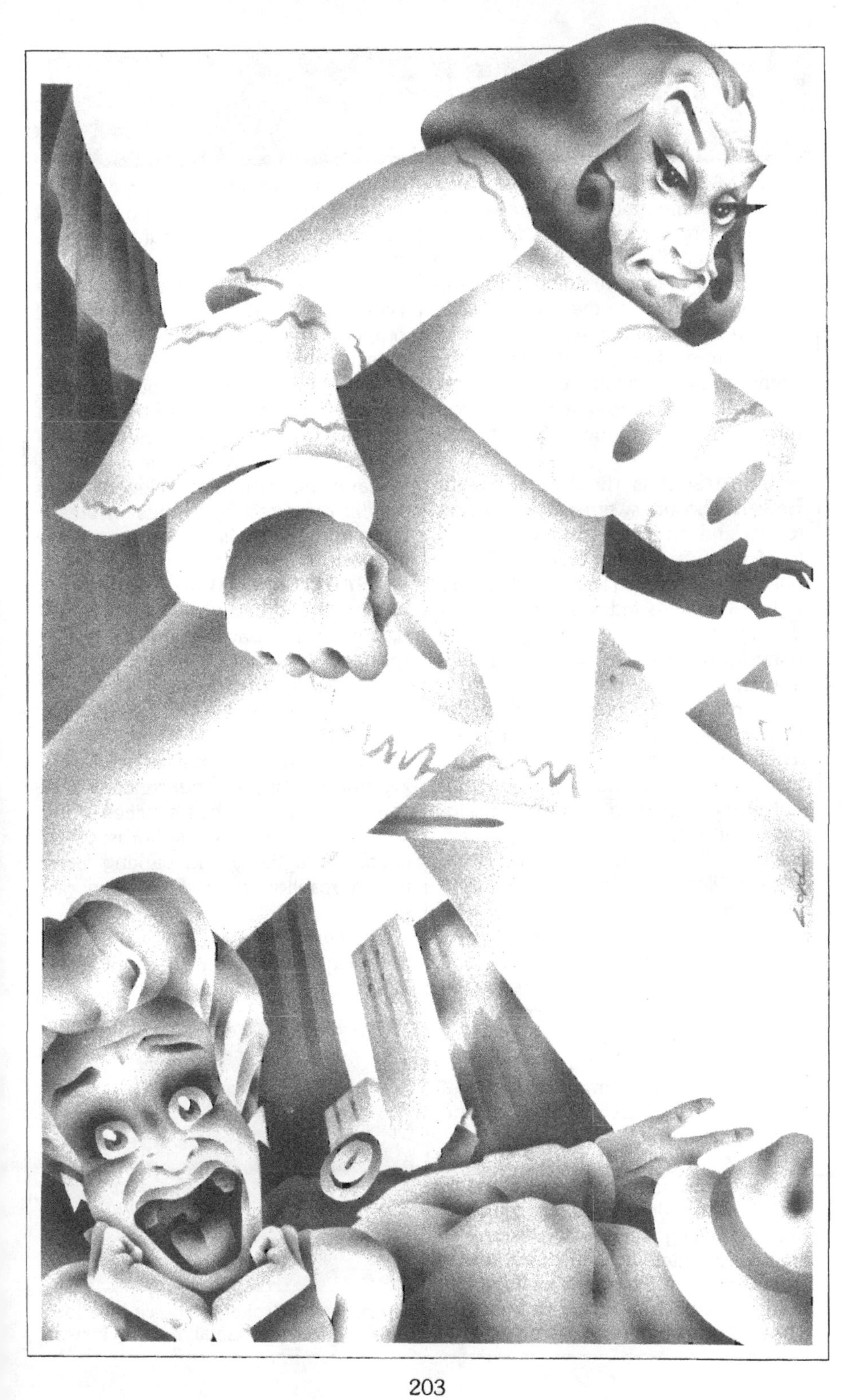

UNREAL ESTATE BROKERS

Vendores condominis fantastica

⊙ **RANGE:** From coast to coast—and several hundred yards off shore—these cunning creatures can be found in almost any direction: down in the boondocks; between sliding hills and eroding beaches; on the side of a cliff; deep in the swamp; in what appears to be an immediately post-blitz neighborhood; off the beaten track; right on the fault line; and always—it says here—convt 2 shpng, scls, chrchs, transp.

◐ **HABITS:** It is the Unreal Estate Brokers who lure swarms of developers to descend on a hick town connected to a city by a defunct railway. Before one can say "zoning law," the Unreal's victims have erected thousands of undistinguished and indistinguishable bungalows. Then, as quickly as they appeared, these mesmerized "developers" *vanish*, only to follow the Unreal Estate Brokers to their next roost: the abandoned lofts of light industry in the inner city, where they install faulty plumbing and picture windows with stunning brick wall exposures, all to the Unreal Estate Broker's specifications. Goosing down payments through the (low, peeling) ceilings, the Unreal's victims then move in, ever at the restless Broker's beck and call. Many of the more spectacular "jokes" (or Urban Renewal Projects, as they are officially called) played upon Americans by the Unreal Estate Brokers could not be accomplished without the help of that architectural elf, the Geodesic Gnome.

★ **HISTORY:** Unreal Estate Brokers had a spectacular career in the Old World, where they filled the minds of hovel-dwelling serfs with visions of Heavenly Cities and inspired aristocrats, from the Pharaohs of Egypt to mad Bavarian monarchs, to construct absurdly expensive habitations, thereby increasing beyond reason the value of adjacent lots, and all without providing to a single soul a suitable place to dwell.

In America, agents of Unreal Estate Brokers have caused the debilitation of property in every state of the Union, most notably in Florida, where many a lot-buyer has found high tide bringing schools of brightly colored tropical fish right in the window of her mobile home, and in Hawaii, where a retiree's volcano-top bungalow view is only *slightly* obscured by clouds of steam rising from the molten rock rivers flowing past the front porch.

☞ **SPOTTER'S TIPS:** Amphibious backhoes. Old barns bulldozed. A sudden craze for barn wood. A plaster shortage. A sudden craze for exposed brick. Old fixtures bought cheap. A sudden craze for adobe. Antique fixtures sold dear. A massive, across-the-board rent increase to offset declining housing starts. The cancelling of commuter rail and bus services in response to the growth of suburbs; vastly improved highway and parking facilities in reaction to a threatened gas shortage.

What was that thing that went bump in the night? Just another Unreal Estate Boom.

Unreal Estate Brokers sell nice little lots, midway between Catalina and Hawaii

FOR SALE
573-5589
856-1084

THE HIGH INTEREST WRAITH

Usurious horribilus

⊙ **RANGE**: Anywhere between inexplicably expensive and temporarily exorbitant, the High Interest Wraith can be found on either the downturn or the upswing. Wherever a small deposit will hold or no serious offer is refused, he makes his mortgaged home.

◐ **HABITS**: He whispers in our ears with unnatural, will-melting charm: Ever think you could own a potentially lucrative and prestigious dew worm ranch? Well, for a limited time only, at a price you can afford! Sound good? That's not all . . . If you buy now, we will throw in that second house you've always dreamed of and never thought you could afford. That's right! A vacation home for you and the family, fabricated of longlasting pressboard, with plenty of air holes for the kids! Originally designed to house prize Labradors, these genuine jerry-built units are selling for just twice the original cost! For customers who act after reading this, we also have available a limited number of US Army surplus jeeps, originally advertised for fifty dollars—now they can be yours at a price so surprising you will be amazed!

A flickering light in the night, he sings to us in a voice full of promise: If after you have taken advantage of these amazing offers you still have any money left wasting away in outmoded savings accounts, we are prepared to give you one year's free investment management! If you are not completely satisfied with your investments after fifty-two weeks, you may file for bankruptcy in any recognized court . . . Just a minute there, friend . . .

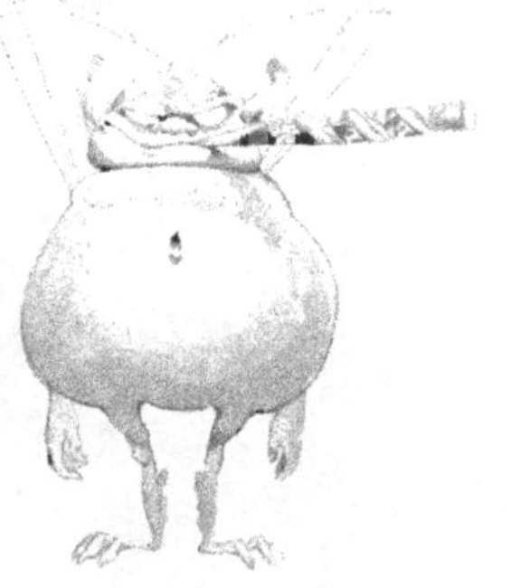

Money-loving High Interest Wraiths are about to foreclose on Oklahoma. Again.

★ **HISTORY**: A European fairy of no fixed nationality, the High Interest Wraith's interest has varied with the times but has always remained a couple of points above prime. His coffers have fattened in many a famine; plagues have contributed to the health of his accounts.

He has been an architect of the American economy ever since arrival here. The High Interest Wraith has constructed Teapot Domes, pyramid schemes, tax shelters, investment houses, decorative financial columns, ground floors to get in on and collapsible financial structures, but never, never, a wage/price ceiling.

Like many fairy folk, he is a shape shifter, and in 1929, he changed himself from a bull into a bear, whereafter thousands of investors came crashing to the street from the sills and ledges of the castles in the air which he had made for them.

Today, he sometimes disguises himself as a tv pitch man, a telephone solicitor, and an economic advisor with a smile as broad as a Laffer curve.

☞ **SPOTTER'S TIPS**: By these signs shall ye know the High Interest Wraith: depressed bond market, men in top hats selling apples, fewer housing starts, station wagons full of farmers heading for California, tightened money supply, big movie musicals featuring aquatic ballet, inventory financing difficulties, and boxcar-riding folksingers.

SAVINGS BANK

THE RITCH DOCTOR

Midas Velbi

⊙ **RANGE**: The Ritch Doctor does not limit his practice to the territory bounded by the first and eighteenth holes; nor does he operate exclusively above the no-parking zones in front of French restaurants. For if his bedside manner is a little brusque at times, you should see him courtside at Wimbledon . . . fireside at St. Moritz . . . poolside at Puerto Vallarta . . . drink-side at the Dorchester, portside out, and starboard home. And all for taking your insides out!

◐ **HABITS**: The Hippocratic Oath, which all newly ordained M.D.s are obliged to recite, sounds, to the layman, like a piece of meaningless mumbo jumbo. But it is actually the sacred invocation by which this Spirit of profitable pathology is invoked.

It is the Ritch Doctor's specific. indicated function to direct physicians toward deductible leisure activities, and to otherwise assure them of the financial rewards they deserve in recompense for their years spent in selfless study carving corpses, chasing nurses, and drinking formalin punch at the Residents' Ball.

If a practicing medico conducts the proper rituals honoring the Ritch Doctor (which include shaving extra close, munching breath mints, going bald in front, and keeping one's hands several degrees below room temperature at all times), then the Spirit of Lucrative Leechcraft will grant said medic certain therapeutic powers.

These include a practice composed of attractive, wealthy hypochondriacs; the ability to obtain transfusions directly from the patient's savings account; the skill to diagnose, cause, and cure psychosomatic illness, and to prescribe for the Body Politic massive, effective antidotes to the threatening plague of Socialized Medicine.

★ **HISTORY**: The full origins of the Ritch Doctor's past are shrouded in medical mystery: recorded in classic sawbone's scrawl on a prescription pad, they are quite indecipherable. (A pharmacological cryptologist who has examined them suggests that the Ritch Doctor either hails from Attic Greece or is a bottle of Nembutal.)

Certainly some benign spirit steered the physicians of old Athens to a better class of client, but then, the magicians of medicine along the Nile and the Druidic faith healers of ancient Britain also seem to have known what strata of their respective societies most needed their compassionate care.

The American Ritch Doctor seems to be a (eugenic) hybrid, whose immigrant ancestors may well have met and mingled at the first-ever A.M.A. convention, a thousand painful, profitable, professional years ago. Regardless of his Old World origins, the Ritch Doctor's practice in the New World dates back to colonial times. Under the benign observation of the Ritch Doctor, all manner of American quacks became wealthy, peddling nostrums, pink pills, patent medicines, and, more recently, holistic life-styles, to (possibly sick but certifiably rich) patients.

After the Civil War, for example, the Ritch Doctor wooed away from the unsavory amputation tents many a lucky young medic to serve as senatorial gout consultants.

During the Industrial Revolution, the Ritch made men famous with all manner of mechanical and electrical cures for the flat feet, aching backs, and thickening waistlines that their electrical machines had caused them.

And even today, R.D., M.D. takes many a struggling intern, seemingly doomed to a career as poorhouse coroner, and inspires him to specialize

in Marin County tennis elbow.

☞ **SPOTTER'S TIPS**: If your family physician listens to your heart through your shirt, guesses your weight, taps his pencil, says "*hmmm,*" refers you to some kind of -ologist, now takes American Express, and has a beeper which reminds him he's late for the wine-tasting, chances are that kindly old "Doc" has been consulting with the Ritch Doctor.

Ethical M.D.'s (Maryland's full of them) consult the professional (accounting) Ritch Doctor.

SMALL BUSINESSMEN

Eine kleine nock muckenstich

⊙ **RANGE:** It is the custom of wealthy celebrities, when they are accepting awards and tributes, to thank "all the Little People behind the scenes." Behind the Little People, in turn, are Small Businessmen. The Little People work for *them.*

These clever wee creatures can be found the world over: haggling over sickly sweet coffee in Middle Eastern cafes, bargaining between puffs of noxious herbs in Oriental bazaars, and, here in America, slamming their tiny fists upon the desks in small (naturally) claims court.

◐ **HABITS:** These diminutive entrepreneurs have frequently been accused (by the small minded) of petty larceny. But while he does, occasionally, sell short, the Small Businessman is much too concerned with his stature in the business community to short change anyone! He often complains (and small wonder) that he is facing extinction as a result of encroachment upon his markets by Corporate Giants and the Tax Burden.

★ **HISTORY:** The American Small Businessman is probably a Red Inkling of (lowland) Scottish extraction, although he might also be descended from the French "*petits* bourgeois," those wizards of "*ledger de main.*" In the Old Days, whenever a dragon's lair was discovered, some warrior Elves would make so bold as to try to steal the dragon's gold hoard. The Small Businessman used to set up a ticket booth at the mouth of the cave.

In the sweatshops of Small Businessmen, the basic fabric of our economy was woven and our money laundered. Two examples of entrepreneurmanship which they recently inspired are "Rural Cottage Industries," a mammoth cartel producing prefab cottages, and "Mom and Pop Stores," in which wealthy urban orphans can purchase a nice new set of parents.

☞ **SPOTTER'S TIPS:** The Small Businessman is seldom far from a telephone. By means of this instrument, he makes *small* talk into the *wee* hours— and a nice *little* profit. Traces of his handiwork can often be detected in *small* print. He is known to be *short* on cash at tax time and a *tiny bit* slow paying bills. His skill at maintaining a *low* overhead *dwarfs* that of a large corporation.

An unsung, heroic Small Businessman, standing up to Big Government and Big Labor, and other big guys from New Jersey to New York.

60

THE TAX BURDEN

Inflatus Stagflatus

⊙ **RANGE:** A creature fond of earth and the home, the Tax Burden naturally hangs around real estate offices looking after his interests—but his awful presence can also be felt quarterly in corporate boardrooms, daily at assessors' offices, and frequently wherever big money changes hands. His only known holiday is April 15th. His presence is, curiously, something of a status symbol, and many people, such as the very rich, complain loudly and incessantly of his torments although in reality he seldom bothers them at all.

He is vast and still growing and totally omnivorous. He is especially fond of paychecks, from which he has been known to take big bites.

◐ **HABITS:** The Tax Burden has been accused, by his detractors, of playing the percentages and other mischievous deeds. They say that he (like many a fairy before him) feeds and clothes the poor—widows and orphans and the like. Nothing could be further from the truth. The Tax Burden is actually a benign and generous goblin, who fills with gold the pockets of needy armaments manufacturers and, all in fun, devotes any of his leftover wealth to funding committees investigating methods of exterminating him.

But the dark shadow which the Tax Burden casts upon the pot of gold at the end of the rainbow is said to sap the get-up-and-go-profit-motivated-energy that Made This Country Great. Many a listless youth would dash from his street corner hangout and rescue a millionaire's daughter on her runaway horse, were it not that the Tax Burden whispers in his ear, "What's the use? It would only put you in a higher tax bracket, anyway."

★ **HISTORY:** "A specter is haunting Europe—the specter of Communism," wrote Karl Marx in 1848. These days, an equally terrifying specter haunts America: the Tax Burden, which, like Communism, takes all your money and gives it to the State, but, unlike Communism, does not supply you with a free pair of rimless spectacles in return.

There is every reason to believe that the Tax Burden, like so many of our woes, is of Russian origin—and is a descendant of the highly un-Orthodox fairy *Ruskali,* once responsible for the Czarist version of the I.R.S.

On a sight-seeing trip through the Gulag, this indomitable fairy wandered across the Aleutians, and arrived just in time to inspire Seward's Folly.

Today, thanks to the arcane Laffer ritual being practiced by Federal exorcists, there is hope of relief from the torments of the Tax Burden—at least, for the very rich.

☞ **SPOTTER'S TIPS:** Like most Evil Spirits, the Tax Burden is usually invisible. But he can be seen clearly—an obese, greedy, grinning monster perched upon the backs of the people—by political candidates to whom he appears every four years.

If we ordinary people keep our eyes open, we, too, can occasionally see a Tax Burden—escaping through a loophole, to join the Gnomes of Zurich.

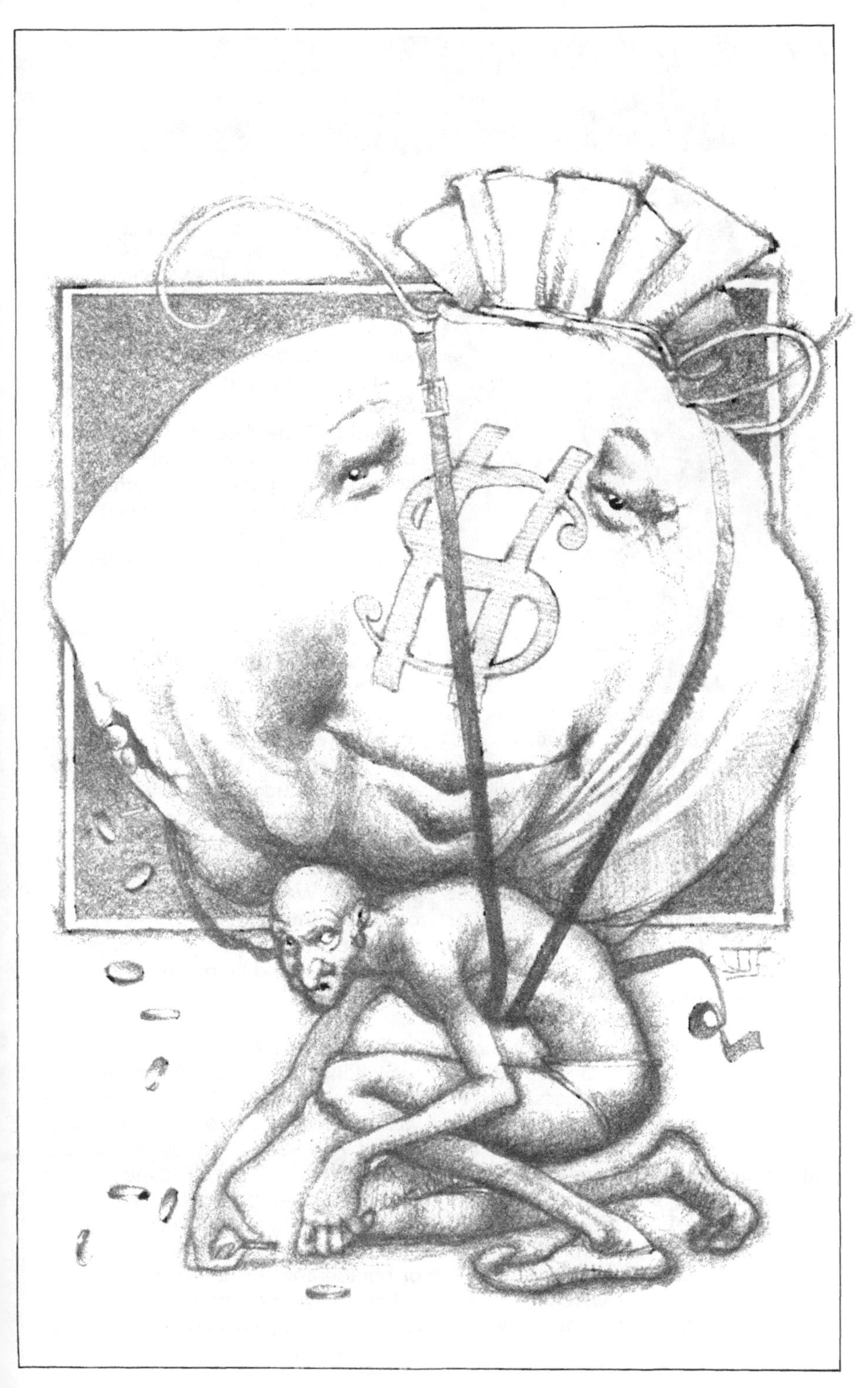

YOUR SIGHTINGS

You are cordially invited to send in your own sightings of the Fair People. The creatures, whose descendants you have just met, may be found in city or country, indoors or out, day or night, in summer's heat or winter's frost. It is up to you to find them, describe them and, if you are quick enough or clever enough, to send us a photograph or illustration of them at play.

IF YOU ARE SUBMITTING TEXT:

The form provided to you at right contains all the information you need to know. Once you have spotted a creature—or having had it described to you by another, perhaps younger member of your family—determine the category into which this Fair Person falls. The categories, as used herein, include: SOCIAL, HOUSEHOLD, CULTURAL, PERSONAL, POLITICAL, ENVIRONMENTAL, REGIONAL, INFORMATIONAL and ECONOMIC. The appropriate category should be entered.

Next, determine the name of your Fair Person. If you have not actually talked to the creature, you may have to make up both its common and formal name (THE PHILHARMONIC ORC is the common name; *Cacophonous gloriosus* is the formal name). This should then be entered on the page.

The *Range*, *Habits*, *History* and *Spotter's Tips* for the Fair Person should then be described. If the space on the form is insufficient, one additional piece of paper in the same size as the form may be used. (Typewritten or printed descriptions, only.) If you are submitting art with your text, check the appropriate box.

IF YOU ARE SUBMITTING TEXT AND ART OR ART ONLY:

Pictures of the Fair People may be submitted as illustrations or photographs. You may submit a photograph or illustration without text. However, you must include a suggested name for your creature in the space provided on the facing page.

NO SUBMISSIONS WILL BE RETURNED. We advise you to send only copies of any photograph or illustration. Do not send original sculptures. All copies should be no larger than 8½ x 11 inches.

ACCEPTANCE:

Sightings describing the most interesting, humorous or beautiful creatures will be selected for use in the next edition of *The Secret;* and those who describe them will be credited in that book. You will be notified by mail if your sighting has been selected, and at that time we will request the original art or photograph for use in the book.

On the back of the facing page is a form to be signed and returned with your sighting.

COMMON NAME ______________________________

FORMAL NAME ______________________________

CATEGORY OF FAIR PERSON ______________________________

⊙ **RANGE:**

◐ **HABITS:**

★ **HISTORY:**

☞ **SPOTTER'S TIPS:**

YOUR SIGHTINGS

My name is ______________________________

My address is: ______________________________

City ______________ State ______________ Zip ____________

Country ____________ Postal Code ____________ Phone ____________

Name of sighted Fair Person ______________________________

I hereby submit my □ Photograph □ Illustration □ Text describing the Fair Person named above.

I understand that if said Fair Person is selected by Byron Preiss Visual Publications for publication in the next edition of *The Secret*, I shall be notified by mail. At that time, I shall be sent a release form to sign which will grant Byron Preiss Visual Publications the right to use my sighting in the next edition of The Secret.

I further understand that Byron Preiss Visual Publications and Bantam Books, Inc. accept no responsibility for any manuscripts, photos, art or other materials sent to them. No original art shall be accepted and no submissions will be returned. I hold Byron Preiss Visual Publications and Bantam Books fully harmless against the use of any submissions similar to mine which may be accepted for use in the next edition of *The Secret*.

Agreed and accepted: ______________________________
Your signature and Date

SEND TO:THE SECRET/SIGHTINGS
Byron Preiss Visual Publications
Box 342
Shelter Island Hts, NY 11965

THE TREASURE

The Fair People's twelve treasures can be found by deciphering the clues in the paintings and the verses in this book.

Each treasure consists of a hand-painted treasure casque, the hand-painted key inside it, and the treasure jewel or jewels. Only the casques and keys are buried. Each key represents the jewel or jewels, which will be given to the person who discovers the hiding place of the casque and key.

The jewels collectively are worth over ten thousand dollars. The treasure casques themselves are of incalculable value, never having been owned by man or woman.

If you believe you have correctly deciphered the clues to any of the Fair People's twelve treasures, you may proceed directly to the site you have determined. *Every* treasure casque is buried underground, at a depth of no more than three to three and one-half feet. The casques are protected by lustrous transparent boxes, and are sealed.

The following places do not hold any treasure:

(a) any life-threatening location, such as a dangerous highway embankment, a contaminated area or active railway track

(b) any cemetery

(c) any public or private flower bed

(d) any property owned by the contributors to the book, their families or friends.

It is not the intention of the Fair People to destroy the beauty of nature or Man through their challenge.If you believe you have correctly determined the location of a treasure, but the treasure is not there, you may write us an inquiry using only the information below. If you have correctly determined the location of a treasure, we will respond to you by mail.

You may also send an inquiry if you believe you have determined the location of a treasure but are unable to explore it in person. If you are correct, and have successfully responded to the options below, *we* will retrieve the treasure casque. You will receive the treasure jewels as described in the next paragraph, but the casque shall remain the property of the Fair People.

If you find a treasure casque: You may notify us by mail or email. The form below should be completed and returned to us with the key that is contained inside the casque. The publisher will use its best effort to locate the treasure jewels for you. (Byron Preiss was killed in an auto accident in 2005.) Your photo and story will appear in the next edition of *The Secret*.

Let the publisher know if you are one of the two people who already unearthed the casques in 1984 and 2004. bricktower@aol.com

My name is:

My address is:

City State
Zip
Country
Postal Code
Phone
email

SEND TO:THE SECRET/SIGHTINGS
Byron Preiss Visual Publications
Box 342
Shelter Island Hts, NY 11965

THE TREASURE

____ I have found a treasure casque. I enclose the key.

____ I think I have found a treasure site, but the treasure is missing.

____ I have determined the site of a treasure, but I am unable to explore it.

This is how I have determined the location of a treasure, using the clues in *The Secret*:

Describe *precisely* the *exact* site of the treasure:

Describe *precisely* the treasure casque (*if found*):

ORIGINS AND WHEREABOUTS OF THE FAIR PEOPLE

Name	Area of origin (Old World)	Area of concentration (New World)
Alibi Elf	French	New Hampshire
American Motor Gremlins	Native American	Michigan
Backyard Barbacreep	Greek	Texas
The Boogie Man	African	ubiquitous
The Bugbear	Western European	Arkansas (and other wilderness)
The Calcubus	Greek	ubiquitous
The Chicago World's Fairy	Polish/Irish/African	Illinois
Corporate Giants	Greek/Persian/ Scandinavian	Delaware
Culture Vultures	Greek	Connecticut
Daemon Runyon	French (Riviera)	Nevada
Devil Dogs	Russian	South Carolina
Dixie Pixie	Irish/Scottish	the North
Djinn Rummy	Middle Eastern/Persian	Kentucky
Don Faun	Italian	all borders
Elf Alpha	Native American	New Mexico
Elf S. Presley	Italian	Tennessee
Energenii	Middle Eastern/Persian	West Virginia
Evil Neckromancers	Eastern European (Transylvanian)	Colorado
The Filthy Hobit	English	Virginia
Foul Sewer Ogres	Native American	Indiana
Freudian Sylphs	Viennese	ubiquitous
Gardengoyle	African	Nebraska, Florida
The Giant (Economy Size)	Scottish	Idaho
Geodesic Gnome	Norse	Arizona
Glitches	Asian	ubiquitous
Gnome Enclature	Arabian	ubiquitous
Handimanticore	German	Vermont
High Interest Wraith	European	Oklahoma
The Hounds of News	Celtic	ubiquitous
Household Unfamiliars	Norse	Oregon
Jack B. Nimbus	ubiquitous	ubiquitous
Jack O'Lectern	European	North Carolina
The Job Goblin	English	Washington
The Joke Fiend	Eastern European	Kansas
Kinderguardians	German	Montana
The Left Wing Symp and The Right Wing Trog	Italian/French	North and South Dakota, Washington D.C.
The Leprachaunman	Irish	Georgia

ORIGINS AND WHEREABOUTS OF THE FAIR PEOPLE

Name	Area of origin (Old World)	Area of concentration (New World)
The Maître D'eamon	French	Washington D.C. Wisconsin
The Mind Boggles	Native American	Ohio
Mira Chimera	Greek	California, New York
Mugwumps	Swedish	Mississippi, Washington D.C.
The Night Mayor	Native American	ubiquitous (urban)
Nymph O'Maine	Celtic	Maine, Maritime Provinces
Paltry Geist	Swiss	Alaska
Passing Fancies	French/German/English	ubiquitous
The Pentagorgon	Greek	Washington D.C.
The Phantasma Glory	German	ubiquitous
The Philharmonic Orc	German/Italian/French	ubiquitous
The Pre-Revolutionary Warlock	French	Northeast
The Pill Grim	English	New England
The Post Monster General	Roman	Louisiana
Preps Ghoul	English	Massachusetts
The Ritch Doctor	Greek	Maryland
Saucier's Apprentices	English	ubiquitous
Screaming Mimi	English	ubiquitous
Scrububus	English/Scottish	Iowa
Small Businessmen	French	New York
The Sophomore Jinx	German/French/English	Pennsylvania
The Spirit of St. Louis	French	Missouri
The Spirit of '76	European/African/Asian	ubiquitous (but rare)
Stylus Devil	Native American	ubiquitous
Sweatsylphs	Greek	ubiquitous
The Tax Burden	Russian	Alberta
Team Spirits	English	Alabama, Quebec
Teen Angels	Native American	New Jersey, California
Tinkerbelles	Native American	ubiquitous
Toll Trolls	Greek	Rhode Island
The Torontogre	English	Ontario
Tupperwerewolves	Dutch	Minnesota
Typographical Terrors	German	ubiquitous
Union Jack	English	British Columbia
Unreal Estate Brokers	Middle Eastern	Hawaii
Werner Von Brownie	Chinese/European	Florida, Texas, California
The West Ghost	Native American	California
The Wooly Bully	German	Wyoming, Wisconsin, New York

PERSONAE

SEAN KELLY
Author

Mr. Kelly was a newspaper reporter, radio actor, advertising agency copywriter, and college teacher of Children's Literature and Victorian History before leaving his native Canada. He joined (and is currently an editor of) the *National Lampoon* magazine, co-wrote and did lyrics for the musical revue, *Lemmings* and edited *Heavy Metal* magazine. He has written comedy for television—Steve Martin, Jonathan Winters, and Robert Klein—and for children's television: *Young People's Concerts* (CBS), the *Drawing Power* series (NBC) and *School House Rock* (ABC). He has contributed to (the Sports and Op-Ed pages of) *The New York Times* and to *Not the New York Times*, to *The 80's: A Look Back, The Quarterly of Joyce Studies, The What's What Book* and *A Treasury of Humor for Children*. He is now editing a collection, *Irish Folk Tales and Fairy Tales,* for W. H. Smith. He is married to Valerie Marchant, and has four children.

TED MANN
Author

Mr. Mann, a native of Canada, is currently a senior editor of *National Lampoon,* for which he has written since 1974. He has written teleplays for ABC's short-lived *Delta House, Behind the Scenes* and NBC's *Drawing Power*. He co-edited *Slightly Higher in Canada* with Mr. Kelly, a frequent collaborator.

JOELLEN TRILLING
Sculptress

Ms. Trilling's sculptures have been the subject of five shows at the Julie Artisans Gallery on Madison Avenue in Manhattan, where such clients as Elton John, Ellen Burstyn, Cher, Julie Christie and Carrie Fisher have purchased them. Her sculptures have appeared in *The Complete Book of Stuffed Work, The Beach Boys, Heavy Metal, The Soho Weekly News, Playboy,* and *Cue*; and in the Renwick Gallery of the Smithsonian Museum in Washington D.C. She has taught soft sculpture in New York and Kentucky, and her work was featured twice on Bill Bogg's *Midday Live* television program in New York. She currently resides in New York.

JOHN PALENCAR
Illustrator

Mr. Palencar's award-winning work has appeared in numerous periodicals such as *Ohio* and the *Cleveland Plain Dealer.* His illustrations have appeared in three shows at the prestigious Society of Illustrators and in *Distant Stars*. He was

PERSONAE

awarded a scholarship to the 1980 Illustrator's Workshop in Paris, and is pursuing careers in both fine art and illustration.

JOHN PIERARD
Illustrator

Mr. Pierard is a graduate of Syracuse University. His fantasy illustrations have appeared in numerous periodicals and at science fiction conventions in the Northeast. He has done thirteen black and white illustrations for Samuel R. Delany's "Prismatica" in *Distant Stars* and illustrations for *Isaac Asimov's Science Fiction Magazine*, Tor Books, and Franklin Watts.

Photo by Betsy Bernfeld

BEN ASEN
Photographer

Mr. Asen's work, which includes editorial and portraiture, has appeared in *Newsweek, The New York Times* and many other publications. He has documented the life of senior citizens and the physically disabled and has exhibited his work at the Wavehill Museum, Soho Photo Gallery and the Wooster Street Gallery in New York. His one-man exhibition, "Living for the City: New York" was shown in London, England and Darmstadt, West Germany in April and May of 1982. He currently resides in New York City with his wife Betsy.

OVERTON LOYD
Illustrator

Mr. Loyd is a Hollywood-based artist whose illustrations have appeared on numerous record albums, in *The National Lampoon, Saturday Review, The New York Times, New York Magazine*, and *The Beach Boys*. He designed two animated short films for the popular groups the Parliaments and the Funkadelics, and a variety of stage and costume designs for Uncle Jam Records.

BYRON PREISS
Editor

Mr. Preiss is the co-author and producer of Bantam's bestselling trade paperback, *Dragonworld*, of which Maurice Sendak said, "*Dragonworld* goes far beyond the flashy pyrotechnics of contemporary fantasy and fantasy illustration." Preiss is considered to be one of the major figures in the renaissance of illustrated fiction in America. He is also the author of *The Art of Leo and Diane Dillon*, a retrospective of the two-time Caldecott Medal winning artists, and *The Beach Boys*, the authorized illustrated biography. He produced and edited Bantam's critically acclaimed trade paperback, *The Dinosaurs*, which was featured in *Life* magazine and was a selection of five book clubs in 1981. He is a graduate of the University of Pennsylvania and Stanford University's Graduate School of Communications.

CPSIA information can be obtained
at www.ICGtesting.com
Printed in the USA
BVHW09*1319200718
522048BV00002B/2/P